AF499247

Göttinger Wirtschaftsinformatik
Herausgeber: J. Biethahn† · L. M. Kolbe · M. Schumann

Band 110

Patryk Zapadka

Digital Innovation in Incumbent Firm Contexts: A Knowledge Integration Perspective

CUVILLIER VERLAG

Herausgeber

Prof. Dr. J. Biethahn† Prof. Dr. L. M. Kolbe Prof. Dr. M. Schumann

Georg-August-Universität
Wirtschaftsinformatik
Platz der Göttinger Sieben 5
37073 Göttingen

Bibliografische Information der Deutschen Nationalbibliothek
Die Deutsche Nationalbibliothek verzeichnet diese Publikation in der Deutschen Nationalbibliografie; detaillierte bibliografische Daten sind im Internet über http://dnb.d-nb.de abrufbar.
1. Aufl. - Göttingen : Cuvillier, 2021
Zugl.: Göttingen, Univ., Diss., 2021

Nonnenstieg 8, 37075 Göttingen
Telefon: 0551-54724-0
Telefax: 0551-54724-21

1. Auflage, 2021
Gedruckt auf umweltfreundlichem, säurefreiem Papier aus nachhaltiger Forstwirtschaft.

ISBN 978-3-7369-7463-0
eISBN 978-3-7369-6463-1

Digital Innovation in Incumbent Firm Contexts: A Knowledge Integration Perspective

Dissertation

zur Erlangung des wirtschaftswissenschaftlichen Doktorgrades

der Wirtschaftswissenschaftlichen Fakultät der Georg-August-Universität Göttingen

vorgelegt von

Patryk Zapadka, M.Sc.

aus Ilawa

Hamburg, 2021

Betreuungsausschuss

Erstbetreuer:	Prof. Dr. Lutz M. Kolbe
Zweitbetreuer:	Prof. Dr. André Hanelt
Drittbetreuerin:	Dr. Sabrina Schneider

Tag der mündlichen Prüfung: 23.04.2021

Abstract

The technological change driven by pervasive digital technologies leads to new requirements on how companies have to design their processes, products and business models in order to maintain their ability to innovate and ensure their competitiveness. Accordingly, firms across contexts need to adjust and renew their existing competencies by integrating new valuable knowledge from the digital sphere into their organizations. However, this poses a significant managerial challenge, especially for incumbent companies, as the convergent and generative nature of digital innovation is not only making the process of knowledge integration more dynamic, but also increases the diversity and amount of knowledge that needs to be integrated across an organization's boundaries.

In order to address this challenge and evaluate possible approaches, four studies have been conducted and compiled in this cumulative dissertation. These studies provide insights into the unique nature of knowledge integration in the context of digital innovation and advance the understanding of how incumbent firms can manage the associated challenges. With regard to this, the utilization of boundary resources is investigated in particular, as it represents an essential mechanism to scale knowledge integration in digital(izing) business ecosystems.

The findings underline that digital technologies increasingly permeate knowledge integration processes and outcomes, making their nature more dynamic and complex. Due to this, incumbent firms require new procedural and technological mechanisms to best manage the new requirements and possibilities for knowledge integration in the digital age. In this context, boundary resources represent a key strategic element, which under certain conditions benefit incumbent firms in leveraging internal as well as external knowledge for digital innovation. Building on these findings, this dissertation draws valuable implications for research as well as practice.

Table of Contents

List of Figures

List of Tables

Acronyms

AI	Artificial Intelligence
API	Application Programming Interface
EAI	Enterprise Application Integration
IS	Information Systems
IT	Information Technology
KMS	Knowledge Management System
M&A	Merger and Acquisition
OEM	Original Equipment Manufacturer
SDK	Software Development Kit

A. Foundation

The first part of this cumulative dissertation is divided into two distinct chapters. The first chapter (A.I) explains the motivation for this work and outlines the research gaps and questions as well as the structure, context, design, and anticipated contributions of this thesis. The second chapter (A.II) then provides the relevant theoretical background.

I. Introduction

The first section of this chapter (A.I.1) highlights the motivation for and relevance of the research conducted in this thesis. Then, the research gaps and questions (A.1.2) addressed in this work are presented, followed by an outline of the thesis' structure (A.I.3) as well as its research context and design (A.I.4). The last section (A.I.5) concludes this chapter with a description of the anticipated contributions to research and practice.

I.1 Motivation

> "*The primary role of the firm, and the essence of organizational capability, is the integration of knowledge.*" (Grant 1996a, p. 375)

According to the knowledge-based theory of the firm, the primary reason for a firm's existence is its superior ability to integrate knowledge from various sources for the purpose of creating goods and services (Grant 1996b). Even if this seems self-evident at first, the ability to integrate knowledge becomes particularly imperative when the existing knowledge base of established companies is devalued in times of disruptive technological change (Christensen 1997; Hill and Rothaermel 2003). To compensate for this loss, incumbent firms require the ability to identify and integrate valuable external knowledge (Cohen and Levinthal 1990). This ability, however, is shaped by past experiences and builds upon previously developed expertise (Sydow et al. 2009; Todorova and Durisin 2007), which is why it is primarily about improving the depth of knowledge in domains in which the established company is already active (Kranz et al. 2016). Consequently, it is challenging for incumbent firms to anticipate and embrace disruptive innovations, as they typically originate from distant and unrelated bodies of knowledge (Lane et al. 2006). Since this is especially the case in times of disruptive change driven by digital technologies, the ability of established companies to integrate new knowledge is required more than ever, not only to maintain their innovativeness, but more importantly, to ensure their survival (Lucas and Goh 2009).

Although technological disruption is typically accompanied by the need for incumbent firms to integrate external knowledge, the associated requirements become more demanding in the era of the digital revolution (Brynjolfsson and McAfee 2011, 2014). Here, apart from the transformative impact on our lives (Yoo 2010), pervasive digital technologies (Bharadwaj et al. 2013) are fundamentally reshaping knowledge integration in organizations that seek to exploit them (Yoo et al. 2010; Yoo et al. 2012). Driven by the force of digital innovation, defined as the creation of or change in market offerings resulting from the use of digital technology (Nambisan et al. 2017), product and industry boundaries are progressively dissolving, thus creating new requirements for firms to integrate increasingly diverse bodies of knowledge (Yoo et al. 2010). As a result, companies have to deal not only with a more dynamic process, but also with a growing diversity and amount of knowledge that needs to be integrated. These consequences stem from the unique nature of digital innovation, which is associated with two fundamental characteristics: *convergence* and *generativity* (Yoo et al. 2012).

On the one hand, the convergence created by pervasive digital technologies is bringing previously separate industries and market offerings together, as experienced in the smartphone industry, where diverse digital capabilities and services (e.g., mobile internet, photo cameras, third-party applications) were combined and integrated within a single device (Yoo et al. 2012). Consequently, as firms across industries increasingly incorporate digital technologies within their innovation processes and outcomes (Tilson et al. 2010; Tiwana et al. 2010), their need to integrate heterogeneous knowledge resources from various fields intensifies and affects their industrial organization (Lee and Berente 2012; Svahn et al. 2017). On the other hand, the need for firms to leverage diverse bodies of knowledge is amplified by the generative and distributed nature of digital innovation and the capacity of digital technology *"to produce unprompted change driven by large, varied, and uncoordinated audiences"* (Zittrain 2006, p. 1980). Based on fundamental characteristics such as *reprogrammability* and a *layered architecture* (Yoo et al. 2010), pervasive digital technologies not only have the capability to add new functions to products after they have been designed and produced (Yoo et al. 2012), they also enable external audiences (e.g., third-party developers) to access certain layers of the product and build complementary innovations (e.g., service applications) on those layers (Ghazawneh and Henfridsson 2013). Although this allows firms to diversify their offerings in an unprecedented way (Boudreau 2012), it further increases the heterogeneity and distributed nature of knowledge resources required to innovate (Yoo et al. 2012).

Consequently, both of these fundamental characteristics of digital innovation mean that "*even though all innovations require successful integration of heterogeneous knowledge, [...] digital technology intensifies the degree of heterogeneity and the need for dynamic balancing and integration of knowledge resources*" (Yoo et al. 2012, p. 1401). While these implications highlight the critical importance and the unique nature of knowledge integration in the context of digital innovation (Yoo et al. 2010; Yoo et al. 2012), the related consequences exacerbate the challenges that established companies face during disruptive technological change (Christensen 1997; Hill and Rothaermel 2003).

In response to the intensifying requirements for integrating knowledge from inside and outside the firm (Yoo et al. 2010; Yoo et al. 2012), recent research has shed some light on two different, though potentially intertwined, paths for incumbent organizations – one addressing the internal and the other the external context of the firm. First, to close knowledge and capability gaps that arise in the context of digital innovation (Henfridsson et al. 2009; Karimi and Walter 2015), affected firms can reconfigure and improve their existing knowledge base through, for example, the realignment of innovation structures and processes (Lee and Berente 2012; Svahn et al. 2017) or the integration of required knowledge through digital mergers and acquisitions (M&As) (Hanelt et al. 2020). Second, concerning the generativity enabled by digital technologies and the new opportunities for distributed innovations (Yoo et al. 2012), incumbent firms can decide to "open up" valuable assets (e.g., digital infrastructures, products, or data) via boundary resources, such as application programming interfaces (APIs), to stimulate outside innovation (Boudreau 2012; Parker et al. 2017). In this context, boundary resources are considered as a means or mechanism for leveraging the heterogeneous innovation capabilities and knowledge resources of outside contributors (Boland et al. 2007; Ghazawneh and Henfridsson 2013) and thus serve as a critical element for resource integration in digital business ecosystems (Eaton et al. 2015; Yoo et al. 2010).

However, despite several conceptual and empirical studies emphasizing the importance of knowledge-based perspectives (Hanelt et al. 2020; Kohli and Melville 2019; Lyytinen et al. 2016) and recognizing knowledge integration as a significant managerial challenge (Henfridsson and Yoo 2014; Piccinini et al. 2015; Svahn et al. 2017; Yoo 2010; Yoo et al. 2012), to date, no attempts have been made to systemize what we know about knowledge integration in information systems (IS) research and how its "*deeper dimensions and processes*" (Hanelt et al. 2020, p. 17) are related to the phenomenon of digital innovation. Similarly, although IS research has generated important qualitative insights into the design, managerial mechanisms, and structural implications of boundary resources in digital contexts (Eaton et al. 2015; Ghazawneh and Henfridsson 2013; Karhu et al. 2018), to date, the factors that drive their adoption and the outcomes of their utilization have not been studied in general, nor from a knowledge-based perspective.

Accordingly, this thesis strives to, first, explore the unique nature of knowledge integration in the context of digital innovation and, second, examine how incumbent firms can manage the associated challenges in their contexts. Consequently, this work aims to shed light on the deeper dimensions and processes of knowledge integration while highlighting those elements that are intertwined with digital innovation (Yoo et al. 2010; Yoo et al. 2012) to advance the understanding of how incumbent firms can dynamically integrate and leverage heterogeneous knowledge resources in the digital era (El Sawy and Pereira 2013; Yoo et al. 2010). With regard to this, the role of boundary resources is investigated in particular, as they enable incumbent firms to leverage knowledge from internal as well external sources in digital(izing) business ecosystems, and thus represent an essential mechanism for knowledge integration (Eaton et al. 2015; Ghazawneh and Henfridsson 2013). Consequently, as illustrated in

Figure A:1, this work relates knowledge integration and boundary resources to the phenomenon of digital innovation in incumbent firm contexts, and aspires to both contribute to specific gaps in IS research and derive important implications for business practice.

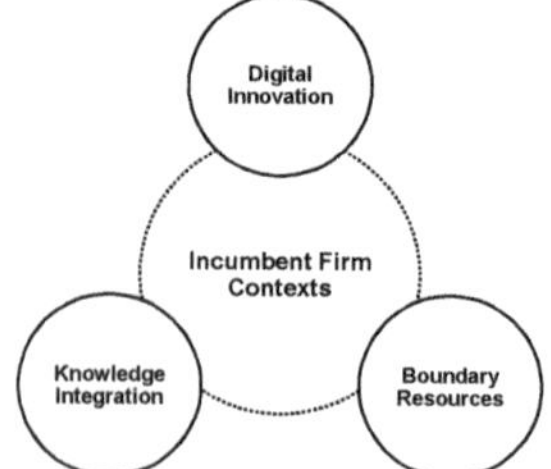

Figure A:1. Research Areas Addressed in the Thesis.

I.2 Research Gaps and Research Questions

As described previously, the essential characteristics of digital innovation have led to a fundamental change in the way and manner in which companies need to integrate and leverage knowledge in their digital(izing) contexts (El Sawy and Pereira 2013; Yoo et al. 2010). Therefore, this thesis intends to improve our understanding of knowledge integration by relating it to the phenomenon of digital innovation and, based on this, it aims to show how incumbent firms can manage the associated requirements and challenges in their digital(izing) business ecosystems. To achieve this, the thesis is divided into four fundamental research questions, which are illustrated in Figure A:2 and which will be outlined in the following.

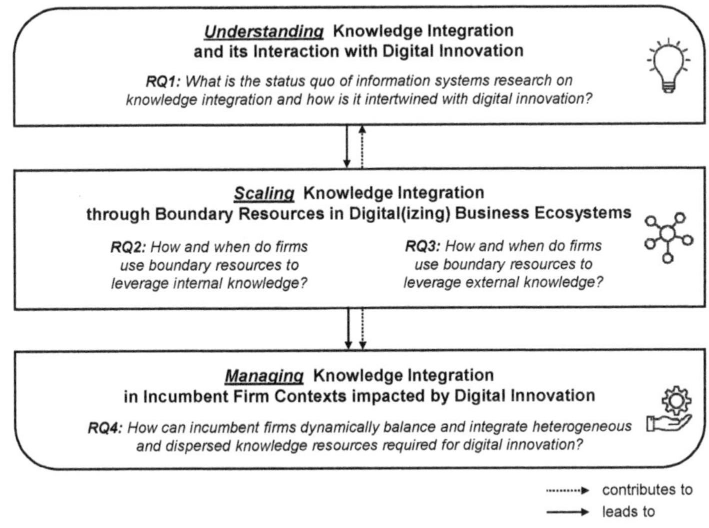

Figure A:2. Overview of the Research Questions.

As innovations that are based on pervasive digital technologies intensify the heterogeneity and need for the dynamic balancing and integration of knowledge resources (Yoo et al. 2012), recent works studying the phenomenon of digital innovation have increasingly adopted knowledge-based perspectives (e.g., Hanelt et al. 2020; Kohli and Melville 2019; Lyytinen et al. 2016). Here, the integration of increasingly heterogeneous bodies of knowledge across distributed disciplines, communities, and their different actors (Henfridsson et al. 2009; Yoo 2010) has been identified as a significant managerial challenge for organizations (Henfridsson and Yoo 2014; Piccinini et al. 2015; Svahn et al. 2017). Nevertheless, particularly the capability of identifying, integrating, and applying valuable knowledge from inside and outside the firm has been considered a fundamental prerequisite when organizations are trying to embrace digital innovation (Kohli and Melville 2019).

Even though the impact of digital innovation has brought the importance of knowledge integration back into focus, the topic is not entirely new to IS research. Previous studies have, for quite some time, examined diverse *determinants* (e.g., digital networks), *processes* (e.g., social interactions), and *outcomes* (e.g., project performance) of knowledge integration in various settings, such as software development or implementation (e.g., Alavi and Leidner 2001; Ejodame and Oshri 2018; Huang et al. 2001; Mehta and Bharadwaj 2015; Mitchell 2006; Robert et al. 2008). However, while a body of knowledge on the topic does exist, it has not been systematically analyzed and related to the recent digital innovation phenomenon. Consequently, this prevents both utilizing established knowledge to resolve current challenges and directing research toward important gaps in our understanding. Thus, it is necessary to explore the current state of IS research on knowledge integration with a particular focus on uncovering how it is intertwined with digital innovation. Accordingly, the following research question was posed:

> *RQ1: What is the status quo of information systems research on knowledge integration and how is it intertwined with digital innovation?*

As firms are increasingly embedded in digital(izing) business ecosystems, they are becoming more dependent on value co-creation and co-capture with heterogeneous and widely distributed players and thus need to reshape their enterprise boundaries (El Sawy and Pereira 2013; Yoo et al. 2012). In response to this, businesses across industries are reflecting on utilizing boundary resources to leverage internal and external knowledge in a manageable and controlled way (Ghazawneh and Henfridsson 2013; Yoo et al. 2010). In general, boundary resources, such as APIs, are considered as a crucial element for enabling resource sharing (Karhu et al. 2018) and facilitating resource integration among heterogeneous actors in digital business ecosystems (Eaton et al. 2015). To this end, depending on the firm's objectives, boundary resources can fulfill two different, partly interconnected objectives.

On the one hand, firms can decide to "open up" and deploy boundary resources to distribute their assets (e.g., digital infrastructures, products, or data) among external audiences (Ghazawneh and Henfridsson 2013; Karhu et al. 2018), which, in the broadest sense, corresponds to leveraging the knowledge that resides inside the firm. Here, firms can instantiate different boundary resources to separately open up assets to distinct target groups (Eisenmann et al. 2008). With regard to this, previous research particularly explored how boundary resources can establish different types of openness, such as controlled interaction with predefined assets (i.e., *access openness*) or less restricted utilization of more valuable core firm resources (i.e., *resource openness*) (Boudreau 2010; Karhu et al. 2018). According to the type of openness, external actors are able to utilize the shared resources either by reusing them in their business activities or by building complementary innovations upon them (Eaton et al. 2015; Parker and van Alstyne 2018).

On the other hand, in contrast to a firm's self-possession of valuable, rare, inimitable, and non-substitutable (VRIN) resources (Barney 1991) or IS capabilities (Bharadwaj 2000; Wade and Hulland 2004), companies can also utilize boundary resources as a channel to access and incorporate valuable assets or capabilities from external actors into their organizational environment (El Sawy and Pereira 2013; Karhu et al. 2018; Lavie 2006b), which, in the broadest sense, corresponds to leveraging knowledge that resides outside the firm. Thus, unlike prior phases that relied on more traditional IS artifacts (Saraf et al. 2007), boundary resources represent a new way for firms to leverage external assets in the context of digital innovation, where some organizational capabilities "*are created and controlled within the firm while others are garnered through the 'cloud'*" (Yoo et al. 2010, p. 732).

Although previous research has generated important qualitative insights into the design (e.g., Ghazawneh and Henfridsson 2013; Wulf and Blohm 2017), managerial mechanisms (e.g., Karhu et al. 2018; Parker et al. 2017; Parker and van Alstyne 2018), and structural implications (e.g., Eaton et al. 2015; Song et al. 2017; Um and Yoo 2016) of boundary resources in digital contexts, factors that drive their adoption and the outcomes of their utilization have not been examined in general, nor from a knowledge-based perspective. However, with the increasing importance and strategic value of boundary resources for knowledge integration, filling the gap in insights about which contextual conditions and influencing factors drive companies to adopt and leverage boundary resources effectively has become increasingly important (Yoo et al. 2010). Consequently, in accordance with the varying objectives of boundary resources, the following two distinct research questions were posed:

RQ2: How and when do firms use boundary resources to leverage internal knowledge?

RQ3: How and when do firms use boundary resources to leverage external knowledge?

Incumbent firms are limited by path dependency (Lane et al. 2006; Sydow et al. 2009) and inertia (Leonard-Barton 1992; Tripsas 2009) when responding to technological discontinuities, which can eventually lead to fateful outcomes (Lucas and Goh 2009). Nevertheless, by integrating new knowledge (Hanelt et al. 2020; Hill and Rothaermel 2003), incumbent firms can close existing capability gaps and leverage new opportunities from technological advancements to their benefit (Henfridsson et al. 2009; Karimi and Walter 2015). Yet, the task of integrating new knowledge, particularly in the digital age, has been highlighted as a significant managerial challenge (Henfridsson and Yoo 2014; Kohli and Melville 2019; Piccinini et al. 2015). This challenge is driven by the convergent and generative nature of digital innovation, which makes the process of knowledge integration more dynamic and increases the required diversity and quantity of knowledge that needs to be integrated (Yoo et al. 2012).

As pervasive digital technologies increasingly permeate the innovation processes and outcomes of organizations (Lee and Berente 2012; Svahn et al. 2017), incumbent firms across industries are forced to face and master the dynamic balancing and integration of increasingly heterogeneous and distributed knowledge resources required for digital innovation (Yoo et al. 2012). In this context, research has already identified different pathways that allow established companies to adapt and improve their existing knowledge base by not only integrating external knowledge to close existing capability gaps (e.g., Hanelt et al. 2020; Lyytinen et al. 2016), but also by leveraging internal and external knowledge via boundary resources in digital(izing) business ecosystems (e.g., Ghazawneh and Henfridsson 2013; Karhu et al. 2018). Nevertheless, despite these insights, we know little about exactly how incumbent firms deal with the intensifying requirements for knowledge integration when embracing digital innovation (Hanelt et al. 2020; Kohli and Melville 2019; Yoo et al. 2012). Therefore, to uncover the interplay of existing insights with those developed in this work, the concluding question is as follows:

> *RQ4: How can incumbent firms dynamically balance and integrate heterogeneous and dispersed knowledge resources required for digital innovation?*

I.3 Structure of the Thesis

This cumulative dissertation consists of three parts. Part A lays the foundation for this thesis by explaining the motivation (A.I.1) and delineating the research gaps and questions (A.I.2). Subsequently, the structure (A.I.3), research context and design (A.I.4), as well as the anticipated contributions (A.I.5) are presented. The next chapter (A.II) provides the theoretical background by delineating the importance of knowledge-based perspectives and the role of boundary resources for digital innovation in incumbent firm contexts.

Part B constitutes the central part of this dissertation and comprises four studies, each of which addresses specific aspects of knowledge integration for digital innovation in incumbent firm contexts (see Table A-1).

Table A-1. Overview of the Studies Included in the Thesis.

No.	Outlet	Status	Ranking (VHB)	Section	RQ	Main contribution
1	Information & Management	Submitted	B	B.I	1	Multi-dimensional framework comprised of determinants, processes, and outcomes of knowledge integration with focused implications for the context of digital innovation.
2	Journal of Strategic Information Systems	Under Review (2nd Round)	A	B.II	1, 2, 3, 4	Assessment of antecedents and performance effects of firms' boundary resources deployments and their role for leveraging internal and external knowledge in the context of digital innovation.
3	International Conference on Information Systems 2020	Published	A	B.II	1, 2, 3, 4	Assessment of antecedents and performance effects of firms' use of external boundary resources for improving organizational capabilities in the context of digital innovation.
4	European Conference on Information Systems 2020	Published (Best Paper Nominee)	B	B.III	4	Insights into contextual conditions, underlying mechanisms, and outcomes of managing knowledge integration for digital innovation in incumbent firm contexts.

Part C summarizes and synthesizes the results of this thesis. Thereby, the implications for research and practice are derived, followed by the limitations of this work as well as future research opportunities. Figure A:3 depicts the structure of this thesis.

A. Foundations

A.I Introduction

A.I.1 Motivation

A.I.2 Research Gaps and Questions

A.I.3 Structure of the Thesis

A.I.4 Research Context and Design

A.I.5 Anticipated Contributions

A.II Theoretical Background

A.II.1 Knowledge-based Perspectives and Digital Innovation

A.II.2 Digital(izing) Business Ecosystems and Boundary Resources

A.II.3 Pre-understanding of Knowledge Integration in Incumbent Firm Contexts

B. Studies on Digital Innovation in Incumbent Firm Contexts from a Knowledge Integration Perspective

B.I Understanding Knowledge Integration and its Interaction with Digital Innovation

RQ1: What is the status quo of information systems research on knowledge integration and how is it intertwined with digital innovation?

Study 1

B.II Scaling Knowledge Integration through Boundary Resources in Digital(izing) Business Ecosystems

RQ2: How and when do firms use boundary resources to leverage internal knowledge?

RQ3: How and when do firms use boundary resources to leverage external knowledge?

Study 2 | Study 3

B.III Managing Knowledge Integration in Incumbent Firm Contexts Impacted by Digital Innovation

RQ4: How can incumbent firms dynamically balance and integrate heterogeneous and dispersed knowledge resources required for digital innovation?

Study 4

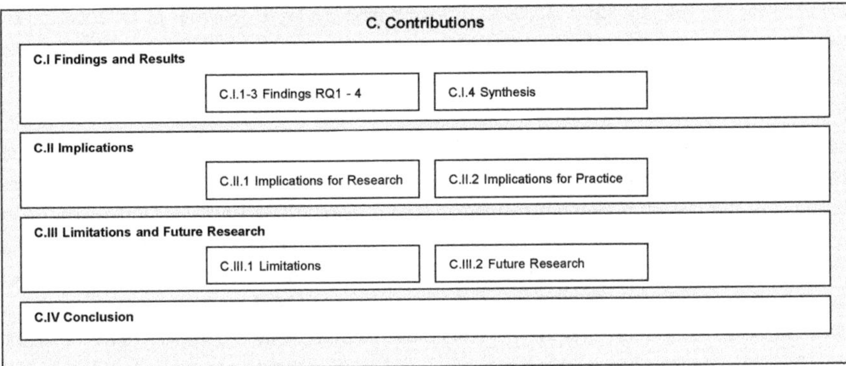

Figure A:3. Structure of the Thesis.

I.4 Research Context and Design

Research in the domain of IS aspires to generate and disseminate knowledge with the purpose of informing researchers and practitioners on "*how to understand, interpret, adapt to, and effectively manage technologies that have been and currently are in use, as well as emerging technologies whose impact are just being felt*" (Banker and Kauffman 2004, p. 294). Given its focus on the interaction between information technology (IT) and human organizations, the IS discipline is associated with the social sciences (Bhattacherjee 2012). The field of IS research, apart from being comparably young and interdisciplinary in nature (Gregor 2006), can be distinguished on the basis of paradigms (Hevner et al. 2004), epistemological stances (Orlikowski and Baroudi 1991), research streams (Banker and Kauffman 2004), applied methods, and theory types (Gregor 2006). In the following, by disclosing its underlying theoretical assumptions in line with the preceding aspects, this thesis will be positioned in IS research.

In terms of research paradigms, the IS discipline is characterized by two distinct approaches: *design science* and *behavioral science* (Hevner et al. 2004). Having its roots in engineering and the sciences of the artificial (Simon 1996), research in design science particularly aims at solving organizational problems in an efficient and effective manner by designing, implementing, and evaluating technology-oriented artifacts (Hevner et al. 2004). In contrast, the behavioral science paradigm descends from natural science research (March and Smith 1995) and aspires "*to develop and justify theories (i.e., principles and laws) that explain or predict organizational and human phenomena surrounding the analysis, design, implementation, management, and use of information systems*" (Hevner et al. 2004, p. 76). Since this thesis investigates the topic of knowledge integration in incumbent firm contexts that are impacted by digital innovation, it corresponds to the described objective of behavioral science and is thus primarily assigned to this research paradigm.

With respect to epistemology, which refers to "*the assessment and justification of knowledge claims*" (Wynn and Williams 2012, p. 788), IS research differentiates between three stances: *positivism*, *interpretivism*, and *critical realism* (see Gregor 2006). Positivist studies rely on the premise of existing "*a priori fixed relationships within phenomena*" (Orlikowski and Baroudi 1991, p. 5) and thus assume an objective reality, in which theories can be tested, confirmed, and falsified to increase the predictability of phenomena (Wynn and Williams 2012). In contrast, research with an interpretivist stance claims that reality is constructed by individuals and their social interactions (Walsham 1995) and thus can only be comprehended through the analysis of the meanings and actions of associated actors (Wynn and Williams 2012). Finally, studies following critical realism presume that "*general elements of an independent reality [...] exist, but our knowledge of specific structures and mechanisms is limited because of the difficulty of accessing them directly through the levels of stratification*" (Wynn and Williams 2012, p. 790). Accordingly, this thesis employs a positivist positioning, as it asserts the existence of an independent, objective reality. In doing so, it investigates the knowledge integration in incumbent firm contexts impacted by digital innovation from a neutral, observer-like position (Orlikowski and Baroudi 1991).

Considering research streams, Banker and Kauffman (2004) differentiate between five directions of research within the IS discipline. The first research stream, *decision support and design science,* deals with the design of decision support systems in conjunction with their human users or related business processes. The second research stream, the *value of information,* is focused on individual decision-makers and technologies in business process contexts, drawing on theories from, for instance, information economics. The third research field, *human-computer systems design,* examines user behavior in interaction with technological artifacts. The fourth research direction, *IS organization and strategy,* investigates diverse organizational and strategic phenomena in relation to IS across multiple levels by drawing upon theories, such as the resource-based view of the firm or technology acceptance models. The last research stream, the *economics of IS and IT*, similarly spans multiple levels of analysis and builds upon theories, such as game theory, which are related to the discipline of economics. Conclusively, according to Banker and Kauffman (2004), this thesis is closely related to the research stream of *IS organization and strategy*, as it explores how incumbent organizations can deal with the requirements and challenges associated with knowledge integration in the context of digital innovation.

Regarding the methodology, the thesis comprises four studies that investigate the topic of knowledge integration in the context of digital innovation by applying a mixed method design with both qualitative and quantitative studies, which is especially suitable for complex social phenomena (Bhattacherjee 2012). With regard to this, Table A-2 provides an overview of the research design as well as the applied methodologies, which were based on established approaches from seminal articles.

Table A-2. Overview of Research Design.

No	RQ	Epistemology	Paradigm	Methodology (Seminal work)	Data collection	Data analysis
1	1	Positivistic	Behavioral science	Systematic literature review (Crossan and Apaydin 2010; Webster and Watson 2002)	Literature review	Coding
2	1, 2, 3, 4	Positivistic	Behavioral science	Longitudinal panel data analysis (Ahuja and Katila, 2001)	Database retrieval, secondary data collection	Panel data regression
3	1, 2, 3, 4	Positivistic	Behavioral science	Longitudinal panel data analysis (Ahuja and Katila, 2001)	Database retrieval, secondary data collection	Panel data regression
4	4	Positivistic	Behavioral science	Grounded theory (Glaser and Strauss 1967)	Interviews	Coding

Furthermore, based on the distinction made by Gregor (2006), IS research can be differentiated between five types of theory: *analysis* ("says what is"), *explanation* ("says what is, how, why, when, and where"), *prediction* ("says what is and what will be"), *explanation and prediction* ("says what is, how, why, when, where, and what will be"), and *design and action* ("says how to do something"). Against this background, Study 1 of this thesis employs a classification based on the existing IS literature on the topic of knowledge integration and thus provides descriptive and analytical insights relating to a Type 1 Theory (i.e., a theory for analysis). However, by employing statistical analysis as well as grounded theory, the remaining studies aim at improving our understanding of the underlying causes and predictions regarding a firm's utilization of boundary resources (Studies 2 and 3) as well as describing the theoretical constructs and relationships of knowledge integration in incumbent firm contexts impacted by digital innovation, which relates them to a Type IV Theory (i.e., a theory for explaining and predicting). Finally, Table A-3 summarizes the positioning of this thesis in IS research with respect to the underlying paradigm (Hevner et al. 2004), epistemological stance (Orlikowski and Baroudi 1991), research stream (Banker and Kauffman 2004), applied methodology, and produced theory type (Gregor 2006).

Table A-3. Positioning of this Thesis in IS Research.

<table>
<tr><td>Epistemology</td><td colspan="2">Positivism</td><td colspan="2">Interpretivism</td><td>Critical Realism</td></tr>
<tr><td>Paradigm</td><td colspan="3">Behavioral Science</td><td colspan="2">Design Science</td></tr>
<tr><td>Theory Type</td><td>Analysis</td><td>Explanation</td><td>Prediction</td><td>Explanation and Prediction</td><td>Design and Action</td></tr>
<tr><td>Research Stream</td><td>Decision Support and Design Science</td><td>Value of Information</td><td>Human-Computer Systems Design</td><td>IS Organization and Strategy</td><td>Economics of IS and IT</td></tr>
<tr><td rowspan="2">Research Method</td><td>Case Study</td><td>Conceptual Model</td><td>Mathematical Model</td><td>Literature Analysis</td><td>Survey</td></tr>
<tr><td>Secondary Data</td><td>Design Science</td><td>Experimental Research</td><td>Interview</td><td>Content Analysis</td></tr>
</table>

I.5 Anticipated Contributions

This work intends to deliver valuable contributions to the IS research community spanning across three key research themes of (1) knowledge integration, (2) boundary resources, and (3) digital innovation and, correspondingly, to derive important implications for practitioners engaged in managing digital innovation in incumbent firm contexts.

Although the topic of knowledge integration has frequently been investigated by IS research (e.g., Huang et al. 2001; Mehta and Bharadwaj 2015; Mitchell 2006) and has become increasingly emphasized in recent studies (e.g., Hanelt et al. 2020; Yoo et al. 2012), to date, no attempt has been made to systematically synthesize what we know about it in relation to the recent digital innovation phenomenon. This prevents both the utilization of established insights to resolve current challenges and impedes directing research toward filling in important gaps in our understanding (Webster and Watson 2002). Therefore, this thesis aims to synthesize the current state of IS research and, in doing so, strives to advance our understanding of knowledge integration by providing an overview of the various theoretical conceptualizations, research streams, and underlying theories. In addition, by evaluating the existing body of knowledge, this work strives to identify the associated research gaps and derive opportunities for future studies. Furthermore, based on the systematic literature review and the development of a multi-dimensional framework (Crossan and Apaydin 2010), the thesis seeks to uncover the "*deeper dimensions and processes*" (Hanelt et al. 2020, p. 17) of knowledge integration while particularly highlighting those that are relevant for and intertwined with the recent digital innovation phenomenon.

Moreover, the work provides an important contribution to the evolving IS literature stream on the topic of boundary resources (Ghazawneh and Henfridsson 2013; Yoo et al. 2010). Building on the qualitative insights regarding the design (e.g., Ghazawneh and Henfridsson 2013), managerial mechanisms (e.g., Karhu et al. 2018), and structural implications (e.g., Eaton et al. 2015) of boundary resources, this thesis aims to shed light on the contextual factors that lead to the adoption and efficient use of specific types of boundary resources across industries. Thus, by highlighting the value of boundary resources in digital(izing) business ecosystems, this work improves our understanding of these resources as an integral part of strategic frameworks in the context of digital innovation (Yoo et al. 2010). Furthermore, the thesis contributes to research by conceptualizing how boundary resources can be used as a technological mechanism for leveraging internal and external knowledge, thus enabling incumbent firms to scale knowledge integration in digital(izing) contexts (Eaton et al. 2015; Yoo et al. 2010).

Since digital innovations merge previously separate industries (i.e., convergence) and increasingly enable others to innovate upon them (i.e., generativity), the dynamic balancing and integration of heterogeneous and distributed knowledge sources has been highlighted as a crucial prerequisite for succeeding in the digital era (Kohli and Melville 2019; Yoo et al. 2012). By following this assessment and responding to the calls for more research in this area (e.g., Hanelt et al. 2020; Piccinini et al. 2015; Yoo 2010), this work seeks to shed light on the specific interplay between contextual conditions, mechanisms, and outcomes of knowledge integration in incumbent firm contexts impacted by digital innovation. In particular, the focused investigation of boundary resources as a technological mechanism for leveraging internal and external knowledge (Eaton et al. 2015; Karhu et al. 2018) contributes to an improved understanding of the dynamic integration of knowledge resources in digital(izing) contexts (Yoo et al. 2010; Yoo et al. 2012). Furthermore, by addressing current research gaps related to the development and realization of digital capabilities (Grover et al. 2018; Loebbecke and Picot 2015), this work derives important insights into how boundary resources can be utilized by firms to close and overcome emerging capability gaps in the wake of digital innovation (Karhu et al. 2018; Karimi and Walter 2015; Yoo et al. 2010).

Finally, this work anticipates valuable contributions for business practitioners engaged in digital innovation activities within incumbent firms. The insights from this work provide managers with a ground-laying overview of the requirements for and mechanisms of knowledge integration that need to at least be considered when they are trying to cope with the challenges and exploit the opportunities of digital innovation. Furthermore, this work informs managers about the internal and external conditions that need to be in place to reap the benefits from the utilization of boundary resources in digital(izing) business ecosystems. In addition, the related insights particularly show how firms can use boundary resources as a technological mechanism to scale knowledge integration and not only stimulate outside innovation, but also close emerging gaps in their digital capabilities. In conclusion, this work helps managers navigate through the increasing complexity and dynamics of knowledge integration in the wake of digital innovation (Yoo et al. 2012) and thus improves their likelihood of success for current and future digital innovation efforts. Table A-4 summarizes the anticipated contributions.

Table A-4. Summary of Anticipated Contributions.

Audience		Anticipated Contribution
Information Systems Research	Knowledge Integration	(1) Overview of the status quo of IS research on the topic of knowledge integration. (2) Synthesis of the determinants and dimensions of knowledge integration within a multi-dimensional framework. (3) Insights into the interaction between knowledge integration and the context of digital innovation.
	Boundary Resources	(1) Improved understanding of boundary resources and their role for knowledge integration in digital(izing) business ecosystems. (2) Insights into the adoption and efficient utilization of boundary resources in digital(izing) business ecosystems.
	Digital Innovation	(1) Improved understanding of the dynamic balancing and integration of heterogeneous knowledge resources in incumbent firm contexts impacted by digital innovation. (2) Insights into building and realizing digital capabilities based on boundary resources in digital(izing) business ecosystems.
Business Practice	Incumbent Firm Manager	(1) Overview of the requirements for and mechanisms of knowledge integration in the context of digital innovation. (2) Insights into internal and external contingencies for effective deployment and utilization of boundary resources in digital(izing) business ecosystems. (3) Improved understanding of managing knowledge integration in incumbent firm contexts impacted by digital innovation.

II. Theoretical Background

As previously described, this cumulative thesis focuses on the investigation of knowledge integration in incumbent firm contexts impacted by digital innovation. To provide an overview of the basic concepts and current state of research relevant to this topic, this chapter presents the theoretical background and related research streams and develops a foundation upon which the individual studies in Part B can build to deliver deeper insights into the phenomena of interest. Consequently, this chapter focuses predominantly on conceptual works and related research streams while trying to minimize redundancies relating to the contents of the studies in Part B.

Accordingly, this chapter develops the theoretical foundation for this thesis by delineating the importance of knowledge-based perspectives for digital innovation in incumbent firms (II.1) and by outlining the role of boundary resources in digital(izing) business ecosystems (II.2). Finally, the theoretical background is synthesized to develop a pre-understanding of knowledge integration in incumbent firm contexts impacted by digital innovation (II.3).

II.1 Knowledge-based Perspectives and Their Importance for Digital Innovation in Incumbent Firms

The emergence of the knowledge-based theory of the firm (Grant 1996b; Nonaka and Takeuchi 1995; Spender 1996a) has directed the attention of researchers and practitioners toward knowledge as a distinctive organizational resource that is largely responsible for the long-term success of companies. Accordingly, by building upon and extending the resource-based view (Barney 1991; Penrose 1959; Wernerfelt 1984), the knowledge-based theory of a firm considers knowledge as the strategically most valuable resource for businesses (Grant 1996b; Spender 1996a). This conclusion is due to the fact that knowledge-based assets are usually difficult to imitate and are socially complex (Alavi and Leidner 2001) and thus possess the greatest potential out of all the firm's resources to generate long-term, sustainable competitive advantages (Coff et al. 2006).

Apart from underscoring the unique role and value of knowledge for organizations, the knowledge-based view reflects upon the firm as a "*dynamic, evolving, quasi-autonomous system of knowledge production and application*" (Spender 1996a, p. 59). In this context, the knowledge-based perspective particularly emphasizes that the firm's primary task is integrating knowledge from multiple streams for the creation of goods and services (Grant 1996b), with the literature differentiating in general between knowledge integration as a process and as an outcome. While the process relates to the activities through which individuals apply, share, combine, or generate knowledge, the outcomes of knowledge integration refer to the results of these activities (Grant 1996a, 1996b), as Okhuysen and Eisenhardt (2002) explain:

> "*The knowledge integration process involves the actions of group members by which they share their individual knowledge within the group and combine it to create new*

> *knowledge. By contrast, knowledge integration is the outcome of these processes, consisting of both the shared knowledge of individuals and the combined knowledge that emerges from their interactions.*" (p. 371)

Despite diverse perspectives, there are different terminologies to the concept of knowledge integration, with some research streams considering knowledge integration as, for example, "*knowledge combination*" (Kogut and Zander 1992) or "*knowledge configuration*" (Henderson and Clark 1990). In the course of this work, however, the focus lies on the commonly applied term of knowledge integration from the seminal work by Grant (1996a). Furthermore, to provide a theoretical basis and develop a pre-understanding for this concept, we consider knowledge integration in the following as the "*process of absorbing knowledge from external sources and blending it with the technical and business skills, know-how, and expertise in the [...] firm*" (Tiwana et al. 2003, p. 256). Unlike conceptualizing knowledge integration, defining the notion of knowledge is particularly challenging due to its complex and unique nature. Consequently, research has not only viewed knowledge differently (e.g., knowledge as a state of mind, object, process, or capability) (Huber 1991; Nonaka 1994; Zack 1998), but has also developed numerous taxonomies for its classification (e.g., tacit vs. explicit, individual vs. collective knowledge) (Grant 1996b; Polanyi 1962, 1967; Spender 1996a, 1996b). However, since the complex nature of knowledge is not in the focus of this thesis and an exact classification is not required, knowledge will be considered herein as an object or an asset that organizations and their employees use to perform tasks and to achieve objectives within the context of knowledge integration (Alavi and Leidner 2001).

The ability of organizations to integrate knowledge is particularly emphasized in research revolving around the impact of disruptive technological change on established companies (Christensen 1997; Hill and Rothaermel 2003; Lavie 2006a). As disruptive innovations typically emerge from distant and unrelated territories, the established knowledge base of incumbent firms usually loses its value (Kranz et al. 2016). As a consequence, the affected companies depend on integrating valuable external knowledge to meet the new technological requirements and changing market demands in their business, as Hill and Rothaermel (2003) illustrate:

> "*The advent of the ultrasound constituted a radical innovation in medical imaging technology. It stemmed from a knowledge base – dynamic continuous imaging based on an understanding of the physics of sound waves – that was novel to incumbent firms in the medical imaging industry, whose prior experience was with static imaging using X-rays.*" (p. 258)

Consequently, related research particularly emphasizes how incumbent firms need to develop so-called dynamic capabilities (Teece et al. 1997) for integrating and reconfiguring their internal and external knowledge to respond to environmental change (Mitchell 2006; Zollo 2002). In this context, research especially points toward an organization's absorptive capacity (Cohen and Levinthal 1990), which is considered to be a knowledge-based dynamic capability (Lane et al. 2006) and is defined as a firm's ability "*to identify, assimilate, transform and apply valuable external knowledge*" (Roberts et al. 2012, p. 625). However, as absorptive capacity is primarily shaped by past experiences and builds on prior knowledge (Lane et al. 2006), this capability is viewed as a double-edged sword (Kranz et al. 2016). Accordingly, although enabling the integration of external knowledge, absorptive capacity is usually closely linked to domains with which the incumbent firms are already familiar. Consequently, as disruptive innovations tend to originate from unrelated and distant bodies of knowledge, established companies are particularly challenged with identifying and integrating the required knowledge appropriately to anticipate market changes and avoid adverse consequences, such as those that resulted in the famous downfall of Kodak (Lucas and Goh 2009).

The challenges associated with knowledge integration have arisen once again for incumbent firms due to a new wave of technological discontinuity driven by ubiquitous and pervasive digital technologies (Bharadwaj et al. 2013; Yoo 2010), which are defined as "*combinations of information, computing, communication, and connectivity technologies*" (Bharadwaj et al. 2013, p. 471). These technologies are fundamentally reshaping the way organizations need to integrate knowledge (Yoo et al. 2012) and thus will be described in the following based on their unique characteristics and specific architecture. In terms of their characteristics, Yoo et al. (2010) attribute three particular traits to digital technologies: *reprogrammability*, *homogenization of data*, and *self-reference*. The first trait, reprogrammablity, stems from the "von Neumann" architecture, which comprises a processing unit and a storage unit, and which offers flexibility in the way data can be manipulated (Langlois 2007). Consequently, as the functional logic is separated from the physical embodiment, digital devices become reprogrammable and thus enable a wide array of digital functions (e.g., web browsing, video editing). The second trait, homogenization of data, refers to the mapping of analog signals into binary numbers (i.e., bits). As a result, all the data (e.g., text, audio, image, video) can be equally stored, processed, transferred, and displayed across digital devices and networks. Finally, the last trait, self-reference, means that digital innovation builds upon and requires digital technologies in a way that creates positive network externalities, thus further accelerating the development and diffusion of digital devices, networks, services, and contents (Benkler 2006; Hanseth and Lyytinen 2010). Based on these characteristics, digital technologies embody a layered architecture comprising four layers: the *device*, *network*, *service*, and *content layers*. While the first two are related to basic components and functions (e.g., computer hardware, operating system, networking capability), the last two are responsible for the application functionality (e.g., creating or processing content, storing data) of the digital device (Yoo et al. 2010). Due to the reprogrammability and layered architecture, it is therefore not only possible to adapt the functionalities of digital technologies even after their design and production, but also to access individual layers separately (based on standards and protocols) and to develop complementary innovations on those layers (Yoo et al. 2012). As a result, completely new opportunities arise for companies outside their traditional boundaries by leveraging the knowledge and innovation capabilities of external actors to further develop and improve their offerings. With regard to this, Yoo et al. (2012) explain:

> *"An illustrative example is smartphones with apps. In this case, the generativity is accomplished through the establishment of a platform, which enables innovations by third-party developers to be integrated into the platform after the fact."* (p. 1399)

Consequently, digital technologies create open and flexible affordances that result in innovations characterized by *convergence* and *generativity* (Yoo et al. 2012), which in turn impact organizational knowledge integration in two fundamental ways. First, digital technologies accelerate the development of convergent products, such as the smartphone, that bring previously separate user experiences (e.g., internet, phone, television) and functions (e.g., calculator, flashlight, camera) together into a single device (i.e., convergence). Thus, as digital technologies permeate market offerings and their respective industries (Bharadwaj et al. 2013), companies have to integrate increasingly heterogeneous knowledge from other unrelated contexts and domains (Yoo et al. 2012). The second important impact on knowledge integration arises from a digital technology's capacity "*to produce unprompted change driven by large, varied, and uncoordinated audiences*" (Zittrain 2006, p. 1980). As illustrated in the example above, the layered architecture of digital technologies enables companies to provide external actors (e.g., third-party developers) access to individual layers of products (e.g., the service or content layers) to develop complementary innovations on those layers (i.e., generativity). Conclusively, the impact of digital innovation, defined as "*the creation of (and consequent change in) market offerings, business processes, or models that result from the use of digital technology*" (Nambisan et al. 2017, p. 224), leads to new requirements for companies to integrate knowledge not only with greater quantity and diversity, but also in a more dynamic way across the firm's boundaries (Yoo et al. 2012).

Even though knowledge integration currently receives more attention and importance in relation to the recent digital innovation phenomenon, the topic itself is not new to IS research. Prior works have developed numerous insights into the interaction and interdependencies between IT and knowledge integration processes and outcomes (e.g., Alavi and Leidner 2001; Huang et al. 2001; Mitchell 2006). Here, the impact of knowledge integration in IT contexts, such as software development, as well as the influence of IT on knowledge integration itself have been studied in IS research. In terms of how knowledge integration influences IT contexts, for instance, Mitchell (2006) investigated the impact of the integrative capabilities of managers (i.e., their ability to access external knowledge and integrate internal knowledge) on the performance of enterprise application integration (EAI) projects. Based on their longitudinal study of 74 EAI projects, they found that the integrative capability of IT managers reduced the duration of IT-related project delays significantly and thus promoted project completion. In another study, Mehta and Bharadwaj (2015) examined the role of sentry and guard processes (i.e., managing the inflow and outflow of information) for team members' knowledge integration in outsourced software development projects. Stemming from their analysis of 139 vendor development teams, they came to the conclusion that, depending on the degree of uncertainty, the calibration of sentry and guard processes could improve knowledge integration and thus overall team performance. Regarding the impact of IT on knowledge integration, for example, Alavi and Leidner (2001) discuss in their theoretical review of IS research related to knowledge management and knowledge management systems (KMS) how diverse IT applications (e.g., workflow automation systems) can enhance knowledge integration in multiple ways within organizations. Respectively, Alavi and Leidner (2001) outline that:

> "*Information technologies allow for organizational knowledge to be applied across time and space. IT can also enhance the speed of knowledge integration and application by codifying and automating organizational routines. Workflow automation systems are examples of IT applications that reduce the need for communication and coordination and enable more efficient use of organizational routines through timely and automatic routing of work-related documents, information, rules, and activities. Rule based expert systems are another means of capturing and enforcing well specified organizational procedures.*" (p. 122)

In another study, apart from theoretical considerations, Robert et al. (2008) investigated how digital networks interact with different dimensions of social capital (i.e., structural, relational, and cognitive) and how this affects knowledge integration and team performance. Based on the investigation of 46 digitally enabled teams, their results indicated that teams that communicated through digital networks relied more on structural and cognitive capital (i.e., patterns of interaction among team members and shared understanding) to improve knowledge integration and achieve a certain quality of team decision-making. In sum, IS research has studied knowledge integration from varying perspectives (e.g., individual vs. collective knowledge integration), in different contexts (e.g., EAI projects), in relation to IT artifacts (e.g., KMSs), and in terms of its outcomes (e.g., team or project performance). More recent studies, however, particularly point toward new digital technologies, such as digital platforms (Tiwana et al. 2010; Yoo et al. 2012) and boundary resources (Eaton et al. 2015; Foerderer et al. 2019), and their role in knowledge integration in the context of digital innovation. Here, boundary resources in particular are highlighted as a new means for resource sharing and integration in digital(izing) contexts (Eaton et al. 2015; Ghazawneh and Henfridsson 2013). Accordingly, firms that decide to "open up" their digital products via boundary resources allow external actors to access, reuse, and eventually innovate upon them. Consequently, as this enables firms to tap into the heterogeneous knowledge and innovation capabilities of external actors, boundary resources serve as a new technological mechanism for knowledge integration in the context of digital innovation (Eaton et al. 2015; Karhu et al. 2018).

Yet, apart from isolated references related to digital technologies (e.g., digital platforms, boundary resources), most of the IS research on knowledge integration comes from pre-digital times. Nevertheless, recent studies with a focus on the phenomenon of digital innovation increasingly employ knowledge-based perspectives and re-emphasize the importance of knowledge integration in the digital age (e.g., Hanelt et al. 2020; Kohli and Melville 2019; Yoo et al. 2012). In addition, several works confirmed that the increasing diversity and amount of knowledge that needs to be dynamically integrated in the context of digital innovation poses significant managerial challenges, especially for established companies (Lyytinen et al. 2016; Piccinini et al. 2015; Svahn et al. 2017). In this regard, Hanelt et al. (2020) particularly emphasize that the "*deeper dimensions and processes of knowledge integration*" (p. 17) are still unclear. However, as the convergent and generative nature of digital innovation increasingly permeates organizations across contexts (Bharadwaj et al. 2013; El Sawy and Pereira 2013), IS scholars agree that knowledge integration represents an integral part of succeeding in the digital age (Kohli and Melville 2019; Yoo et al. 2012).

II.2 Digital(izing) Business Ecosystems and the Role of Boundary Resources

With the increasing adoption and diffusion of pervasive digital technologies accompanied by the emergence of flexible and scalable digital infrastructures (Tilson et al. 2010), companies across contexts have become increasingly digital and interconnected in terms of products, processes, and services (Yoo et al. 2012). Accordingly, as industry and product boundaries are changing, firms are facing new competitive and cooperative dynamics (Yoo et al. 2010). As a result, organizations are not only forced to adjust their strategies (Bharadwaj et al. 2013), business processes (Lyytinen et al. 2016), organizational capabilities (Kohli and Melville 2019), and products (Yoo et al. 2010), but are also becoming increasingly embedded in digital(izing) business ecosystems, which can be defined as a "*collective of firms that is inter-linked by a common interest in the prosperity of a digital technology*" (Selander et al. 2013, p. 184). These digital(izing) business ecosystems, however, are driven by the generative and distributed nature of digital innovation and making firms increasingly dependent on value co-creation and co-capture with heterogeneous and distributed actors (El Sawy and Pereira 2013; Yoo et al. 2012).

In response to this, companies are increasingly incorporating digital technologies into their offerings to enhance them with new digital capabilities that have the potential to stimulate the development of complementary and combinatorial innovations (Yoo et al. 2012). While the former relates to complementary products or services (e.g., applications), the latter refers to the development of new offerings based on the recombination and connection of existing modules with digital capabilities (Yoo et al. 2010; Yoo et al. 2012). Hence, as firms decide to allow external actors access to certain layers of their digitally enhanced products, new opportunities for distributed and combinatorial innovation emerge. With regard to this, Yoo et al. (2012) illustrate:

> "*When Google Maps API was first introduced, for example, the designers at Google did not know that it would be combined with thousands of location-based databases to create so-called 'mash-ups'*" (p. 1402)

Thus, as the locus of innovation shifts toward the periphery of organizations, embracing digital innovation increasingly requires the enabling of others to innovate (Yoo et al. 2012). Especially in digital(izing) business ecosystems, leveraging the firm's own knowledge base and the external knowledge and innovation capabilities of distributed partners is considered to be mandatory for innovation and growth (Boudreau 2012; Gawer and Cusumano 2014). Therefore, companies utilize the help of external participants and contributors to scale and diversify their offerings over a broad range of application areas (Boudreau 2012; Parker et al. 2017). To achieve this, firms must "open up" by allowing external actors access to valuable assets or infrastructures (Boudreau 2010; Parker and van Alstyne 2018; Yoo et al. 2010). Opening up, however, is particularly challenging for established companies, as they usually want to protect their knowledge and resource base from external access and exploitation (Karhu et al. 2018; Yoo et al. 2010). Consequently, the incumbent firm's need to share resources in digital(izing) business ecosystems goes hand in hand with the need to control them (Ghazawneh and Henfridsson 2013). This results in a managerial tension between openness and control that established companies try to solve in the context of digital innovation (Eaton et al. 2015; Karhu et al. 2018). One possible strategy for resolving this tension resides in the utilization of boundary resources, which are viewed in IS research as a means or mechanism for "*resourcing and controlling external contributions*" (Karhu et al. 2018, p. 482). In practice, this refers to "*the development of novel technological resources such as open data, APIs, and SDKs [that] are simultaneously intertwined with certain social norms, organizational principles, and role divisions*" (Yoo et al. 2012, p. 1402). Thus, according to their definition, boundary resources serve two distinct purposes: On the one hand, they are enabling participation and contributions from external parties, stimulating the development of complementary or combinatorial applications (Boudreau 2012; Gawer 2014; Ghazawneh and Henfridsson 2013). On the other hand, they also represent control points (Pagani 2013) through which focal companies determine what is allowed and how value is created and captured (Karhu et al. 2018; Tilson et al. 2010; Tilson et al. 2012). Consequently, the use of boundary resources can be viewed as an intermediary strategy for triggering innovation by multiple and dispersed third-party developers in a manageable and controlled manner (Ghazawneh and Henfridsson 2013).

Despite being considered an important topic in the general debate on openness vs. control in digital business ecosystems (Ghazawneh and Henfridsson 2013; Tilson et al. 2010), boundary resources have also been examined by IS research in terms of their varying purposes. For example, depending on the firm's requirements and objectives, boundary resources can be designed and instantiated to separately open up varying assets to distinct participating and contributing groups (Eisenmann et al. 2008). Furthermore, companies can also establish different forms of openness via boundary resources by either relaxing or tightening the restrictions associated with the use of the assets made available through them (Eaton et al. 2015). Accordingly, companies can design boundary resources in such a way that they, on the one hand, strongly regulate the use of valuable core resources and, on the other hand, simplify access to less valuable ones (Boudreau 2010; Karhu et al. 2018). As a result, external participants and complementors can utilize the firm's assets provided through boundary resources either by reusing them in their own business activities or by building complementary or combinatorial innovations upon them (Eaton et al. 2015; Parker and van Alstyne 2018). Consequently, with the utilization of boundary resources, companies are defining their openness and facilitating complementors' work (Karhu et al. 2018).

Apart from making resources available to outside participants and contributors (Ghazawneh and Henfridsson 2013), firms can also be on the user side of boundary resources and, for example, integrate the capabilities of external players into their own internal environment or operations (Karhu et al. 2018; Yoo et al. 2010). Compared to prior phases that were dependent on more traditional IS artifacts (Saraf et al. 2007), boundary resources are considered a more ready-to-use infrastructure for accessing external resources in the context of digital innovation (Yoo et al. 2012). Thus, in contrast to a firm's self-possession of valuable, rare, inimitable, and non-substitutable (VRIN) resources (Barney 1991) or IS capabilities (Bharadwaj 2000; Wade and Hulland 2004), boundary resources represent a new channel for leveraging valuable assets from external players in networked settings (Karhu et al. 2018; Lavie 2006b). This is particularly important in digital(izing) business ecosystems (Eaton et al. 2015; Selander et al. 2013), where complex and dynamic developments are challenging companies to close capability gaps faster than ever to adapt to rapidly changing market demands (El Sawy et al. 2010; Karimi and Walter 2015). For instance, Johnson Controls' facility management division developed a smart thermostat that integrates the digital capabilities from Google's and Amazon's voice assistants to meet recent customer demands (Johnson Controls 2021). With regard to this, Yoo et al. (2010) emphasize that some digital capabilities that companies require in the context of digital innovation *"are created and controlled within the firm while others are garnered through the 'cloud'"* (p. 732).

In summary, the evolving IS literature stream has already generated valuable qualitative insights for the design (e.g., Ghazawneh and Henfridsson 2013), managerial mechanisms (e.g., Karhu et al. 2018), and structural implications (e.g., Eaton et al. 2015) of boundary resources. Accordingly, boundary resources enable companies not only to leverage their own knowledge by distributing their assets and stimulating innovation among external audiences (Ghazawneh and Henfridsson 2013), but also to leverage external knowledge (e.g., digital capabilities) from other players to quickly close capability deficits and respond to changing business requirements (Karimi and Walter 2015; Selander et al. 2013; Yoo et al. 2010). Thus, boundary resources represent a key element for organizing and integrating knowledge resources in digital(izing) business ecosystems (Eaton et al. 2015) and can be considered a new technological mechanism for scaling knowledge integration across the boundaries of the firm. Consequently, as knowledge integration becomes increasingly complex and dynamic, especially in incumbent firm contexts impacted by digital innovation, the strategic relevance and importance of boundary resources continues to increase for both research and practice (Yoo et al. 2010; Yoo et al. 2012).

II.3 Pre-understanding of Knowledge Integration in Incumbent Firms Impacted by Digital Innovation

Building on the previously described background, it is clear that even though the topic of knowledge integration is particularly relevant for incumbent firms affected by disruptive change, it is gaining even more importance in the context of digital innovation. Here, due to the convergent and generative nature of digital innovation, the scope and scale of knowledge that needs to be dynamically integrated by incumbent firms is increasing considerably (Yoo et al. 2012). In this context, previous research provides initial guidance based on established perspectives, such as the knowledge-based theory of the firm (Grant 1996b; Nonaka and Takeuchi 1995; Spender 1996a), which outlines and emphasizes the importance of knowledge integration for businesses in general (Grant 1996a), as well as in times of disruptive technological change (Hill and Rothaermel 2003; Kranz et al. 2016). In addition, IS research provides specific insights into individual determinants and dimensions of knowledge integration in IT contexts (e.g., Alavi and Leidner 2001; Mitchell 2006). However, most of these findings have been generated in pre-digital times. Therefore, with the increasing importance of current phenomena in the context of digital innovation, attention has once again been drawn to the topic of knowledge integration, as incumbent firms are particularly dependent on it in times of disruptive change driven by digital technologies. To this end, emerging studies provide conceptual evidence for the interdependency of digital innovation and knowledge integration (e.g., Kohli and Melville 2019; Yoo et al. 2012), the associated managerial challenges (e.g., Piccinini et al. 2015; Svahn et al. 2017), and approaches to solve them (e.g., Hanelt et al. 2015; Lyytinen et al. 2016). However, to comprehensively understand the complexity and central components of knowledge integration, it is necessary to initially synthesize the already existing knowledge in the research field of IS and connect it with the recent digital innovation phenomenon.

Furthermore, as incumbent firms become increasingly embedded in digital(izing) business ecosystems (Bharadwaj et al. 2013; Selander et al. 2013; Tilson et al. 2010), research emphasizes the strategic role and value of boundary resources as a new mechanism for resource sharing (Ghazawneh and Henfridsson 2013) and integration (Eaton et al. 2015) among increasingly heterogeneous and distributed players (El Sawy and Pereira 2013). In this context, boundary resources not only enable leveraging internal knowledge by distributing the firm's assets to outside participants and contributors (Eaton et al. 2015; Ghazawneh and Henfridsson 2013), but they also facilitate leveraging external knowledge by integrating knowledge-based and digital capabilities from external partners into the firm's internal context and operations (Selander et al. 2013; Yoo et al. 2010). Thus, boundary resources serve as a crucial element for organizing and integrating heterogeneous knowledge and innovation capabilities in digital(izing) business ecosystems (Karhu et al. 2018; Yoo et al. 2010). However, although research has already found valuable insights into the design (e.g., Ghazawneh and Henfridsson 2013), managerial mechanisms (e.g., Karhu et al. 2018), and structural implications (e.g., Eaton et al. 2015) of boundary resources, there are relevant gaps about the conditions under which companies can utilize boundary resources beneficially, both from the provider and the user side. Accordingly, since boundary resources can be considered an important mechanism for knowledge integration, it is necessary to address these gaps, especially from a knowledge-based perspective.

Finally, emerging studies accentuate the increasing importance of and requirements for knowledge integration in the context of digital innovation (e.g., Kohli and Melville 2019; Yoo et al. 2012) while simultaneously highlighting the significance of the associated managerial challenges (e.g., Lyytinen et al. 2016; Piccinini et al. 2015). However, even though initial approaches suggest how knowledge integration can help to master digital innovation, there are still relevant gaps in terms of its "*deeper dimensions and processes*" (Hanelt et al. 2020,

p. 17), which are particularly relevant for incumbent firms. Therefore, to better understand the unique nature of knowledge integration in incumbent firm contexts impacted by digital innovation, the existing knowledge base needs to be synthesized and complemented by explorative in-depth insights. Accordingly, the development of an updated perspective on knowledge integration allows for both solutions to be provided to managerial challenges in practice and for future research to be guided toward improving our understanding of this, though elusive, highly relevant topic.

Figure A:4 summarizes the theoretical foundations and illustrates the relevant concepts and primary interactions that were described in the section above and will be investigated in the course of this thesis.

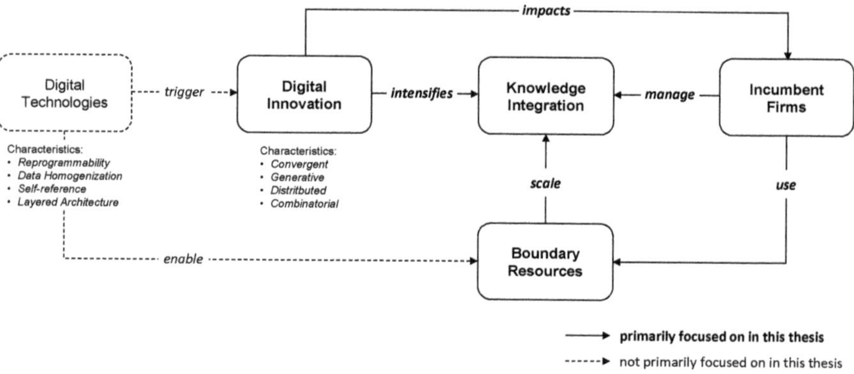

Figure A:4. Conceptual Overview of the Theoretical Foundation.

B. Studies on Digital Innovation in Incumbent Firm Contexts from a Knowledge Integration Perspective

As described in Part A, this cumulative dissertation aims to improve our understanding of how knowledge integration needs to be managed by incumbent firms in the context of digital innovation. To address this overall research goal, four distinctive questions were derived and will be answered in the four studies included in Chapters I, II, and III of Part B.

The first Chapter (B.I) contains Study 1, which, based on the systematic literature review, systemizes the existing insights in IS research on knowledge integration and examines them with respect to the recent digital innovation phenomenon. This answers RQ1 regarding the status quo of IS research on knowledge integration and its interaction with digital innovation.

Subsequently, the second Chapter (B.II) comprises Studies 2 and 3, which provide detailed insights into how companies can utilize boundary resources to leverage internal and external knowledge and, thus, allow them to scale knowledge integration in digital(izing) business ecosystems. Furthermore, the studies also provide insights into the conditions under which boundary resources can be successfully utilized – both from the provider and user side. Therefore, this chapter answers RQ2 and RQ3. In addition, Studies 2 and 3 provide complementary insights to RQ1 and RQ4, which will be presented in Part C of this thesis.

Finally, the third Chapter B.III contains Study 4, which builds on and extends the results from the previous studies by delivering in-depth insights into how incumbent firms can dynamically balance and integrate increasingly heterogeneous and dispersed knowledge in the context of digital innovation. Thus, it provides answers to RQ4.

The studies included in this thesis were adjusted to a small degree where necessary to ensure a consistent layout.

I. Understanding Knowledge Integration and Its Interaction with Digital Innovation

Since this thesis aims to investigate knowledge integration in incumbent firm contexts that have been impacted by digital innovation, the existing knowledge base must first be reviewed with regard to aspects relevant to this topic. Here, even though research increasingly emphasizes the importance of knowledge integration in the context of digital innovation, the field has not yet been systematically reviewed for already existing and relevant insights (Yoo 2010; Yoo et al. 2012).

Thus, to close this gap, Study 1 involves a systematic literature review (Webster and Watson 2002) of the IS research on the topic of knowledge integration. Furthermore, building upon the approach by Crossan and Apaydin (2010), the study derives a multi-dimensional framework that organizes the existing findings according to the determinants and dimensions of knowledge integration to highlight those elements that are particularly relevant for the context of digital innovation.

1 Study 1: Knowledge Integration and Digital Innovation – Towards a Multi-Dimensional Framework

Table B-1. Fact Sheet of Study No. 1.

Title	Knowledge Integration and Digital Innovation – Towards a Multi-Dimensional Framework
Authors	Patryk Zapadka*, Lutz M. Kolbe Chair of Information Management, University of Goettingen, Platz der Göttinger Sieben 5, 37073 Göttingen *Corresponding author. Tel.: +49 551 3924440. E-mail address: patryk.zapadka@stud.uni-goettingen.de
Outlet	Information & Management
Abstract	The generative and convergent nature of innovations building upon pervasive digital technologies increases the heterogeneity of required knowledge resources. Therefore, firms that embrace digital innovation are obliged to identify and integrate valuable knowledge across distributed disciplines and communities held by diverse actors. Consequently, knowledge as a firm's most valuable resource has recently gained more attention in information systems (IS) research on digital innovation. This paper consolidates the state of IS research on the specific topic of knowledge integration. By employing a systematic review of literature published in leading journals, theoretical foundations are synthesized into a comprehensive multi-dimensional framework of knowledge integration in the digital era – linking knowledge integration determinants and dimensions. Furthermore, this study provides conceptual approaches towards knowledge integration and derives implications for both research and managerial practice.
Keywords	Knowledge integration, knowledge management, digital innovation, literature review, multi-dimensional framework

1.1 Introduction

"Even though all innovations require successful integration of heterogeneous knowledge [...], the convergence of pervasive digital technology intensifies the degree of heterogeneity and the need for dynamic balancing and integration of knowledge resources" (Yoo et al. 2012).

This opening quote by Yoo et al. (2012) underscores both the critical importance as well as the unique nature of knowledge integration when it comes to digital innovation. Besides conceptual works (e.g., Yoo 2010), recent empirical studies have pointed to the value of knowledge integration for digital innovation success (Hanelt et al. 2020; Zapadka 2020). Albeit these insights, to date, no attempt has been made to systemize what we know about knowledge integration and relate this wisdom to the current phenomenon of digital innovation in order to progress theoretically and give informed guidance to managerial practice.

Recent works on the topic of digital innovation (i.e., creations of or changes in market offerings that result from the use of digital technologies (Nambisan et al. 2017) have emphasized the importance of knowledge-based perspectives (e.g., Hanelt et al. 2020; Kohli and Melville 2019; Lyytinen et al. 2016). Accordingly, the identification, assimilation and application of valuable knowledge from inside and outside the firm is seen as a fundamental requirement when embracing digital innovation (Kohli and Melville 2019). In this context, integrating knowledge from inside and outside the firm has been defined as "*the process of absorbing knowledge from external sources and blending it with the technical and business skills, know-how, and expertise that reside in the business and IS units of a firm*" (Tiwana et al. 2003). This process of knowledge integration is particularly important as to the generative and convergent nature of innovations building upon digital technologies. Since digital innovations tend to merge previously separate industries (i.e., convergence) and enable others to innovate upon them (i.e., generativity) (Yoo et al. 2010; Yoo et al. 2012), the dynamic integration and balancing of heterogeneous knowledge sources is considered as an integral part of succeeding in the digital era (Lyytinen et al. 2016; Yoo et al. 2012; Zapadka 2020).

However, integrating increasingly heterogeneous and distributed bodies of knowledge from inside and outside the firm has been recognized as a significant managerial challenge for organizations (Henfridsson and Yoo 2014; Piccinini et al. 2015; Svahn et al. 2017) and is particularly emphasized by Yoo (2010) in his call for research to investigate "*how do organizations manage the heterogeneity of required knowledge resources in producing new products and services.*" Furthermore, the crucial role of knowledge and its management is highlighted by recent IS studies and claimed as critically important for achieving digital innovation outcomes. For instance, Kohli and Melville (2019) particularly emphasize that organizations need to develop new managerial capabilities to learn, apply, and creatively recombine knowledge in order to generate digital innovation outcomes.

While digital innovation gives new impetus to the focus on knowledge integration, the topic itself is not new. Prior IS research has been investigating knowledge integration for quite a long time (e.g., Alavi and Leidner 2001; Huang et al. 2001; Mitchell 2006; Newell et al. 2000).

While a body of knowledge on the topic exists, it has not been systematically analyzed with regard to recent phenomena of digital innovation. This current state prevents both utilizing established insights to resolve present challenges and directing research to important gaps in our understanding.

In this paper, we respond to this research opportunity by conducting a systematic literature review to explore and synthesize the current state of insights on the process of knowledge integration and its outcomes in IS research. Therefore, we have searched and collected 56 articles from leading journals in IS research, i.e., the AIS Senior Scholars' Basket of Journals, and developed a multi-dimensional framework comprising determinants and dimensions of knowledge integration. As a result, this study contributes to the literature on knowledge management in the IS discipline and derives conceptual insights for the management of digital innovation in organizations (Kohli and Melville 2019; Svahn et al. 2017; Yoo 2010; Yoo et al. 2012). For this purpose, the paper is structured as follows: First, the design of the literature review will be described. Second, the diverse definitions and conceptualizations of knowledge integration will be presented. Then, building upon the approach by Crossan and Apaydin (2010) and their literature synthesis on the topic of organizational innovation, a multi-dimensional framework consisting of determinants and dimensions of knowledge integration will be derived. Afterwards, contributions and limitations of this study will be discussed. The paper concludes with avenues for future research.

1.2 Design of Literature Review

We followed the guidelines of Webster and Watson (2002) to conduct a concept-centric literature review. A review itself does not present new results, rather describes, summarizes, assesses or integrates previous research insights to the topic of interest. In order to develop a multi-dimensional framework of knowledge integration, it is necessary to analyze and synthesize relevant literature (Levy and Ellis 2006; Webster and Watson 2002). We limited our systematic literature review to knowledge integration in the IS discipline. To examine the current state of research on knowledge integration processes and outcomes, we conducted an in-depth topic-based review following the principles of Webster and Watson (2002). They suggest a three steps approach to orderly identify relevant literature. The following list outlines the respective steps:

1. Start in leading journals, as major contributions are likely to be found there.
2. Backward search citations for the articles identified in step (1).
3. Forward search articles, that cites the key articles identified in the previous two steps.

Following the first principle of Webster and Watson (2002) and considering the identified area of interest, we focused our selection on leading outlets in IS research, i.e., the AIS Senior Scholars' Basket of Journals. Then, we prepared keywords regarding our topic to identify relevant knowledge integration literature. We used 'wildcards', marked with an asterisk *, to automatically alter keywords. This resulted in three keyword groups: (1) "integration of knowledge", (2) "integrat* knowledge", and (3) "knowledge integrat*." By using the wildcards, the database search engines automatically altered integrat* to integrating, integrate and so forth. Table B-2 illustrates the search results in the corresponding outlets and databases.

Table B-2. Article Results by Journals.

Outlet	Vendor database	Hits	Selected
ISR	InformsPubsOnLine	18	11
MISQ	JSTOR	34	7
JMIS	EbscoHost	6	5
JAIS	AIS eLibrary	11	5
JIT	ProQuest	17	4
ISJ	WileyOnlineLibrary	11	5
JSIS	ScienceDirect	11	8
EJIS	ProQuest	35	7
Sum		**143**	**52**

Forward- and backward search	4
Total	**56**

After collecting the identified literature, we reviewed the articles manually and filtered them according to an iterative set of exclusion criteria (e.g., relevant title, abstract, or content). Articles that included any theoretical conceptualizations, definitions, or considerations of and were related to knowledge integration were considered as relevant. Articles that did not address or evaluated any aspects of knowledge integration were excluded. Consequently, we eliminated 91 articles, which resulted in 52 relevant articles. Once we had the set of 52 relevant articles, we again followed Webster and Watson's (2002) principles on backward and forward search. Initially, we scanned cited literature based on titles, followed by abstract. This procedure added 4 articles, which resulted in a final sample of 56 relevant articles.

In the next step, each researcher coded the final sample of articles independently according the following pre-defined concepts:

- *Determinants:* Individual, organizational, and technological elements that influence knowledge integration processes and outcomes.
- *Processes:* Dimensions and characteristics of knowledge integration processes.
- *Outcomes:* Dimensions and characteristics of knowledge integration outcomes.

After initially coding the articles independently, both researchers discussed their outcomes and consolidated their results.

1.3 Findings

This paper will review the 56 studies we selected in our literature research and synthesize their content, theoretical implications, similarities, differences, and their overall contributions towards the topic of knowledge integration. Building upon the approach by Crossan and Apaydin (2010) and their synthesis of literature on organizational innovation, we similarly develop a multi-dimensional framework by evaluating determinants and dimensions of knowledge integration in the collected body of literature. Consequently, we identified a multitude of determinants and dimensions of knowledge integration processes and outcomes. Further, we matched and categorized the identified determinants and dimensions of knowledge integration. In the following, we will briefly show descriptive results and findings on theoretical conceptualizations of knowledge integration. Afterwards, we will present the derived determinants and dimensions of knowledge integration.

1.3.1 Descriptive Results

Table B-3 shows that the publications are somewhat consistently distributed between 1999 and 2018 with some high points and a slightly increasing trend. Considering the extant body of research on knowledge management (Yoo 2010), we assume that the specific topic of knowledge integration has been more or less continuously embedded and investigated.

Table B-3. Article Results by Publication Year.

Year	1999 - 2002	2003 - 2006	2007 - 2010	2011 - 2014	2015 - 2018
Results	12.5% (7)	21.4% (12)	26.8% (15)	16.1% (9)	23.2% (13)

Furthermore, we examined the applied research method as well. A brief overview is presented in Table B-4. Almost 50% of the research conducted employed quantitative methods (e.g., structural equation modeling, panel data regressions) to test specified hypotheses. The second most frequent type of publication were exploratory case studies (~30%), followed by publications that developed a conceptual theory (~13%). Only a few literature reviews were primarily focusing on the broader notion of knowledge and its management.

Table B-4. Article Results by Research Method.

Research method	Literature review	Meta-analysis	Theoretical	Quantitative	Qualitative	Multi-method
Results	5.4% (3)	1.8% (1)	12.5% (7)	46.4% (26)	30.4% (17)	3.6% (2)

Table B-5 summarizes the most frequent theoretical concepts that were found in the identified literature. Most commonly, the concepts of knowledge-based view (Grant 1996b), resource-based view (Barney 1991), dynamic capabilities (Teece et al. 1997), absorptive capacity (Cohen and Levinthal 1990), and social capital theory (Nahapiet and Ghoshal 1998) were adopted by researchers as theoretical lenses on the topic of knowledge integration.

Table B-5. Theoretical Lenses.

Theoretical lenses	Authors
Knowledge-based view (Grant 1996b)	Alavi and Leidner 2001; Armstrong and Sambamurthy 1999; Dibbern et al. 2008; Huang et al. 2001; Jayatilaka et al. 2003; Saraf et al. 2007; Srivardhana and Pawlowski 2007; Wang et al. 2008; Wu and Hu 2012
Resource-based view (Barney 1991)	Armstrong and Sambamurthy 1999; Jayatilaka et al. 2003; Mitchell 2006; Peppard and Ward 2004; Tanriverdi 2005

Dynamic capabilities (Teece et al. 1997)	Bittner and Leimeister 2014; Carlo et al. 2012; Cooper and Molla 2017; Joshi et al. 2010; Prieto and Easterby-Smith 2006; Srivardhana and Pawlowski 2007; Wu and Hu 2012
Absorptive capacity (Cohen and Levinthal 1990)	Carlo et al. 2012; Cooper and Molla 2017; Datta and Roumani 2015; Dibbern et al. 2008; Gold et al. 2001; Joshi et al. 2010; Srivardhana and Pawlowski 2007
Social capital theory (Nahapiet and Ghoshal 1998)	Daniel et al. 2018; Patnayakuni and Ruppel 2006; Peppard 2007; Preston and Karahanna 2009; Robert et al. 2008; Wang and Haggerty 2009

1.3.2 Theoretical Conceptualization of Knowledge Integration

The analysis of the selected articles revealed that knowledge integration has been theorized as either a process or an outcome. Regarding the process of knowledge integration, the employed definitions vary between rather simplistic ones (Majchrzak et al. 2013) and more niche descriptions that consider social interactions (Huang et al. 2001) or the firm's external environment (Ejodame and Oshri 2018) (see Table B-6).

Table B-6. Knowledge Integration as a Process.

Focus	**Exemplary definition**
Integration of existing knowledge	Majchrzak et al. (2013): "Knowledge integration refers to the recombination of knowledge by merging, categorizing, reclassifying, and synthesizing existing knowledge."
Collective knowledge integration	Huang et al. (2001): "Knowledge integration is defined [...] as an ongoing collective process of constructing, articulating and redefining shared beliefs through the social interaction of organizational members."
Integration of external and internal knowledge	Ejodame and Oshri (2018): "Knowledge integration has been defined as the process of absorbing knowledge from external sources and blending it with the technical and business skills, know-how, and expertise that reside in the business and IS units of a firm."

Regarding the outcomes of knowledge integration, researchers differentiated between the establishment of shared understanding and beliefs within a group of organizational actors or the development of new knowledge (see Table B-7).

Table B-7. Knowledge Integration as an Outcome.

Focus	**Exemplary definition**
Establishment of shared understanding	Goh et al. (2013): "achieve, and refine a shared understanding among all project stakeholders through interaction, sense-making, and collective learning."
Creation of new knowledge	Kearns and Sabherwal (2006): "knowledge being applied or combined with other knowledge to create new knowledge."

Although some articles employed multiple perspectives on and theoretical conceptualizations of knowledge integration, the evaluated studies predominantly focused on internal knowledge integration from knowledge sources inside the firm. This preliminary finding indicates and confirms the need for further research with particular emphasis on the dynamic integration and management of heterogeneous knowledge resources required for digital innovation (Yoo 2010; Yoo et al. 2012).

1.3.3 Determinants of Knowledge Integration

In the first step of developing a multi-dimensional framework, we assessed the articles in order to consolidate determinants that influence the processes and outcomes of knowledge integration. Table B-8 presents the identified determinants, their definitions, and exemplary references.

Table B-8. Determinants of Knowledge Integration.

Determinant	Definition	Exemplary reference
Knowledge management activities	Organizational activities related to knowledge integration	Carlo et al. (2012): "Sensing routines affect how firms acquire external knowledge through scanning and focused searches, through seeking to understand its value through interpretation, and through assimilating it by integrating it into its knowledge structure."
Intra-organizational linkages	Organizational linkages between units and their pockets of specialized knowledge	Mitchell (2006): "Where organizational units hold specialized knowledge, inter-unit linkages are the primary means of transferring that knowledge [...] such knowledge transfer permits knowledge reuse, and the recombination of existing knowledge."
Process formalization	Degree of organizational processes being formalized and structured	Patnayakuni and Ruppel (2006): "Formalized structures embed knowledge into stringent routines, institutionalize behaviors (including behaviors related to the creation and use of knowledge) and suppress collaboration."
Innovation culture	Org. culture that supports the dexterity to assimilate various types of acquired knowledge	Datta and Roumani (2015): "An innovation culture increases the diversity of the [firm's] own innovation knowledge base that can be leveraged when integrating and absorbing a wide range of acquired innovation knowledge."
Knowledge management systems	Class of IS applied to managing org. knowledge	Alavi and Leidner (2001): "IT-based systems developed to support and enhance the organizational processes of knowledge creation, storage/retrieval, transfer, and application."
Digital networks & platforms	Collaborative technologies that support knowledge-related activities	Zhang et al. (2011): "important objective of [...] collaborative technologies is to facilitate knowledge sharing and integration among distributed team members."
Digital boundary resources	Software tools (e.g., APIs) that serve as an interface between diverse entities	Foerderer et al. (2019): "employed by [firms] in order to overcome knowledge boundaries and enable effective product development outcomes."
System complexity	Degree of interdependency between software elements	Daniel and Stewart (2016): "When a [software] design allows completion of smaller tasks without understanding the entire product, developers can integrate [knowledge] more quickly."
Social interactions & activities	Set of interactions and activities (e.g., interactive discussion) between org. actors	Daniel and Stewart (2016): "Interactive discussion among individuals facilitates knowledge generation, combination, and transfer."
Social networks & relationships	Set of networks and relationships among org. actors	Robert et al. (2008): "The set of resources embedded within the relationships among actors within a network."
Communication channels	Informal/formal communication channels among org. actors	Mitchell (2006): "The knowledge integration process involves social interactions among individuals using internal communication channels for knowledge transfer to arrive at a common perspective for problem solving."
Shared understanding & beliefs	Shared mental models, group cognition and sense-making among org. actors	Bittner and Leimeister (2014): "the ability of multiple agents to coordinate their behaviors with respect to each other in order to support the realization of common goals or objectives."

While consolidating the determinants, we derived three distinctive meta-theoretical constructs: Social mechanisms, technological mechanisms, and managerial levers.

The first construct social mechanisms is primarily related to social capital theory (Nahapiet and Ghoshal 1998) and consists of all social aspects, such as social interactions and activities, social networks and relationships, communication channels as well as shared understanding and beliefs. The identified social mechanisms are predominantly affecting knowledge integration on an individual or group level. The second construct technological mechanisms comprises all technological elements, such as knowledge management systems, digital networks and platforms, digital boundary resources, and system complexity.

These technological mechanisms are closely related to the firm's IT capabilities and reflect all technological artifacts that have an influence on knowledge integration. The third construct managerial levers is comprised of knowledge management activities, intra-organizational linkages, innovation culture, and process formalization. These influencing factors were commonly linked to dynamic capabilities (Teece et al. 1997). Here, the identified determinants were affecting knowledge integration from a broader, organizational level.

All constructs, however, were influenced by the underlying knowledge bases and resources of the firm and were conceptualized through the knowledge-based view. Depending on the focus of analysis, these knowledge resources were linked either to individuals or as an accumulation to the organization itself. Due to the varying and partly contradictory theoretical conceptualization of absorptive capacity (Roberts et al. 2012) as a determinant, process and outcome of knowledge integration, it was excluded in the model development to ensure clarity and comprehensibility of the derived findings.

1.3.4 Process and Outcome Dimensions of Knowledge Integration

Knowledge integration can be considered as a process or an outcome. Knowledge integration processes reflect the activities and measures through which individuals or systems utilize, share or combine specific knowledge (Grant 1996b; Kearns and Sabherwal 2006). Knowledge integration outcomes refer to knowledge being shared, combined, synthesized or applied to create shared understanding or new knowledge. During the systematic review of the literature, we coded each paper according process and outcome dimensions of knowledge integration. Here, we derived seven dimensions that surfaced during the coding of the articles. Four of them were related to the process of knowledge integration ("explaining the how") and the other three were pertaining to the outcomes of knowledge integration ("explaining the what"). Table B-9 illustrates the process dimensions, their definitions, and exemplary references.

Table B-9. Process Dimensions of Knowledge Integration.

Dimension	Definition	Exemplary reference
Level	The level (individual, group, org.) on which the knowledge integration process takes place.	Newell et al. (2000): "where IT cuts across departmental and geographical boundaries within an organization [...] there is a need to integrate the dispersed internal organizational knowledge that is implicated."
Actor	The participating entities, such as individuals, groups, organizations or technological artifacts, that carry out the knowledge integration process.	Tiwana and McLean (2005): "organizational entities such as project teams as vehicles for integrating [...] knowledge."
Source	The internal and external paths through which knowledge is sourced and integrated.	Carlo et al. (2012): "an internal path where innovation is spawned relying knowledge from an internal source and an external path where innovation is generated using an external knowledge source."
Form	The way how knowledge is being integrated: 1. Social interaction with focus on establishing shared understanding or beliefs; 2. Synthesis of knowledge with focus on creating new knowledge.	1. Huang et al. (2001): "ongoing collective process of constructing, articulating and redefining shared beliefs through the social interaction of organizational members." 2. Kearns and Sabherwal (2006): "Knowledge integration refers to the outcomes of that knowledge being [...] combined with other knowledge to create new knowledge."

The process dimension level explains in which context the knowledge is being integrated. This can happen on the individual, group or organizational level. The process dimensions actor and source relate to who conducts the knowledge integration (individuals or technological artifacts) and from where is the knowledge sourced (inside or outside the firm). The last process dimension form describes whether knowledge integration is carried out without the need of extensive social interaction (e.g., through technological artifacts like APIs) or requires, for instance, interactive discussions in order to achieve shared understanding.

Regarding outcomes of knowledge integration, we identified the dimensions locus, novelty, and type. Table B-10 illustrates the outcome dimensions, their definitions, and exemplary references.

Table B-10. Outcome Dimensions of Knowledge Integration.

Dimension	Definition	Exemplary reference
Locus	The organizational knowledge base (product, process, or business model) that benefits from the knowledge integration.	Carlo et al. (2012): "keeping the organization in a state of change by trying out technologies, applications, business models, or organizational processes."
Novelty	The nature of the knowledge that has been created through the knowledge integration: 1. Shared knowledge; 2. New knowledge.	1. Goh et al. (2013): "achieve, and refine a shared understanding among all project stakeholders through interaction, sense-marking, and collective learning." 2. Kearns and Sabherwal (2006): "knowledge being applied or combined with other knowledge to create new knowledge."
Type	The type of knowledge (tacit, explicit) that has been created through the knowledge integration.	Patnayakuni and Ruppel (2006): "While collaborative exchange enhances individual learning by expanding participants' individual tacit knowledge through the process of sharing and transfer, individuals also generate explicit knowledge in the form of development artifacts [...] that integrate knowledge across the application and technical domain."

Concerning the dimension locus, the integration of knowledge can lead to outcomes related to product, process or business model knowledge. The outcome dimension novelty differentiates between shared knowledge (e.g., shared understanding or beliefs) between individuals and newly created or combined knowledge. The dimension type displays whether the integrated knowledge reflects rather tacit or explicit knowledge.

1.4 Discussion and Implications

This study provides insights on how scholars conceptualized and utilized the theme of knowledge integration. Therefore our main contribution in this paper is the consolidation of the body of knowledge in IS research into a parsimonious, theoretically grounded, multi-dimensional framework of knowledge integration, connecting social mechanisms, technological mechanisms, and managerial levers – and viewing knowledge integration as a process and an outcome (see Figure B:1).

Relating the analysis of current insights on knowledge integration to the recent topic of digital innovation, several interesting insights emerge. First, the multi-dimensional model highlights that new technological elements such as digital boundary resources (e.g., APIs) and system complexity are gaining relevance in shaping processes and outcomes of knowledge integration in the digital era. With digitalizing products and the emergence of layered modular architectures (Yoo et al. 2010), organizations are employing boundary resources to enable generativity and exploit external knowledge sources and capabilities from complementors. This, in turn, hints at a fundamental shift in organizational knowledge management from developing and maintaining control over the firm's own knowledge base to enabling others to innovate upon it and orchestrating heterogeneous and distributed knowledge capabilities (Boudreau 2012; Ghazawneh and Henfridsson 2013).

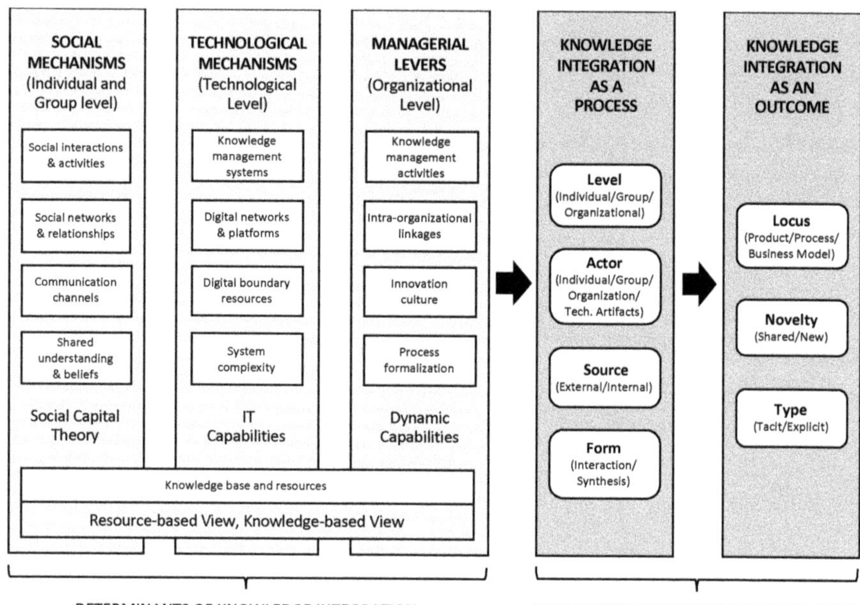

Figure B:1. Multi-dimensional Framework for Knowledge Integration.

Regarding social mechanisms, pervasive digital technologies are increasingly embedded in social activities and interactions among organizational actors. Here, for instance, digitally enhanced or enabled teams increasingly carry out knowledge integration in the virtual space of digital networks and platforms. These interactions are particularly important in the context of digital innovation and its convergent nature, as heterogeneous and constantly changing actors are required to interact dynamically with each other (Yoo et al. 2012). Consequently, with the increase in availability and feasibility of virtual interactions potentially in any place at any time with any one, the process of knowledge integration becomes more flexible and dynamic and thus requires new knowledge management capabilities by organizations.

As to managerial levers, knowledge integration in the digital era depends increasingly upon individual and organizational linkages between distributed pockets of knowledge as sharing and learning among partners, internally and externally, drives the recognition and exploitation of opportunities related to digital innovation (Kohli and Melville 2019). This is further reinforced by the distributed nature of digital innovation, where more and more actors need to innovate together. Thus, managerial levers, such as organizational linkages (within and outside the firm) and innovation culture, become increasingly important to knowledge integration in digital contexts (Datta and Roumani 2015; Mitchell 2006; Yoo et al. 2012).

Furthermore, due to the combinatorial and generative nature of digital innovation, knowledge integration becomes a more permanent, dynamic, and multifaceted topic. The multiplicity and complexity of knowledge integration processes and outcomes take on a greater scale in the digital era, which is why more investigations into this evolving and highly dynamic topic are required (Kohli and Melville 2019; Yoo et al. 2010; Yoo et al. 2012).

In conclusion, our review suggests that there is a solid platform of insights about knowledge integration that is valuable and can be used in the context of digital innovation. However, a substantial part of these insights were generated in pre-digital times. Therefore, in what follows, we identify necessary extensions to cater to most recent phenomena. These potential extensions mark important avenues for future work.

First, emerging aspects of digital innovation, such as digital networks, boundary resources, and digitally enabled teams, are somewhat represented in the current state of research on knowledge integration and deliver valuable insights to managers for coping with current digitalization challenges related to internal and external knowledge management. However, due to the distributed nature of innovations with pervasive digital technologies, there is currently a lack of insights on strategies and frameworks on the development of appropriate knowledge management capabilities for dealing with increasingly heterogeneous and dispersed knowledge resources required for digital innovation (Kohli and Melville 2019; Yoo et al. 2012; Zapadka 2020).

Second, albeit the existent knowledge on knowledge integration, current literature in this area has not yet dealt in depth with the particularities of digital knowledge (as opposed to other types of knowledge), which is subject to knowledge integration in contexts of digital innovation. Recent research shows that these particularities might render knowledge integration a different process (Hanelt et al. 2020). Furthermore, the loose coupling between different elements in digital innovation, afforded by standardized interfaces, points to the necessity of differentiating the degree of knowledge integration. Recent case study research suggests that in digital innovation, diverse knowledge might be utilized without deep integration and that balancing different kinds of knowledge integration might be a key managerial challenge in the digital age (Zapadka 2020).

Apart from these necessary extensions, the derived framework delivers practitioners a ground-laying set of significant activities and aspects that should be at least considered when they are trying to exploit and integrate heterogeneous knowledge resources for effective digital innovation. Moreover, the overview of the numerous determinants, process and outcomes dimensions can provide managers with crucial knowledge on how to improve the likelihood of success for current and future digital innovation efforts.

1.5 Limitations

We followed the methodological research design of Webster and Watson (2002) in terms of review and analysis design. In addition, the practical guidance by Levy and Ellis (2006) applying Webster and Watson (2002) was also considered. We assumed that although a significant body of literature for knowledge integration is incorporated in studies related to knowledge management, the conceptualization and theoretical consideration would be heterogeneous across different research streams. Our findings confirmed this and synthesized the various perceptions and approaches towards knowledge integration in IS research. However, we still have to consider limitations in our research design and methodology.

Although Webster and Watson (2002) provide a common framework for reviewing a body of knowledge, we could have choose other methodological designs for our literature review (e.g., Rowe 2014; Schryen 2015). Furthermore, the choice of our literature potential database vendors might have impacted our results. Webster and Watson (2002) suggested starting in leading journals. Reducing the research scope to top quality journals might have also limited our results, since relevant literature can potentially be also found in less qualitative journals or conference proceedings, and other disciplines. Another limitation might have occurred in the choice of keywords. We derived keywords based on our understanding of knowledge integration. The construct of keyword groups between "integrat*" and "knowledge" may have led to missing crucial literature. For future research we suggest to include more variations and terms like assimilation, transformation or combination.

Even though we were able to review a significant amount of literature, there was only little or partial research effort towards an integrated process framework of knowledge integration. In general, we can approve, based on our findings that until today the body of knowledge with particular emphasis on the integration of heterogeneous knowledge resources still requires fundamental investigation. Consequently, we suggest that researchers should put more emphasis on the analysis of the integration of heterogeneous and distributed knowledge resources in the context of digital innovation in order bring more light into this, though elusive, highly significant topic.

1.6 Appendix A: Literature Review Concept Matrix

No.	Outlet	Author	Year	Publication type	Level of analysis	Level of Theory[1]	Type of Integration[2]
1	ISR	Armstrong and Sambamurthy	1999	Quantitative	Organization	2	Internal
2	JSIS	Gray	2000	Theoretical	Group/team	1	Internal
3	ISJ	Newell et al.	2000	Theoretical	Organization	3	Both
4	MISQ	Alavi and Leidner	2001	LitRev	Multi-level	2	Internal
5	JMIS	Gold et al.	2001	Quantitative	Organization	2	Both
6	EJIS	Huang et al.	2001	Qualitative	Organization	3	Internal
7	MISQ	Chatterjee et al.	2002	Quantitative	Organization	2	External
8	JSIS	Pan and Leidner	2003	Qualitative	Organization	1	Internal
9	EJIS	Jayatilaka et al.	2003	Qualitative	Organization	2	External
10	JSIS	Peppard and Ward	2004	Theoretical	Organization	2	Internal
11	MISQ	Tanriverdi	2005	Quantitative	Organization	1	Internal
12	ISR	Majchrzak et al.	2005	Quantitative	Individual	1	Internal
13	JMIS	Tiwana and McLean	2005	Quantitative	Group/team	2	Internal
14	EJIS	Prieto and Easterby-Smith	2006	Qualitative	Organization	1	Internal
15	ISR	Slaughter and Kirsch	2006	Quantitative	Individual	1	Internal
16	JMIS	Kearns and Sabherwal	2006	Quantitative	Individual	2	Internal
17	MISQ	Mitchell	2006	Quantitative	Multi-level	3	Both
18	EJIS	Howard-Grenville and Carlile	2006	Qualitative	Organization	3	Both
19	JAIS	Patnayakuni and Ruppel	2006	Quantitative	Organization	3	Internal
20	JSIS	Srivardhana and Pawlowski	2007	Meta-Analysis	Multi-level	2	Both
21	ISR	Saraf et al.	2007	Quantitative	Organization	2	Both
22	EJIS	Peppard	2007	Theoretical	Individual	2	Internal
23	MISQ	Dibbern et al.	2008	Qualitative	Organization	1	External
24	EJIS	Wang et al.	2008	Qualitative	Organization	1	External
25	ISJ	Oshri et al.	2008	Qualitative	Group/team	1	Internal
26	JSIS	Andersson et al.	2008	Qualitative	Organization	2	Internal
27	ISR	Robert et al.	2008	Quantitative	Group/team	3	Internal
28	ISJ	Wang and Haggerty	2009	Theoretical	Individual	1	Internal
29	ISR	Preston and Karahanna	2009	Quantitative	Individual	2	Internal
30	JSIS	Sedera and Gable	2010	Quantitative	Organization	1	Internal
31	JIT	van den Hooff et al.	2010	Quantitative	Individual	1	Internal
32	MISQ	Yoo	2010	Theoretical	Organization	2	External
33	ISR	Gopal and Gosain	2010	Quantitative	Organization	2	External
34	ISR	Joshi et al.	2010	Quantitative	Organization	2	Both
35	JAIS	Zhang et al.	2011	Quantitative	Group/team	2	Internal
36	JAIS	Wu and Hu	2012	Quantitative	Organization	2	Both
37	MISQ	Carlo et al.	2012	Quantitative	Organization	3	Both
38	JAIS	Javadi et al.	2013	Theoretical	Group/team	1	Internal
39	MISQ	Majchrzak et al.	2013	Quantitative	Individual	2	Internal
40	JAIS	Goh et al.	2013	Qualitative	Multi-level	2	Internal
41	JMIS	Bittner and Leimeister	2014	Qualitative	Group/team	1	Internal
42	JIT	Lempinen and Rajala	2014	Qualitative	Organization	2	Internal
43	EJIS	Vermerris et al.	2014	Qualitative	Organization	2	Internal
44	JIT	Newell	2015	LitRev	Multi-level	1	Internal
45	ISR	Tiwana and Kim	2015	Quantitative	Organization	2	Both
46	EJIS	Datta and Roumani	2015	Quantitative	Organization	3	External
47	JMIS	Mehta and Bharadwaj	2015	Quantitative	Group/team	3	Both
48	JSIS	Daniel and Stewart	2016	Qualitative	Group/team	3	External
49	ISR	Lindberg et al.	2016	Qualitative	Group/team	3	Internal
50	ISR	Ravichandran et al.	2017	Quantitative	Organization	1	External
51	ISJ	Cooper and Molla	2017	Multi-method	Organization	2	External
52	JSIS	Daniel et al..	2018	Quantitative	Individual	2	External
53	JSIS	Liu et al.	2018	Multi-method	Organization	2	Internal
54	ISJ	Peppard	2018	LitRev	Organization	2	Internal
55	JIT	Ejodame and Oshri	2018	Qualitative	Organization	3	Both
56	ISJ	Foerderer et al.	2018	Qualitative	Organization	2	External

Note: [1]*Level of theory reflects the degree of theoretical conceptualization of knowledge integration - "1" means knowledge integration provides basic theoretical support, "2" means knowledge integration is theorized in hypotheses, propositions or model, and "3" means knowledge integration is in the focus of theoretical analysis.* [2]*Type of integration reflects whether knowledge from inside or outside the firm has been integrated.*

II. Scaling Knowledge Integration through Boundary Resources in Digital(izing) Business Ecosystems

While the previous chapter provided a foundation by synthesizing existing insights on the topic of knowledge integration and reviewing them in the context of digital innovation, the next chapter specifically focuses on the technological mechanism of boundary resources. To this end, the chapter aims at examining, first, how firms can scale knowledge integration through boundary resources as they leverage internal and external knowledge in digital(izing) business ecosystems and, second, under which internal and external conditions this utilization is beneficial for them.

Accordingly, Study 2 employs panel data regressions to a longitudinal, cross-industry dataset to explore how and when firms deploy own boundary resources to leverage internal as well as external knowledge in their digital(izing) business ecosystems. In contrast to that, although Study 3 also employs panel data regressions in a large-scale quantitative investigation, it primarily focuses on how and when firms utilize external boundary resources to close internal capability gaps in the context of artificial intelligence (AI). Together, the studies provide insights into how firms utilize boundary resources to scale knowledge integration in digital(izing) business ecosystems and under which conditions this is beneficial for them.

1 Study 2: Digital at the Edge – Antecedents and Performance Effects of Boundary Resources Deployment

Table B-11. Fact Sheet of Study No. 2.

Title	Digital at the Edge – Antecedents and Performance Effects of Boundary Resources Deployment
Authors	Patryk Zapadka*[a], André Hanelt[a], Sebastian Firk[b] [a] Chair of Digital Transformation Management, University of Kassel, Kleine Rosenstr. 3, 34109 Kassel, Germany [b] Department of Accounting, University of Groningen, Nettelbosje 2, 9747 AE Groningen, Netherlands *Corresponding author. Tel.: +49 561 804 3902. E-mail address: patryk.zapadka@uni-kassel.de
Outlet	Journal of Strategic Information Systems (JSIS)
Abstract	With business environments digitalizing by the force of digital innovation, the deployment of boundary resources such as application programming interfaces (APIs) becomes a strategic option across contexts. We differentiate boundary resources that provide access and resource openness and theorize the antecedents and consequences of their deployment. Employing panel data regressions to a longitudinal, cross-industry dataset, we find that the digital knowledge base of the focal firm and the existence of potential digital complementors drive boundary resources deployment. Such deployment benefits firm performance depending on the firm's market power. From our empirical analysis, we derive important implications for research and practice.
Keywords	Boundary resources, application programming interfaces, digital business ecosystem, firm performance, panel data regression

1.1 Introduction

The top five largest companies by market value, namely *Apple, Amazon, Alphabet, Microsoft* and *Facebook* (Forbes 2019) excel at leveraging their own digital knowledge as well as that of other actors in their digital business ecosystems by deploying boundary resources such as application programming interfaces (APIs) (Boland et al. 2007; Parker and van Alstyne 2018; Song et al. 2018; Yoo et al. 2010). Microsoft and Facebook, for instance, are constantly integrating new innovations into their platforms and exposing them to third parties by opening up new APIs (Parker and van Alstyne 2018). Through these APIs, external participants and contributors are allowed to access the assets made available by the deploying firms to either utilize them in their own contexts or develop new digital offerings building upon them (Boudreau 2012; Ghazawneh and Henfridsson 2013). The benefits and the growing strategic value of boundary resources is not only being recognized and leveraged by firms from the digital space (Iyer and Subramaniam 2015a, 2015b). Companies across industries, such as retail (Best Buy 2020; Macys 2020; Walmart 2020), transportation (FedEx 2020; UPS 2020), and manufacturing (Ford 2020; John Deere 2020; Svahn et al. 2017), eager to create innovative digital offerings, are increasingly leveraging their digital assets by enabling external participation and contribution through APIs. As a result, through the force of digital innovation, business environments are increasingly moving towards distributed co-creation and co-capture of value, a development that also is questioning enterprise boundaries (El Sawy and Pereira 2013; Yoo et al. 2012).

Therefore, managers throughout industries are increasingly reflecting upon deploying boundary resources to leverage their own digital innovation by exposing them to larger audiences and trigger outside contributions in a manageable and controlled way (Ghazawneh and Henfridsson 2013; Yoo et al. 2010). For instance, the industrial-age car manufacturer *Ford* is providing an API for developers with the goal of facilitating the creation of voice-activated services within vehicle technology (ProgrammableWeb 2019). Another example is the online travel booking platform *Expedia* that allows external actors to source its booking functionalities through APIs and, thus, invokes their integration in other contexts such as third-party websites (Iyer and Subramaniam 2015b). However, despite the fact that boundary resources are associated with certain advantages in digital business ecosystems, they also, like any other technological infrastructure, incur significant costs through their development and administration (Eaton et al. 2015). Therefore, the decision of a company to opt for deploying and utilizing boundary resources permanently is far from trivial and depends on whether the expected benefits from such a strategy exceed the associated costs (Boudreau 2012; Karhu et al. 2018).

Gaining momentum in business practice, boundary resources have also been in the focus of research within the last decade. In the evolving IS literature stream, boundary resources are considered as an important means by which firms "open up" to external audiences to enable the utilization of their assets and by this stimulate innovation and growth in the respective digital business ecosystem (Ghazawneh and Henfridsson 2013; Yoo et al. 2010). Despite being dynamically adjusted through co-creative and distributed dynamics (Eaton et al. 2015), previous research particularly investigated how boundary resources can be instantiated by firms to fulfill specific objectives, such as managing external participation (Ghazawneh and Henfridsson 2013) or preventing hostile exploitation (Karhu et al. 2018). In particular, firms can deploy and design boundary resources to provide two types of openness, that is, *access* and *resource openness* (Karhu et al. 2018). *Access openness* refers to leveraging the firm's existing assets by allowing external audiences to utilize and integrate them in other contexts. For instance, *eBay* deploys a broad range of APIs for *access openness* that let external parties utilize its transaction services (e.g., managing auctions) or incorporate its data (e.g., bidder information) in other contexts – all of which drives the exposure of *eBay*'s assets and thus increases revenues (eBay 2020; Iyer and Subramaniam 2015b). By contrast, *resource openness* relates to leveraging external innovation capabilities by providing capable resources to complementors that enable them to diversify the firm's offerings. As an example, the agricultural and construction manufacturer *John Deere* has deployed diverse APIs for *resource openness* that provide distinct capabilities (e.g., access to machine data) for developing new services in the context of logistics management and agronomic solutions (John Deere 2020). Therefore, boundary resources allow firms to either create and capture more value out of their existing assets by generating network effects (Gawer 2014; Gawer and Cusumano 2014; Karhu et al. 2018) or diversifying their offerings through external development (Boudreau 2012; Ghazawneh and Henfridsson 2013).

Yet, while previous research generated important qualitative insights on the design, managerial mechanisms and structural implications of boundary resources in business ecosystems in digital contexts (Eaton et al. 2015; Ghazawneh and Henfridsson 2013; Karhu et al. 2018), factors that drive their adoption are as unclear as the performance outcomes of boundary resources, especially empirically. However, with the increasing business relevance and strategic value of boundary resources, filling such research gaps becomes increasingly important (Yoo et al. 2010). From a research perspective, to achieve a more comprehensive understanding, it is necessary to extend the existing knowledge on the functioning of boundary resources by complementing it with insights on important internal and external contingencies that lead organizations to effectively deploy particular types of boundary resources in the first place and, thereby, shedding light on the conditions that lead to their manifestation. From the perspective of managerial practice, as digital innovation is progressively dissolving industry and product boundaries, companies are in need of strategic guidance on how to cope with the new competitive requirements and mechanisms of digital ecosystems (Iyer and Subramaniam 2015b; Jacobides et al. 2018; Yoo et al. 2010). Insights about whether and when the benefits of deploying boundary resources as one particular strategic option outweigh the associated costs is of vital importance.

Accordingly, our research is concerned with the following research questions:

(1) How do firm- and context-related factors influence boundary resources deployments and

(2) when are these deployments beneficial for the firm?

In order to provide answers to these questions, we create a specific theoretical framework by drawing on contingency theory (Weill and Olson 1989), a lens that has proven valuable to investigate antecedents and consequences of deployment decisions in multiple contexts several times in IS research (e.g., Shao et al. 2016; Sharma and Yetton 2007; Teo and Pian 2003), and derive a set of hypotheses. To investigate our predictions, we employ a panel data regression to a longitudinal dataset of Standard & Poor's 500 (S&P 500) firms between 2010 and 2018. To this end, we utilized the ProgrammableWeb API database for any API listings that matched our S&P 500 firms and were introduced in the respective timeframe – steering us towards the choice of APIs as our operationalization of boundary resources. Furthermore, following Karhu et al.'s (2018) distinction, we differentiate two types of boundary resources deployments: (1) APIs for *access openness* and (2) APIs for *resource openness*. Our findings suggest that digital knowledge and the presence of potential digital complementors in the industry positively affect the decision to deploy boundary resources. Moreover, we find that the firm's digital knowledge is particularly driving the deployment of APIs for *access openness*, while potential digital complementors in the industry particularly drive the deployment of APIs for *resource openness*. Regarding the performance implications of boundary resources deployments, we could not find a positive impact on firm performance per se. However, we observe that boundary resources deployments can increase firm performance for firms with high market power. Differentiating between the types of boundary resources deployments, we find that the positive performance effects for firms with high market power are primarily driven by the deployment of APIs for *access openness*.

Our work contributes to boundary resources research by providing to date missing empirical large-scale evidence shedding light on the contextual factors that lead companies across industries to the adoption and beneficial deployment of specific types of boundary resources (Eaton et al. 2015; Ghazawneh and Henfridsson 2013; Karhu et al. 2018). In addition, we contribute to research by highlighting the value of boundary resources in digitalizing business ecosystems and thus accentuate their crucial role in strategic frameworks for the context of digital innovation (Bharadwaj et al. 2013; Yoo et al. 2010). Furthermore, our research has important implications for managerial practice by informing managers reflecting upon the relevant contextual conditions as well as potential consequences of deploying boundary resources.

1.2 Theoretical Background

1.2.1 Digital Innovation and Digital(izing) Business Ecosystems

Owing to the force of digital innovation, defined "*as the creation of (and consequent change in) market offerings, business processes, or models that result from the use of digital technology*" (Nambisan et al. 2017, p. 224), product and industry boundaries are progressively dissolving and thus forcing firms to cope with new competitive as well as cooperative dynamics (Yoo et al. 2010). These dynamics are reshaping business ecosystems and the way how firms need to operate within them. Driven by the generative and distributed nature of digital innovation, companies are increasingly dependent on value co-creation and co-capture with heterogeneous and widely dispersed players (El Sawy and Pereira 2013; Yoo et al. 2012).

Moreover, as companies increasingly incorporate digital technologies, a new hybrid form of product design – the layered modular architecture – is emerging and creating new opportunities for generative and distributed innovations (Yoo et al. 2010). Products with a layered modular architecture embody the layered design of digital technologies comprising a device, network, service and contents layer. Each layer fulfills a specific objective, such as providing application functionality (i.e., service layer) or managing stored and shared data (i.e., contents layer). Furthermore, based on loose couplings between and heterogeneous design hierarchies of components in a layered modular architecture, companies are able to focus on one layer (e.g., device layer) and let others generate contributions on other layers (e.g., content layer) by using firm-controlled boundary resources such as APIs (Ghazawneh and Henfridsson 2013; Yoo et al. 2010). For instance, external developers can connect a tracking program of a running shoe with either map APIs to visualize the running path, or social network APIs for sharing the running information with the individuals' friends (Yoo et al. 2012).

As a result, digital innovation exhibits two particular key traits, that is, its distributed and combinatorial nature (Yoo et al., 2012). Regarding the former, innovation within a layered modular architecture can be characterized as *"distributed because the primary source of value creation is the generativity that comes from the unbounded mix-and-match capability of heterogeneous resources across layers [and] doubly distributed because (a) the control over product components is distributed across multiple firms, and (b) the product knowledge is distributed across heterogeneous disciplines and communities"* (Yoo et al. 2010, p. 730). Furthermore, digital innovation is combinatorial in that new digital products or services are increasingly created based on the recombination or connection of existing modules with digital capabilities, which, in turn, has become a new source of innovation (Yoo et al. 2010; Yoo et al. 2012). For example, at the introduction of the Google Maps API, the developers could not predict that external actors would combine numerous location-based databases and, by doing that, develop new services upon their product (Yoo et al. 2012). Moreover, as digitized products and services become even more interdependent and connected in the so-called Internet of Things (IoT), so are the organizations increasingly embedded in digital business ecosystems and thus are obliged to co-create and co-capture value with customers, competitors and complementors (El Sawy and Pereira 2013; Jernigan et al. 2016; Porter and Heppelmann 2014).

In business ecosystems (re-)shaped by the force of digital innovation, value co-creation and co-capture amongst distributed partners with diverse capabilities and knowledge resources is mandatory for innovation and growth (Boudreau 2012; Gawer and Cusumano 2014). Accordingly, on the one hand, firms need to consider how to leverage their own resources through distribution among participants and complementors in their respective digital business ecosystem (Ghazawneh and Henfridsson 2013). On the other hand, firms need to discern how to scale and diversify their offerings over a broad range of application areas through the help of external actors (Boudreau 2012; Parker et al. 2017). One possible strategy to achieve both resides in the deployment of boundary resources, which can be utilized as a means that "*enables resource sharing and permits contributions*" (Karhu et al. 2018, p. 482). Thus, these boundary resources allow, on the one side, distributing chosen assets to external audiences, and on the other side, stimulating external contributions (Boudreau 2012; Ghazawneh and Henfridsson 2013; Karhu et al. 2018).

1.2.2 Boundary Resources

Boundary resources, according to their definition, fulfill an essential function in digital business ecosystems: Enabling resource sharing and stimulating external contribution (Ghazawneh and Henfridsson 2013; Parker et al. 2017). With regard to this, scholars revealed valuable qualitative insights towards the design (e.g., Ghazawneh and Henfridsson 2013; Wulf and Blohm 2017), associated managerial mechanisms (e.g., Karhu et al. 2018; Parker et al. 2017; Parker and van Alstyne 2018) and structural implications (e.g., Eaton et al. 2015; Song et al. 2017; Um and Yoo 2016) of boundary resources in their respective digital business ecosystems. From a holistic perspective, however, there are to date no insights in IS research on contextual conditions serving as antecedents that lead companies to deploy boundary resources as well as how such whether and when such decisions pay off in terms of financial benefits. Additionally, previous studies were predominantly carried out in the IT-industry and thus paid less attention to investigating other contexts that are affected by digital innovation, even though the decision to adopt boundary resources is becoming more and more relevant across industries in times of digitalization. Addressing these gaps is particularly important as previous research delineated different types of boundary resources, which, depending on the firm's assessment and strategic decision, can be instantiated with varying purposes and, for instance, separately open assets to distinct participating and contributing groups (Eisenmann et al. 2008). To this end, previous research examined different forms of openness that boundary resources help to establish, such as controlled interaction with chosen assets or less restricted utilization of more valuable core resources of the firm (Boudreau 2010; Karhu et al. 2018). These different types of openness allow external participants or complementors to leverage the provided assets either by employing them in their business operations or utilizing them for more innovation-oriented development activities (Eaton et al. 2015; Parker and van Alstyne 2018). Hence, by deploying boundary resources, firms are able *"to define openness and facilitate complementors' work"* (Karhu et al. 2018, p. 493). Relatedly, Karhu et al. (2018) delineate two forms of openness: *access openness* that relates to distributing a firm's assets and enabling external actors to interact with them and *resource openness*, which refers to opening up more valuable resources by forfeiting their IPR.

In the spirit of Karhu et al. (2018), two types of boundary resources can be discerned by relating to the different forms of openness towards external actors they provide: (1) Boundary resources for *access openness* enable firms to distribute their existing digital offerings to external audiences, which then can be utilized or integrated by them in other business activities or contexts. Consequently, this type of boundary resources primarily drives the distribution and exposure of the deploying firm's existing assets among external parties. As an example, *Visa* provides multiple of its financial service solutions through APIs in order to distribute them among users and complementors in their digital business ecosystem (Visa 2020). Similarly, *Citrix* allows external audiences to integrate the functionality of their online conferencing tools with other services and applications (ProgrammableWeb 2020b). By contrast, (2) boundary resources for *resource openness* refer to opening up assets that enable external parties to diversify the deploying firm's offerings through their heterogeneous development activities (Boudreau 2012; Ghazawneh and Henfridsson 2013). Thus, firms that deploy boundary resources for resource openness aim to exploit the heterogeneous innovation capabilities and knowledge resources of external complementors (Boland et al. 2007; Yoo et al. 2010). In the context of their digital business ecosystems, these firms embrace resource openness in order to diversify their offerings through external development (Boudreau 2012; Parker et al. 2017). For instance, *Apple* is providing dedicated access for external developers to the iPhone's camera functionality (e.g., control of exposure or focus) in order to build new services and diversify the user's experience while capturing photo and video material (Apple 2020). *Amazon,* as an additional example, allows external complementors to tap into distinct capabilities of its voice assistant *Alexa* (e.g., managing voice commands) in order to encourage and enable developers to create new and diverse voice-driven "skills" (e.g., services activated through voice commands) for its digital assistant's service ecosystem (Amazon 2018).

Conclusively, boundary resources can be either facilitating *access openness* that focuses on increasing the distribution and exposure of the deploying firm's existing offerings or *resource openness* that provides dedicated assets to leverage external innovation capabilities towards the development of novel offerings. Yet, the antecedents and implications of deploying these different types of boundary resources effectively are still unexplored. Such insights would be particularly relevant as catering to the different forms of openness that are provided (i.e., access vs. resource openness) can yield a more comprehensive and differentiated perspective on boundary resource deployments.

1.3 Theoretical Framework and Hypotheses Development

Boundary resources provide two specific benefits – leveraging internal digital knowledge through the distributing activities of third parties and leveraging external digital knowledge through the creative contributions of external actors. At the same time, the development and provision of boundary resources, as any other large-scale technological infrastructure, causes expenses such as upfront development and continuous administrative costs (Eaton et al. 2015; Karhu et al. 2018). Following a contingency perspective (e.g., Shao et al. 2016; Sharma and Yetton 2007; Teo and Pian 2003; Wang and Benbasat 2013; Yayla and Hu 2011), the decision to deploy boundary resources could be determined by contingencies that create a particular need for these inherent benefits of boundary resources that may be perceived to outweigh the costs, specifically (1) internal digital knowledge that can potentially be leveraged (2) complementors that can potentially contribute as carriers of external digital knowledge.

1.3.1 Leveraging Internal Digital Knowledge

In general, a firm's knowledge base indicates its technological capabilities (Grimpe and Hussinger 2014; Vermeulen and Barkema 2001). The ability to deploy boundary resources as digital technological artifacts (Yoo et al. 2012) should therefore be related to a firm's digital knowledge base. Furthermore, firms possessing digital knowledge have been found to also significantly drive digital innovation (Hanelt et al. 2020; Kohli and Melville 2019). In particular, as to its combinatorial and distributed nature, digital innovation requires complementarities with other parties, which can be eased by boundary resources such as APIs (Yoo et al. 2012). Consequently, firms possessing digital knowledge may seek to deploy APIs to enable that other actors may access and utilize their components within the loosely coupled modular layered architecture (Yoo et al. 2010). More specifically, firms with superior digital knowledge bases may use boundary resources to provide access openness to the digital innovations, which they have developed drawing on internal digital knowledge, in an attempt to foster network effects and distribution (Karhu et al. 2018). In addition, as firms with superior digital knowledge bases probably have incurred greater expenses (e.g., financial and technological resources) in the past to build up their digital expertise, they also might be more inclined to commercialize it and thus opt for using boundary resources for access openness (Eaton et al. 2015; Hanelt et al. 2020). In sum, it seems likely that firms with elaborated digital knowledge bases are comparatively more capable of deploying boundary resources and that they especially aspire to utilize them to distribute and scale their digital innovations.

Accordingly, we propose the following hypothesis:

H1: Internal digital knowledge is positively associated with the likelihood of boundary resources deployments, particularly those targeted at access openness.

1.3.2 Leveraging External Digital Knowledge

Boundary resources do not only serve as a means to foster the distribution of existing digital innovations, but also to unleash generativity in the development of new digital innovations (Yoo et al. 2012). However, in order to profit from this generativity, potential complementors have to be available. Probably more than any other form of innovation, digital innovation relies on the combination of heterogeneous knowledge brought in by diverse actors (Yoo et al. 2010). Here, digital ventures seem particularly relevant as they, on the one hand, exhibit elaborated digital capabilities (Tumbas et al. 2017b). These firms, on the other hand, regularly draw on existing digital infrastructures (Tilson et al. 2010) to build their services, and are therefore keen to use accessible boundary resources (Eaton et al. 2015; Huang et al. 2017). Offering boundary resources might attract the creative and rapidly scaling streams of digital innovation towards the deploying company (Parker et al. 2017). In particular, firms may use boundary resources to provide resource openness to their digital innovation practices in an attempt to profit from the creative inputs by external actors (Karhu et al. 2018). Thus, these external contributions may help firms to diversify their current offerings on a much greater scale and meet the continuously changing customer demands through a constant flow of new services (Boudreau 2012; van de Ven 2005; Yoo et al. 2010). In sum, it seems likely that firms might decide for boundary resources deployments when they observe the availability of potential complementors and that they especially aspire to utilize them to develop new digital innovations.

Accordingly, we propose the following hypothesis:

H2: The presence of external digital complementors is positively associated with the likelihood of boundary resources deployments, particularly those targeted at resource openness.

1.3.3 Performance Implications

From an economic perspective, the deployment of boundary resources can influence firm performance via two different paths. First, contributions from external parties that are enabled by boundary resources for resource openness are often less costly than self-development (Boudreau 2012; Boudreau and Jeppesen 2015). Large groups of external developers may help to keep an existing product fresh and attractive by a continuous flow of new functionality being added (Boudreau 2012; van de Ven 2005; Yoo et al. 2010). This can lead to stabilizing or even increasing revenues. For example, external developer communities are constantly releasing new applications on Apple's operating system (iOS), which results in constant evolution of functionalities on existing devices (e.g., iPhone or iPad). In addition, second, boundary resources for access openness allow to extend the reach and commercialization of existing offerings (Boudreau 2012). This was the case as the pharmacy retail chain *Walgreens* allowed external audiences to access its photo printing services through APIs and integrate them in other contexts – resulting in greater exposure and higher overall engagement as well as revenues per customer (Iyer and Subramaniam 2015b). In sum, the deployment of boundary resources for access openness as well as for resource openness might positively influence firm performance via several direct and indirect effects on costs and revenues.

Accordingly, we propose the following hypothesis:

H3: The deployment of boundary resources, including those targeted at access as well as resource openness, is positively associated with performance implications.

Apart from that, there might be a further nuance regarding the performance implications of boundary resources deployments. In particular, how deployed boundary resources translate into firm performance is also dependent on how it is received by the external environment. In an era of digital innovations that grow substantially based on direct and indirect network effects (Gawer 2014), a powerful market position on the one hand makes the deploying firms attractive for potential complementors. For instance, digital ventures might perceive an established firm's position, brand or customer base as a way to rapidly scale up or accelerate their innovation activities (Huang et al., 2017). On the other hand, a powerful market position gives deploying firms the opportunity to readily leverage digital knowledge and capabilities on a larger scale and scope. For example, Apple's diverse technological platforms (e.g., iPhones or iPads) and integrated distribution channels (e.g., iOS App Store) are able to attract a wide range of developer communities and thus effectively leverage their heterogeneous knowledge resources and competencies (Eaton et al. 2015; Ghazawneh and Henfridsson 2013). In sum, firms that rank high in market power seem likely to profit from upstream and downstream potentials in the utilization of boundary resources, which may further strengthen the positive performance effects.

H4: Market power positively moderates the relationship between the deployment of boundary resources and performance implications.

1.4 Methodology

1.4.1 Sample Selection

To gain large-scale empirical insights, we focus on a longitudinal sample of firms listed in the S&P 500 index. To create a longitudinal sample covering the diffusion of boundary resources deployment, we decided to investigate the years 2010 to 2018 and focused on the index constituents of our starting year 2010. We collected data for boundary resources deployment by systematically collecting information from the ProgrammableWeb API directory in April 2019, which is the internet's most complete account of information about public APIs (Evans and Basole 2016; Um and Yoo 2016; Wulf and Blohm 2017; Yu and Woodard 2008). Financial and ownership data were retrieved from Datastream, board, TMT and CEO data from the BoardEx database, and data on digital start-ups from the CrunchBase database. From potentially 4,500 firm-years, we could only include firm-years with available financial and other relevant data for our regressions yielding in a final sample of 3,720 firm-years. For the analysis of performance implications, we needed to exclude the year 2018 due to lacking data availability (i.e., future performance) reducing the sample to 3,307 firm-years.

1.4.2 Variables

1.4.2.1 Main Variables

Boundary resources deployment. To measure boundary resources deployment, we utilized the ProgrammableWeb API directory (Evans and Basole 2016; Yu and Woodard 2008) as we choose APIs as our operationalization of boundary resources. The API directory contains all relevant information about company APIs that are described by pre-defined criteria such as category, type, provider, introduction date and other interaction-related and technical properties. In order to collect all the required information for our analysis, we searched the ProgrammableWeb directory for any API listings that matched our S&P 500 firms and were introduced in the timeframe between the year 2010 and 2018.

After hand collecting all relevant API information, we coded the content of each API entry (e.g., description and related properties) according our previously defined conceptualizations of openness: *access openness* and *resource openness*. On the one side, an API that was providing access to digital offerings (e.g., software solutions or modules) with the purpose of distribution among external actors and integration in other contexts was considered to be an API for *access openness*. Here, keywords like "provides service", "offers solution", or "allows integration of software" indicated an API for *access openness.* On the other side, an API that was providing assets capable of diversifying the deploying firm's offerings and thus being utilized for the development of novel services or products was considered to be an API for *resource openness*. Accordingly, terms like "build applications", "develop services", or "support development activities" indicated an API for *resource openness*. After conducting an initial pilot coding of 100 randomly selected APIs by two authors, an intercoder-reliability score of over 85% was achieved. The remaining disagreements among the coders were discussed among all the authors until consensus was reached.

Based on the collected API information and our coding results, we created three variables to measure boundary resources deployment. First, we created a binary variable *API* that takes the value of 1 if a firm adopted at least one API in the given year and zero otherwise. Second, we created a binary variable *API access* that takes the value of 1 if a firm adopted at least one API for access openness in the given year and zero otherwise. Third, we created a binary variable *API resource* taking the value 1 if a firm adopted at least one API for resource openness in the respective year.

Digital knowledge. To capture the digital knowledge of firms, we focus on digital patent fillings. We follow prior literature in the view that patents can reflect the knowledge-base of a firm (Prabhu et al. 2005) and that this view holds also true when it comes to digital knowledge (Hanelt et al. 2020). Specifically, we assume similar to Hanelt et al. (2020) that the number of digital patent fillings can proxy for a firm's digital knowledge base. We focus on data from the USPTO (Graham et al. 2015; Marco et al. 2015) for a firm's patenting activities. We focus on initial filings in patent classes that reflect digital technologies. Specifically, we consider the following technological classes of the U.S. Patent Classification (USPC) scheme as related to digital technologies. First, we consider the technological domain of "Communications & Computers" similar to Hall et al. (2001). Second, we consider technological classes that were newly created after the initial year of defining this technological domain in 2001 and that are clearly associated with digital technologies such as "Data processing: software development, installation, and management." The table of Appendix A provides a full list with the USPC classes used for our operationalization. Finally, to construct our measure for digital knowledge, we considered the number of digital patent filings over the last two years. Moreover, to reduce the influence of outliers we follow prior studies (e.g., Balsmeier et al. 2017; Custódio et al. 2019; Hanelt et al. 2020) by log transforming the *digital knowledge* variable.

Digital complementors. We suggest that boundary resources deployment can help to unleash the generativity in digital innovation. The presence of potential digital complementors is crucial to realize this benefit. To proxy for the presence of potential complementors, we constructed a measure for the level of digital ventures per industry incumbent. We extracted all start-ups in the CrunchBase database founded between 2008 and 2018 (Ghezzi et al. 2016; Spiegel et al. 2016). Based on the industry description provided by CrunchBase, we then classified each start-ups industry affiliation into one Fama and French 48 industry. We also checked whether each start-up was indeed a digital venture. Specifically, we evaluated the description of the start-ups and classified start-ups as either digital or not based on a list of digital keywords. Next, we counted the number of digital ventures in the industry and divided it by the number of sample firms in the industry. This procedure results in a ratio reflecting the number of digital ventures by each industry incumbent. We then calculated the two-year average of this number to construct our final *digital complementors* variable.

Firm performance. We decided to use a market-based as well as an accounting-based measure for firm performance. We use the firm's total shareholder return (TSR) as a market based performance measure reflecting the shareholder stock and dividend returns over a certain period. Specifically, it is calculated as the share price at the end of a period minus the share price at the beginning of the period, plus dividends paid, all divided by the beginning share price. To capture long-term effects of boundary resources deployment, we decided to measure TSR over a two-year period t and t+1 (*TSR 2y*). As an accounting based performance measure, we use return on assets (ROA). We use the ROA as defined by DataStream. Again, we consider that performance effects of API adoption might have longer lead times and measured ROA over a two-year period t and t+1 (ROA 2y).

1.4.2.2 Control Variables

We selected several variables to control for confounding effects. First, we selected control variables on the ownership, board, CEO, and TMT level to capture the parties potentially involved in the decision to deploy boundary resources. We include *ownership concentration* as large blockholders might drive or prevent the decision to employ boundary resources. We further include information on technology expertise in the board (*IT board expertise)* and TMT (*IT TMT expertise)* that could encourage the decision to deploy boundary resources. Moreover, we include *CEO age* as a control as older CEO are frequently considered to be less willing engage in new project and generally to innovate. Second, we include several financial and organizational controls to account for potential confounding effects. We include firm *size* as larger firms are considered to adopt new technologies earlier. Similarly, a better economic situation of the firm is often associated with more innovative activities. Hence, we include *ROA* to account for the firm's profitability and *TSR* to account for the capital market perception. For a similar reason, we include *leverage*, *sales growth* and *firm risk*. We also consider the firm's *diversification* as more diversified firms could have more various opportunities to deploy boundary resources. In addition to diversification, we also account for the degree of which a firm's targets businesses and consumers as their customers (*B2B-B2C mix*) because such firms may have more options to deploy various boundary resources. We further included the firm's *intangible assets* and the *R&D intensity* as this may be related to a firm's general innovation activities that may drive benefits of boundary resource employment. Finally, we also considered five industry dummies according to Fama and French. For the analyses of the performance implications, we used the same set of control variables but excluded the two performance measures ROA and TSR as controls. A detailed explanation of the calculation of each control variable and the data source is provided in the table of Appendix A.

1.4.3 Empirical Methods

To analyze both the antecedents and the performance implications of the deployment of boundary resources, we need to address different empirical challenges in our empirical analyses. We first elaborate on our reasoning behind choosing an estimation procedure for analyzing the antecedents of boundary resources deployment and, second, on our reasoning behind choosing an estimation procedure for analyzing the performance implications of boundary resources deployment.

1.4.3.1 Estimating the Antecedents of Boundary Resources Deployment

To analyze the antecedents of boundary resources deployment, we have to account for the binary nature of our dependent variables regarding API adoption. The panel structure of our data further allows us to control for unobserved heterogeneity in our empirical analysis. We decided for a general estimating equations (GEE) regression with a logit link function as it enables us to account for both within and between firm variance to calculate robust estimates, thus tackling the issue of unobserved heterogeneity (Ballinger 2004; Liang and Zeger 1986). Specifically, the GEE corrects for the correlation in the dependent variable across firms over time by estimating the correlation structure of the error terms (Gupta and Misangyi 2018). We preferred a GEE model over alternative panel logit models with random or firm-fixed effects for several reasons. First, logit fixed effects models would drop out all observations of firms that did not adopt any API during our time frame. Second, the assumption of random effects models that error terms are uncorrelated over time may be questioned in our panel data set. Third, the GEE fits a population-average model allowing the coefficient to be interpreted as the influence averaged across the population of firms aligning well with our antecedents hypotheses targeting population differences.

To operationalize the GEE, we considered the *xtgee* command in Stata 15. The command requires to specify a correlation structure of the dependent variable. As the efficiency of the GEE depends on the selection of an appropriate correlation structure, we followed a careful selection process. We started by running a Wooldridge test for autocorrelation to check whether choosing an autoregressive correlation structure is appropriate. As the test did not show evidence of autocorrelation, we decided to select among the remaining options (i.e., exchangeable, unstructured or independent) by applying the quasi-likelihood under the independence model criterion (QIC) measure (Cui 2007). Based on the smallest-QIC criteria, we selected an exchangeable correlation structure as it yielded the best fit for all three variables of boundary resources (Gupta and Misangyi 2018; Quigley and Hambrick 2012). Next, we specified a logit link function of the binomial family and the robust option considering the Huber–White standard error correction. Finally, we lagged all our independent and control variables to tackle reverse causality issues. Specifically, we test the following model to analyze our first and second hypothesis:

I. $$Boundary\ resources\ deployment_{i,t+1} = a + \beta_1(digital\ knowledge)_{i,t} + \beta_2(digital\ complementors)_{i,t} + + \gamma(CONTROLS)_{i,t} + Y_t + I_i + \varepsilon_{i,t}$$

where t indexes time periods and i the firms. *Boundary resources deployment* stands for the three dependent variables API, API access and API resource that are each tested separately. *Digital knowledge* is the independent variables used to test our first hypothesis, while *digital complementors* is the independent variables used to test our second hypothesis. The item $CONTROLS$ represents a matrix reflecting the selected control variables. The item Y_t represent year fixed effects. Industry fixed effects are represented by the item I_i. The remaining items are the constant term (α) and the random error term $\varepsilon_{i,t}$.

1.4.3.2 Estimating the Performance Implications of Boundary Resources Deployment

To examine performance implications of boundary resources deployment, we need to consider potential sources of endogeneity. First, there might be systematic differences between firms that employ and do not employ boundary resources that drive performance differences. To address this issue, we decided to run a firm-fixed effects regression that assigns each firm an individual effect. Thereby, the firm-fixed effects model controls for time-invariant firm-specific unobservable factors and estimates only time-variant effects within a firm. Prior IS research, therefore, highlights the importance of firm-fixed effects in capturing unobserved firm heterogeneity when studying IS performance implications (Joshi et al. 2019; Mithas et al. 2012; Pan et al. 2018).

Second, as boundary resources deployment is an endogenous choice and also time-variant unobservable factors could drive the decision for boundary resources deployment and firm performance at the same time, we still could face a self-selection bias. To account for this, we decided to include a correction factor as suggested by Shaver (1998). Specifically, Shaver (1998) proposes to include an additional control variable in the model that is based on a first-stage probit model estimating the propensity to engage in a particular strategy (e.g., boundary resources deployment). Following this suggestion, we estimated the probability to decide for boundary resources deployment while accounting for our second-stage control variables and an exclusion criterion. The exclusion criterion should be correlated with the decision for boundary resources deployment but not correlated with firm performance. We chose the average diffusion of boundary resources deployment in the industry as this should be related to boundary resources deployment of the focal firm, but should not affect the performance of the focal firm other than through the impact on deciding for boundary resources deployment or not. Finally, we used the predicted values of the probit regressions to calculate an inverse Mills ratio (Heckman 1979), which we included as an additional control variable in our firm-fixed effects regressions (i.e., λ boundary resources deployment).

Finally, we lagged all our independent and control variable to tackle reverse causality issues. Specifically, we used the *xtreg* command in Stata 15 and specified the Huber-White standard error correction to estimate the following firm-fixed effects regression to test hypothesis 3:

II. $$Firm\ performance_{i,t+1} = \alpha + \beta_1(boundary\ resources\ deployment)_{i,t} + \gamma_2(CONTROLS)_{i,t} + (\lambda\ boundary\ resources\ deployment)_{i,t} + Y_t + \eta_i + \varepsilon_{i,t}$$

For Hypothesis 4, we further added market power as moderator variable and interacted this variable with our boundary resources deployment proxies.

III. $$Firm\,performance_{i,t+1} = \alpha + \beta_1(boundary\,resources\,deployment)_{i,t} + \beta_2(boundary\,resources\,deployment * market\,power)_{i,t} + \beta_3(market\,power)_{i,t} + \gamma_2(CONTROLS)_{i,t} + (\lambda\,boundary\,resources\,deployment)_{i,t} + Y_t + \eta_i + \varepsilon_{i,t}$$

In both equations II and III *t* indexes time periods and *i* the firms. *Firm performance* stands for our two performance measures ROA2y and TSR 2y and $boundary\,resources\,deployment$ for the three variables API, API access and API resource adoption that are each tested separately. $Market\,power$ reflects our moderator variable and the item $CONTROLS$ a matrix reflecting the selected control variables. The items beside the dependent, independent, moderator and control variables comprise the self-selection correction($\lambda\,boundary\,resources\,deployment$), year dummies ($Y_t$), the constant term ($\alpha$), the firm-specific effects (η_i), and the error term (ε_{it}).

1.5 Findings

1.5.1 Descriptive Results

To illustrate the presence of boundary resources deployment in listed firms, we provide an overview of the development of API use and adoption within our sample. Panel A of Table B-12 displays the API use in our sample by year as well as industry. The overview provides at least two interesting findings: First, the results indicate a rapid diffusion of API use in recent years. While in our starting year less than 4 % of the firms had an API installed, 15 % installed at least one API in 2018. This supports the relevance of boundary resources deployment and the need to better understand the antecedences and implications of this decision. Second, the results support the idea that API use is not limited to technology firms. Specifically, while the Services sector including many technology firms such as Alphabet or Salesforce has the highest diffusion rate, we also find a considerable amount of API users in the Manufacturing (e.g., automotive) and Wholesale & Retail industry. Panel B of Table B-12, further illustrates the frequency of adoptions of APIs over time as well as the differences in this development for the two types of APIs. The results indicate that in each year around 4% of the sample firms adopted at least one API. Moreover, the results indicate that many firms adopted APIs in more than just one year as the sum of all API adoption exceeds the API users. Regarding APIs for access or resource openness, we observe a more frequent adoption of APIs for access openness than of APIs for resource openness. Similar to that, in 2018 users of APIs for resource openness account for only 7% of our sample while around 12% use at least one API for access openness.

Table B-12. Descriptive Statistics on API Adoption and Users.

Panel A: *API users by industry and time*						
YEAR	Mining & Construction	Manufacturing	Transportation	Wholesale & Retail	Finance & Insurance	Services
2010	0%	7%	1%	0%	0%	17%
2011	0%	7%	1%	5%	0%	24%
2012	0%	9%	2%	7%	0%	31%
2013	0%	13%	4%	7%	7%	33%
2014	0%	13%	7%	9%	7%	39%
2015	0%	15%	8%	9%	7%	41%
2016	0%	15%	9%	11%	10%	41%
2017	0%	15%	9%	11%	10%	41%
2018	0%	15%	9%	13%	10%	44%
Total	0%	12%	6%	8%	5%	35%
Obs.	*234*	*1539*	*495*	*414*	*552*	*486*

Panel B: *API adoptions and users by API type* over time						
YEAR	API adoptions	API users	API access adoptions	API access user	API resource adoptions	API resource user
2010	2%	4%	1%	3%	2%	2%
2011	4%	6%	4%	5%	1%	2%
2012	5%	8%	4%	6%	3%	4%
2013	4%	10%	3%	8%	1%	5%
2014	5%	12%	5%	9%	2%	6%
2015	5%	13%	5%	11%	2%	6%
2016	5%	14%	5%	11%	3%	7%
2017	3%	14%	3%	11%	3%	7%
2018	4%	15%	4%	12%	3%	7%
Total	4%	10%	4%	8%	2%	5%

Notes: The industry categories reflect the Standard Industrial Classification (SIC) industry divisions. We further subsumed Mining and Construction under one category as well as Wholesale Trade and Retail Trade. Note that sum of API adoptions can exceed the percentage of API users as some firms adopt multiple APIs. Due to this, the sum of API access and API resource users also exceeds the percentage of API users

In Table B-13, we provide means, standard deviations, 25th and 75th percentile values and the pairwise correlations of all our regression variables. The correlations are below critical thresholds hence alleviating multicollinearity concerns. We further checked variance inflation factors (VIF). However, the highest average VIF for one of our regression models (1.76) as well as the highest individual VIF (3.05) were below critical thresholds.

Table B-13. Descriptive Statistics and Correlation Matrix of All Regression Variables.

No	Variable name	Mean	SD	P25	P75	(1)	(2)	(3)	(4)	(5)	(6)	(7)	(8)	(9)	(10)	(11)	(12)
(1)	API $_{(t+1)}$	0.04	0.20	0.00	0.00	1.00											
(2)	API access $_{(t+1)}$	0.04	0.19	0.00	0.00	0.93	1.00										
(3)	API resource $_{(t+1)}$	0.02	0.14	0.00	0.00	0.67	0.50	1.00									
(4)	Digital knowledge[a]	0.56	1.21	0.00	0.41	0.15	0.14	0.11	1.00								
(5)	Digital complementors[b]	44.28	90.06	2.31	31.50	0.19	0.20	0.13	0.09	1.00							
(6)	CEO age	57.27	6.50	53.00	61.00	-0.12	-0.11	-0.11	-0.06	-0.16	1.00						
(7)	IT board expertise	0.70	1.12	0.00	1.00	0.18	0.17	0.13	0.04	0.23	-0.08	1.00					
(8)	IT TMT expertise	1.54	0.70	1.00	2.00	0.16	0.14	0.13	0.19	0.18	-0.02	0.18	1.00				
(9)	Size[a]	16.38	1.40	15.39	17.20	0.10	0.10	0.10	0.13	-0.23	0.12	-0.03	0.19	1.00			
(10)	R&D intensity[b,c]	2.07	14.24	0.00	0.04	0.18	0.16	0.15	-0.01	0.12	-0.15	0.25	0.22	-0.21	1.00		
(11)	Intangibles[b]	2.23	3.34	0.03	3.03	0.06	0.07	0.02	0.01	0.32	-0.09	0.14	0.16	-0.14	0.23	1.00	
(12)	Market power[b,c]	17.49	24.50	2.76	19.11	0.08	0.07	0.10	0.22	-0.16	0.10	0.02	0.08	0.54	-0.17	-0.16	1.00
(13)	Leverage[b,c]	26.63	17.68	13.66	37.06	-0.09	-0.08	-0.06	0.01	-0.10	0.06	-0.07	-0.06	-0.01	-0.20	-0.05	0.06
(14)	B2B-B2C mix	0.08	0.21	0.00	0.00	0.02	0.02	0.02	0.19	-0.01	0.02	-0.01	0.08	0.02	0.00	0.11	0.03
(15)	Diversification	0.14	0.27	0.00	0.10	0.00	0.00	0.00	0.24	0.02	0.12	0.02	0.08	0.06	-0.05	0.11	0.07
(16)	ROA[b,c]	6.97	6.90	3.29	10.46	0.05	0.05	0.04	0.03	0.13	-0.01	0.06	-0.01	-0.29	0.13	0.09	-0.07
(17)	TSR[b,c]	13.42	31.76	-3.08	30.88	0.02	0.03	0.01	0.03	0.05	0.00	0.02	0.06	0.00	0.03	0.04	-0.01
(18)	Sales growth[b,c]	7.27	13.23	-0.25	12.18	0.15	0.12	0.13	0.09	0.12	-0.14	0.04	0.06	-0.03	0.14	0.17	-0.07
(19)	Firm risk[b]	9.00	13.65	1.97	9.16	0.01	0.01	0.00	0.04	0.06	-0.02	-0.02	0.04	-0.10	0.02	-0.04	-0.03
(20)	Ownership conc.[c]	5.47	10.19	0.31	5.70	0.06	0.06	0.04	0.02	0.02	-0.02	0.00	-0.11	-0.13	-0.05	-0.02	-0.05
(21)	TSR 2y[b,c] $_{(t+1)}$	17.85	26.61	1.85	28.66	0.04	0.04	0.04	0.05	0.03	-0.07	0.01	0.00	-0.05	0.08	0.03	-0.01
(22)	ROA 2y[b,c] $_{(t+1)}$	7.02	6.37	3.45	10.27	0.04	0.03	0.03	0.02	0.12	0.01	0.07	-0.01	-0.33	0.16	0.08	-0.09
(23)	Margin 2y[b,c] $_{(t+1)}$	15.75	15.02	8.09	22.79	0.05	0.05	0.03	-0.06	0.05	0.01	0.02	-0.07	0.12	0.07	0.09	-0.07
(24)	Sales 2y[b,d] $_{(t+1)}$	14.08	17.58	3.27	15.54	0.21	0.21	0.20	0.28	-0.10	0.09	0.06	0.26	0.65	-0.11	-0.12	0.68

No	Variable name	Mean	SD	P25	P75	(13)	(14)	(15)	(16)	(17)	(18)	(19)	(20)	(21)	(22)	(23)	(24)
(13)	Leverage[b,c]	26.63	17.68	13.66	37.06	1.00											
(14)	B2B-B2C mix	0.08	0.21	0.00	0.00	0.05	1.00										
(15)	Diversification	0.14	0.27	0.00	0.10	0.06	0.55	1.00									
(16)	ROA[b,c]	6.97	6.90	3.29	10.46	-0.03	0.00	-0.05	1.00								
(17)	TSR[b,c]	13.42	31.76	-3.08	30.88	-0.02	0.00	0.00	0.21	1.00							
(18)	Sales growth[b,c]	7.27	13.23	-0.25	12.18	-0.13	-0.04	-0.09	0.23	0.10	1.00						
(19)	Firm risk[b]	9.00	13.65	1.97	9.16	0.32	-0.01	0.00	0.11	0.03	-0.06	1.00					
(20)	Ownership conc.[c]	5.47	10.19	0.31	5.70	-0.04	-0.05	-0.07	0.06	-0.05	0.00	0.02	1.00				
(21)	TSR 2y[b,c] $_{(t+1)}$	17.85	26.61	1.85	28.66	-0.03	-0.03	-0.04	0.04	-0.20	0.06	0.00	0.05	1.00			
(22)	ROA 2y[b,c] $_{(t+1)}$	7.02	6.37	3.45	10.27	0.02	-0.01	-0.04	0.72	0.11	0.15	0.13	0.08	0.22	1.00		
(23)	Margin 2y[b,c] $_{(t+1)}$	15.75	15.02	8.09	22.79	0.06	-0.07	-0.11	0.30	0.06	0.11	0.00	0.00	0.18	0.52	1.00	
(24)	Sales 2y[b,d] $_{(t+1)}$	14.08	17.58	3.27	15.54	-0.03	0.09	0.13	-0.04	0.02	0.02	-0.01	-0.04	-0.01	-0.04	-0.07	1.00

1.5.2 Regression Results

1.5.2.1 Antecedents of Boundary Resources Deployment – Results for Hypotheses 1 and 2

In Table B-14, we run GEE logit regressions that estimate the influence of *internal digital knowledge* as well as *external digital complementors* on boundary resources deployment. In Model 1, we test the influence on the adoption of APIs, in Model 2 on the adoption of APIs for access openness and in Model 3 on the adoption of APIs for resource openness.

Table B-14. Antecedents of API Adoption.

Model	**1**	**2**	**3**
Method	**GEE logit**	**GEE logit**	**GEE logit**
Dependent variable	**API**	**API access**	**API resource**
Digital knowledge (H1)	0.318**	0.354**	0.271
	(0.013)	(0.011)	(0.156)
Digital complementors (H2)	0.294**	0.391***	0.665***
	(0.011)	(0.001)	(0.000)
Controls			
CEO age	-0.146	-0.140	-0.078
	(0.274)	(0.312)	(0.733)
IT board expertise	0.189*	0.215**	0.255*
	(0.059)	(0.033)	(0.100)
IT TMT expertise	0.519***	0.439***	0.975***
	(0.001)	(0.002)	(0.002)
Size	0.406**	0.312*	0.280
	(0.022)	(0.080)	(0.270)
R&D intensity	0.630***	0.479***	0.886***
	(0.000)	(0.000)	(0.000)
Intangibles	0.092	0.080	-0.165
	(0.416)	(0.511)	(0.397)
Market power	0.473**	0.573**	1.104***
	(0.042)	(0.017)	(0.001)
Leverage	-0.054	-0.085	0.053
	(0.694)	(0.533)	(0.809)
B2B-B2C mix	0.215**	0.221**	0.393**
	(0.047)	(0.041)	(0.012)
Diversification	-0.163	-0.217	-0.365**
	(0.225)	(0.153)	(0.048)
ROA	0.204*	0.103	0.002
	(0.088)	(0.463)	(0.991)
TSR	-0.117	-0.103	-0.182
	(0.273)	(0.411)	(0.200)
Sales growth	0.085	-0.005	0.265
	(0.485)	(0.973)	(0.261)
Firm Risk	0.154	0.150	0.155
	(0.108)	(0.145)	(0.244)
Ownership concentration	0.282***	0.272***	0.334**
	(0.001)	(0.003)	(0.019)
Constant	-4.690***	-5.675***	-6.497***
	(0.000)	(0.000)	(0.000)
Industry effects	yes	yes	yes
Year effects	yes	yes	yes
Chi-square	202.46	200.91	244.75
N	3720	3720	3720

Notes: *p<0.10; **p<0.05; ***p<0.01. Two-tailed p-values are reported in the parentheses. To facilitate the comparison of the coefficients all independent variables are standardized. Detailed information on all regression variables is provided in the Appendix.

Regarding the influence of internal digital knowledge on API adoption, we find a positive and significant coefficient for our internal digital knowledge variable in Model 1. In practical terms, Model 1 suggest that a 1-standard deviation (SD) increase of internal digital knowledge from its mean value relates to a 37% higher probability of adopting an API. Moreover, the results of Model 2 and Model 3 indicate that the positive and significant influence of internal digital knowledge is restricted to the adoption of APIs for access openness. Specifically, while Model 2 suggests that a 1-SD increase of internal digital knowledge from its mean is associated with a 42% higher probability of adopting APIs for access openness, internal digital knowledge does not significantly affect adoption of APIs for resource openness. Hence, the results displayed in Table B-14 provide support for Hypothesis 1 suggesting that a digital knowledge base is an important driver of API adoption and, in particular, of APIs for access openness that are used to distribute and commercialize digital innovations.

Regarding the influence of external digital complementors on API adoption, we find a positive and significant coefficient for our digital complementors variable in all Models 1 to 3. However, we also observe that the influence of digital complementors is particularly strong when it comes to the adoption of APIs for resource openness. Specifically, while we find that a 1-SD increase of digital complementors from its mean value relates to a 47% higher probability of adopting APIs for access openness, a similar increase is associated to a 94% higher probability in the adoption of APIs for resource openness. Hence, the results support the idea of Hypothesis 2 that external digital complementors drive the use of API adoption and, in particular, of APIs for resource openness that aim to integrate digital innovations of external complementors.

1.5.2.2 Performance Implications of Boundary Resources Deployment – Results for Hypothesis 3 and 4

In Table B-15, we run firm-fixed effects regressions estimating the performance consequences of boundary resources deployment. We therefore test the influence of API adoptions on the firm's TSR and ROA over the adopting and the next year. We also separately test the influence of access and resource APIs on firm performance.

With regard to the adoption of APIs per se, we do not find a significant and positive effect on one of the firm performance variables in Panel A of Table B-15. However, when considering market power as a moderator in Model 2 and Model 4 of Panel A of Table B-15, we find a positive and significant moderating effect of market power on the relation between API adoption and both performance variables. These results suggest a positive performance effect of API adoption for firms with relatively high market power. Specifically, Model 2 indicates that API adoption for a firm with high market power (1-SD above the mean) is associated with a 21% increase in market-based performance (TSR 2y) and a 17% percent increase in accounting-based performance (ROA 2y). Hence, we find support for our fourth hypothesis suggesting that the performance effect of API adoption increases with the firm's market power. However, we could not find support that API adoption has a positive influence on performance on average as suggested in Hypothesis 3.

Table B-15. Performance Implications of API Adoption.

***Panel A:** The influence of API adoption on firm performance*				
Model	1	2	3	4
Method	Firm-fixed effects	Firm-fixed effects	Firm-fixed effects	Firm-fixed effects
Dependent variable	TSR 2y	TSR 2y	ROA 2y	ROA 2y
API	1.478 (0.573)	0.465 (0.868)	-0.121 (0.724)	-0.310 (0.367)
API * Market Power		3.225* (0.092)		0.799** (0.040)
Market Power		-8.758*** (0.007)		0.767 (0.312)
Control variables	yes	yes	yes	yes
Year effects	yes	yes	yes	yes
Firm fixed effects	yes	yes	yes	yes
Adjusted R-square	0.181	0.184	0.139	0.141
N	3307	3307	3307	3307
***Panel B:** The influence of API access adoption on firm performance*				
Model	1	2	3	4
Method	Firm-fixed effects	Firm-fixed effects	Firm-fixed effects	Firm-fixed effects
Dependent variable	TSR 2y	TSR 2y	ROA 2y	ROA 2y
API access	0.732 (0.815)	-0.303 (0.927)	0.044 (0.914)	-0.143 (0.720)
API access * Market Power		4.544** (0.031)		0.939** (0.020)
Market Power		-8.839*** (0.006)		0.770 (0.311)
Control variables	yes	yes	yes	yes
Year effects	yes	yes	yes	yes
Firm fixed effects	yes	yes	yes	yes
Adjusted R-square	0.181	0.184	0.139	0.142
N	3307	3307	3307	3307
***Panel C:** The influence of API resource adoption on firm performance*				
Model	1	2	3	4
Method	Firm-fixed effects	Firm-fixed effects	Firm-fixed effects	Firm-fixed effects
Dependent variable	TSR 2y	TSR 2y	ROA 2y	ROA 2y
API resource	4.545 (0.328)	3.928 (0.501)	0.052 (0.944)	0.041 (0.956)
API resource * Market Power		1.766 (0.658)		-0.049 (0.937)
Market Power		-8.659*** (0.007)		0.838 (0.278)
Control variables	yes	yes	yes	yes
Year effects	yes	yes	yes	yes
Firm fixed effects	yes	yes	yes	yes
Adjusted R-square	0.182	0.184	0.139	0.140
N	3307	3307	3307	3307

Notes for Panel A-C: *p<0.10; **p<0.05; ***p<0.01. Two-tailed p-values are reported in the parentheses. The moderator variable Market power is standardized. The included control variable comprise: *CEO age, IT board expertise, IT TMT expertise, Size, R&D intensity, Intangibles, Leverage, BSB-BSC mix, Diversification, Sales growth, Firm Risk, Ownership concentration* and the selection correction factor *λ boundary resources deployment.* Detailed information on all regression variables is provided in the Appendix.

Moreover, we also tested the performance implications of the adoption of APIs for access openness in Panel B of Table B-15 and the adoption of APIs for resource openness in Panel C of Table B-15. The results indicate that the performance effect observed for both types of API adoptions in Panel A of Table B-15 is mainly determined by adoption of APIs for access openness. Similar to general API adoptions, adoptions of APIs for access openness do not increase firm performance on average, but they do for firms with a relatively high market power. Specifically, Model 2 of Panel B of Table B-15 indicates that the adoption of APIs for access openness for a firm with high market power (1-SD above the mean) is associated with a 25% increase in market-based performance (TSR 2y) and a 22% percent increase in accounting-based performance (ROA 2y). In contrast, Panel C of Table B-15 indicates that the adoption of APIs for resource openness is not significantly associated with a performance increase on average and also not for firms with a higher market power.

1.5.3 Robustness of Results

We run several (untabulated) robustness tests. With regard to the antecedents of boundary resource employment, we alternatively run a panel logit with random effects and also tested alternative correlation structure in the GEE model and found similar results. We further tested whether changing the link function to a probit model would affect our results and found again similar results. Finally, we considered that some firms may adopt multiple APIs in one year and tested alternatively the impact on the number of API adoptions and found results similar to the ones with the binary proxies. With regard to the performance effect of API adoptions, we also tested the number of API adoptions in a year and found consistent results. Moreover, we considered even longer lead times for the performance effect and tested the impact of API adoptions over three years. We found again similar results to those reported.

1.5.4 Additional Test – Drivers of the Performance Effects

In an additional test, we further aimed to investigate the drivers of the performance effect of API adoptions. Based on our arguments in the hypotheses, we expected that APIs could, for example, serve as an efficient distribution channel that increases revenues and profits. While we would particularly expect increases in revenue on average, gaining superior profits might be more difficult. Specifically, adopting and employing APIs is certainly associated with considerable administrative costs that need to be compensated by additional margins. In the context of APIs for resource openness, this might be particularly difficult as also the external contributors aim to benefit from their participation. We hence decided to investigate the impact of API adoption on net sales as well as the operating margin in the next two years. Market power could help in the acceptance of APIs and thus increase their sales impact. It may also affect how firms are able to translate additional revenue into profits. Hence, we also consider the moderating effect of market power in the additional analysis. Table B-16 presents the results of the additional analyses.

Table B-16. Drivers Behind the API Performance Relation.

Panel A: *The influence of API adoption on the operating margin and sales*				
Model	1	2	3	4
Method	Firm-fixed effects	Firm-fixed effects	Firm-fixed effects	Firm-fixed effects
Dependent variable	Margin 2y	Margin 2y	Sales 2y	Sales 2y
API	0.251	-0.224	1.220*	0.892*
	(0.649)	(0.706)	(0.052)	(0.085)
API * Market Power		1.223*		1.556*
		(0.071)		(0.053)
Market Power		-7.626***		3.399***
		(0.003)		(0.002)
Control variables	yes	yes	yes	yes
Year effects	yes	yes	yes	yes
Firm fixed effects	yes	yes	yes	yes
Adjusted R-square	0.181	0.184	0.139	0.141
N	3307	3307	3307	3307
Panel B: *The influence of API access adoption on the operating margin and sales*				
Model	1	2	3	4
Method	Firm-fixed effects	Firm-fixed effects	Firm-fixed effects	Firm-fixed effects
Dependent variable	Margin 2y	Margin 2y	Sales 2y	Sales 2y
API access	0.415	-0.020	1.654**	1.307**
	(0.457)	(0.974)	(0.014)	(0.019)
API access * Market Power		1.715**		1.838**
		(0.026)		(0.035)
Market Power		-7.646***		3.385***
		(0.003)		(0.002)
Control variables	yes	yes	yes	yes
Year effects	yes	yes	yes	yes
Firm fixed effects	yes	yes	yes	yes
Adjusted R-square	0.181	0.184	0.139	0.142
N	3307	3307	3307	3307
Panel C: *The influence of API resource adoption on the operating margin and sales*				
Model	1	2	3	4
Method	Firm-fixed effects	Firm-fixed effects	Firm-fixed effects	Firm-fixed effects
Dependent variable	Margin 2y	Margin 2y	Sales 2y	Sales 2y
API resource	0.896	1.317	3.341***	1.507*
	(0.527)	(0.531)	(0.006)	(0.072)
API resource * Market Power		(0.120)		2.904**
		(0.932)		(0.047)
Market Power		-7.560***		3.407***
		(0.004)		(0.002)
Control variables	yes	yes	yes	yes
Year effects	yes	yes	yes	yes
Firm fixed effects	yes	yes	yes	yes
Adjusted R-square	0.182	0.184	0.139	0.140
N	3307	3307	3307	3307

Notes for Panel A-C: *p<0.10; **p<0.05; ***p<0.01. Two-tailed p-values are reported in the parentheses. The moderator variable Market power is standardized. The included control variable comprise: *CEO age, IT board expertise, IT TMT expertise, Size, R&D intensity, Intangibles, Leverage, BSB-BSC mix, Diversification, Sales growth, Firm Risk, Ownership concentration* and the selection correction factor *λ boundary resources deployment.* Detailed information on all regression variables is provided in the Appendix.

The results in Table B-16 indicate that API adoptions are associated with a sales increase on average. Interestingly, we find that both types of APIs are associated with significant increases in sales. We also find that market power positively moderates the relationship between API adoption and sales. The positive moderation is again significant for both API types. With regard to the impact of API adoption on the operating margin the results show a more nuanced picture. Specifically, we do not find a positive influence on the operating margin on average. Only for firms with a relative high market power API adoptions are associated with a slightly significant increase in the operating margin. Moreover, we find that this effect is driven by adoptions of APIs for access openness. Specifically, we find a positive and significant impact of the adoption of APIs for access openness on the operating margin for firm with a higher market power, while the influence of the adoption of APIs for resource openness is not significant irrespective of the firm's market power. In sum, the additional analysis suggests that APIs are effective in increasing revenues, but also that it is difficult to extract superior margins from APIs. While market power could help to increase the margin effect of APIs, this holds only true for access APIs. In the following, we discuss our results in more detail.

1.6 Discussion of Findings

Boundary resources are an essential element of vibrant digital business ecosystems (Boudreau 2012; Ghazawneh and Henfridsson 2013; Yoo et al. 2010). Prior IS research has created valuable knowledge about the design of boundary resources such as APIs, the ecosystem interactions revolving around them as well as the mechanisms by which value is created (Eaton et al. 2015; Ghazawneh and Henfridsson 2013; Karhu et al. 2018). The antecedents and performance implications of boundary resources from the perspective of the deploying firm, however, are less understood. In this paper, building upon a theoretical framework comprising specific contingencies and drawing on a cross-industry and longitudinal dataset, we present empirical insights on these topics.

Our findings suggest that firms with pre-existing digital knowledge opt to deploy APIs. This finding supports absorptive capacity theory in that past knowledge helps to develop new related knowledge in the future as well as to realize technological outputs building upon that knowledge (Lane et al. 2006; Roberts et al. 2012). On the one hand, since they themselves represent digital technology artifacts, it is likely that firms that have digital capabilities are better prepared to build APIs. One might expect that such firms already build substantially upon IS (Zmud et al. 2010) and are therefore particularly ready to greatly deploy APIs. From case studies in digital industries (Eaton et al. 2015; Ghazawneh and Henfridsson 2013; Parker et al. 2017), we know that the respective firms make great use of APIs. On the other hand, the finding indicates that firms possessing digital knowledge do not perceive boundary resources as unnecessary or even a potential threat to their own competence, but pro-actively seek to leverage and expose their internal digital knowledge. In this regard, we know that firms that are rich in digital knowledge are particularly apt to pursue digital innovation (Hanelt et al. 2020; Kohli and Melville 2019). As to the distributed and combinatorial nature of digital innovation (Yoo et al. 2012), the development of boundary resources might be an important step in this direction. This aspect is also underscored as our empirical analysis revealed that firms that rank high in digital knowledge tend to particularly deploy those boundary resources that provide access openness (Karhu et al. 2018). Accordingly, APIs might be perceived as a measure of exploitative learning (March 1991) from the perspective of firms that have already progressed on the digital maturity curve. These firms seem to utilize such boundary resources particularly in the commercialization (West and Bogers 2014) or implementation and exploitation (Kohli and Melville 2019) phase of innovation.

Here, in an attempt to achieve network effects (Boudreau 2012; Boudreau and Jeppesen 2015), APIs may be used to increase the reach of specific offerings with help of others. Accordingly, the contributions of external actors making use of such boundary resources may be more distributive in nature.

Apart from that, we found that the existence of digital ventures in the field is positively associated with boundary resource deployments. At least two potential explanations emerge. First, the presence of digital ventures might threaten established firms based on a perception that these firms could be potential competitors or disruptors (Karimi and Walter 2015; Lucas and Goh 2009). Driven by that perception, firms may feel especially alerted to engage in digital innovation to defend against disruption (Henfridsson and Yoo 2014), which could drive the decision to deploy APIs (Svahn et al. 2017). Second, it might be that established firms see digital ventures as potential complementors and want to steer them towards their direction by setting up APIs as, in digital innovation, "*a firm's ability to attract heterogeneous and unexpected firms to build various components has become strategically important*" (Yoo et al. 2010, p. 731). Since digital business ecosystems are regularly characterized by the notion of coopetition (El Sawy and Pereira 2013), it is likely that both aspects are true. However, our analysis further revealed that firms that face the existence of digital ventures in their field tend to deploy particularly those boundary resources that allow for resource openness (Karhu et al., 2018). Thus, using boundary resources to enable co-creation might represent a measure of explorative learning (March, 1991). The experiences of an incumbent automobile manufacturer embracing digital innovation provide an illustrative example: To explore new design options, APIs were used to "*give third-party developers the opportunity to use in-car resources, such as sensor data, screens, and loudspeaker systems, for developing applications.*" (Henfridsson and Yoo 2014, pp. 938-939). Here, such boundary resources may particularly support rather the initiation and development (Kohli and Melville 2019) or obtaining and integration (West and Bogers 2014) phases of innovation where firms attempt to profit from widespread and diverse knowledge of others to create new offerings. Thus, the contributions of external actors are rather creative in nature.

As to the consequences of boundary resources deployments, on the one hand, we can derive the insight from our data that deploying APIs, on average, does not have a significant performance implication per se. This finding could indicate that companies deploy APIs but are not necessarily capable of managing such new technologies properly, which might result in lower realization of the potential economic benefits. For instance, incumbent automotive manufacturers struggle to realize the potentials of APIs: "*Leveraging connectivity by exposing the car to external developers, such as through open APIs, was expected to generate a new level of functional diversity in the automotive industry. This bold vision, however, stood in stark contrast to existing innovation practices and business models.*" (Svahn et al., 2017, p. 241). Apart from that, some firms might invest in API deployment not for rational reasons but to follow management fashions (Abrahamson 1991; Baskerville and Myers 2009) emerging from the omnipresent discourse and uncertainty related to digitalization (Tumbas et al. 2018).

On the other hand, our findings suggest that firms with higher market power significantly profit from boundary resources deployments. The nature of boundary resources lends some interpretation. Boundary resources deployments are just a first step to profit from co-creation and co-capture of value. The second step is represented by external actors that actively utilize boundary resources to, for instance, leverage the provided assets in their contexts (Parker et al. 2017). Firms that rank high in market power might represent attractive partners for external audiences due to their established brands, customer bases, and quality of products or services (Eaton et al. 2015). External stakeholders might project that they could themselves profit from these assets or ultimately reach larger audiences within their contexts and related business activities (Karhu et al. 2018). In addition, our findings provide a differentiated picture in terms of the specific effects of the two types of boundary resources deployments (i.e., APIs for access and resource openness). Interestingly, our results suggest that firms with high market power profit only from deploying APIs for access openness. The following reasoning stemming from the distinct purposes and requirements of the two types of boundary resources could provide an explanation. A key function of APIs for access openness is distributing readily available digital innovations to external parties that utilize them in their contexts. Consequently, these digital assets need to constitute a certain degree of maturity and quality in order to provide added value to the targeted audiences, thus providing inherently greater commercialization opportunities. In contrast, in the case of APIs for resource openness, the commercialization phase might be still far away. Moreover, with regard to the associated costs, developing and maintaining APIs for resource openness probably requires, in comparison to APIs for access openness, greater financial and technological resources, due to the more complex coordination and governance of the heterogeneous complementors' activities and contributions (Eaton et al. 2015; Karhu et al. 2018) – limiting potential financial benefits. In addition, complementors strive to capture parts of the generated revenues stemming from their contributions (Eaton et al. 2015; Karhu et al. 2018), what might further lower the probabilities of realizing significant performance-related benefits from APIs for resource openness.

Furthermore, as to our additional findings on the drivers of performance effects, we find that both types of boundary resources deployments are effective for increasing revenues, which is also further augmented by a firm's market power. This insight confirms our predictions that boundary resources support firms in commercializing and diversifying their digital offerings (Boudreau 2012; van de Ven 2005; Yoo et al. 2010) – all of which stabilizes and increases revenues. However, our results also suggest that it is difficult for firms to realize superior margins through the deployment of boundary resources. More specific, although being just slightly significant, only firms with higher market power are able to extract operational margins as they deploy APIs for access openness. Presumably, firms with less market power might be obliged to offer their products at lower price levels in order to convince audiences of their offerings and thus intend to increase their respective market shares, which in turn makes it difficult to extract higher operational margins from the deployment of APIs. In contrast, firms with relative high market power, once again, might benefit from, one the one side, infrastructural control (Eaton et al. 2015) as well as lock-in effects of customers (Zhu and Zhou 2012), and on the other side, from technological infrastructures that unlock economies of scale and thus have greater potential to extract higher operational margins (Tilson et al. 2010).

1.7 Implications

The era of digital business ecosystems and digital innovation is said to require increased openness in a firm's business and innovation activities (El Sawy and Pereira 2013; Yoo et al. 2012). At the same time, opening up reduces the firm's ability to control its assets and the operations of external actors (Parker and van Alstyne 2018). In business practice, firms that are trying to cope with the new competitive dynamics of growing and diversifying business ecosystems are confronted by the strategic decision whether they need to open up towards external contribution, and if they do so, how they can maintain control over their strategic assets (Yoo et al. 2010). This decision reflects a managerial tension since firms are increasingly dependent on outside heterogeneous capabilities and resources in the context of digital innovation, but simultaneously need to protect their assets from external exploitation (Karhu et al. 2018; Yoo et al. 2010). In this regard, the concept of boundary resources has been suggested as a theoretical device to deal and mitigate this tension (Eaton et al. 2015; Ghazawneh and Henfridsson 2013). Therefore, the deployment of boundary resources can be understood as an intermediate strategy residing between complete openness and tight control, which reflects the firm's balancing act of stimulating external contribution while simultaneously maintaining control over strategic assets (Ghazawneh and Henfridsson 2013).

While prior works have revealed important insights about what happens inside firms or ecosystems in the time after boundary resources deployment, the strategic reasoning to do so as well as the consequences for the deploying firm received less attention. In this regard, our study provides valuable extensions. Our findings suggest that firms that possess digital knowledge are driven toward this intermediate strategy. On the one hand, these firms want to leverage their knowledge. On the other, they are likely to also want to retain some kind of control. Furthermore, firms surrounded with digital ventures opt for the middleground strategy. These firms might perceive advantages in opening up to some degree to allow cooperation, while they also might be aware of giving away too much to the potential competitors. Boundary resources are a viable strategy to exert some kind of control over external actors that do not fall into the traditional realm of suppliers or partners that might be controlled via contracting. In sum, as indicated by our findings, particularly when firms possess digital knowledge and face digital ventures in their fields, the middle-ground strategy of deploying boundary resources seems to be attractive as it enables openness, yet also affords exerting soft power in leveraging internal and external knowledge. Thus, firms in such constellations open up gradually, yet also in a confined manner to secure important assets. This strategy, however, does only pay off financially for some firms, that is, those that rank high in market power. Firms lacking such a position might potentially profit more from an alternative strategy that pursues an even higher degree of openness to reach larger audiences, e.g., by providing open source licenses (Karhu et al. 2018). Following this train of thought, the decision to open up for co-creation and co-capture of value with external actors as well as the implementation of technical artifacts such as APIs that allow to do so are as important as the potential assets (brands, customers, platforms etc.) that a firm can bring in to the relationships with these actors.

Apart from that, our study further illuminates the dynamics of coopetition in the digital age (El Sawy and Pereira 2013). Traditionally, potential competitions between internal and external sources of innovation were described (West and Bogers 2014). The nature of digital technologies, including an architecture consisting of loosely coupled layers (Yoo et al. 2010), as well as the traits of digital innovation, including its combinatorial and distributed characteristics (Yoo et al. 2012), indicate the particular value of combining and integrating both internal and external knowledge. Accordingly, we find that firms that generate a high amount of digital knowledge themselves also engage in gathering further knowledge from external parties (without contracting or formally acquiring it). Therefore, boundary resources, on the one hand, might be viewed as technical support of external knowledge acquisition in digital(izing) business environments. This view provides a valuable extension to IS research related to absorptive capacity (Roberts et al. 2012) and knowledge recombination. With regard to the latter, prior works have found that IT significantly drives knowledge recombination (Dong and Yang 2019). However, such existing studies were mostly focusing more traditional IT systems that were used either internally or externally concerning very specific business partners. Boundary resources such as APIs with their external orientation and low barriers to usage might therefore significantly drive knowledge recombination, particularly with regard to its diversity (i.e., the scope of knowledge that is recombined by a firm) (Dong and Yang 2019). On the other hand, boundary resources might be viewed as a viable strategy to expose internal digital knowledge. That is, they strengthen a firm's desorptive capacity as an important capability in achieving technology transfer across organizational boundaries (Müller-Seitz 2012; Ziegler et al. 2013), a perspective missing so far in the IS discourse. The bi-directional nature of boundary resources renders a simultaneous view on inflows and outflows of knowledge particularly relevant (West and Bogers, 2014).

Apart from that, our findings provide an interesting contextual differentiation in boundary resources research. Prior literature has predominantly dealt with purely digital contexts. For instance, the study by Karhu et al. (2018) was situated in the context of digital platform business. In the context of digitalization across industries (Tilson et al. 2010), however, the topic of boundary resources deployment is becoming relevant in all types of business contexts. Our study revealed the widespread dissemination of boundary resources across a broad range of industries and different contexts. Particularly in contexts that do not belong to IT or digital industries, the decision to adopt boundary resources might be embedded in a larger process of digital transformation. Firms that are yet to explore and develop their digital business strategies (Bharadwaj et al. 2013) might learn in parallel or through the deployment of APIs. Furthermore, based on inexperience and uncertainty, they might also follow trends and hypes in deploying APIs. These aspects might then influence their decisions to deploy APIs. Relatedly, history might be influential in this regard in a variety of ways, e.g., due to socio-technical or socio-cognitive inertia (Besson and Rowe 2012). For instance, firms that achieved to be successful in the past in in non-digital contexts might strongly adhere to a supply chain logic, which might run against the platform logic in digital(izing) business environments (Gawer and Phillips 2013). Accordingly, the particular organizational surroundings of boundary resources deployment become more relevant in the era of digitalization and provide valuable insights into managerial decisions about and the effectiveness of boundary resources deployment.

Additionally, our study has important implications for managerial practice. In the discourse revolving around digital transformation, managers might reflect about the deployment of boundary resources such as APIs. First, our study informs managers about the internal and external factors that drive firms to deploy boundary resources – an insight that is relevant both to assess the strategic moves of competitors and to reflect on the firm's own situation and potential development with regards to openness. Second, our study reveals that setting up APIs does not have a performance effect per se. When the goal is to economically profit from APIs, the right conditions should be in place. Here, particularly firms with superior market power can expect positive returns. This, however, is primarily driven by deploying APIs for access openness. More specific, although both types of APIs are effective in increasing revenues, only APIs for access openness allow firms with high market power to extract operational margins. Consequently, it is vital that firms take their market position and bargaining power into account when they assess whether benefits from deploying boundary resources have the potential to outweigh the costs. Lastly, firms need to understand that, in digital(izing) business environments, they are embedded in an ecosystem of increasingly heterogeneous and diverse actors with various requirements and demands. Accordingly, they should focus on optimizing the quality of co-creation on their part and be extra-sensitive to hubris and false assumptions. Furthermore, managers should not perceive APIs as a means to substitute their own R&D efforts but as a means to gather valuable complements and profit from knowledge (re-)combination (Dong and Yang 2019). Here, digital entrants should not only be viewed as threats, but as potential co-creators.

1.8 Limitations and Future Research

The results of our study offer valuable theoretical and practical contributions. However, there are some caveats worth mentioning. First, we restricted our sample to publicly listed companies on the US market based on the S&P 500 stock index. Although the S&P 500 stock index represents a widespread set of companies across various industries on a renowned market, the generalizability of our findings is limited. The adoption and intensity of boundary resources deployment can be influenced by the fact that the most valuable and impactful tech companies in the world (e.g., Google or Amazon) originate from and are headquartered in the US. Future research in other international markets could thus help to validate and expand our empirical findings.

Further, we focused on APIs as boundary resources and considered only a certain amount of companies (S&P 500). Therefore, further research is needed to understand boundary resources deployment more comprehensively. A potential area of future research would be to repeat the study with a larger scale of companies for the purpose of developing more general insights. In addition, the analysis of additional boundary resources like SDKs might promise fruitful insights that could expend our understanding of different deploying strategies related to other types of boundary resources. To this end, future studies could also deep-dive and focus on the empirical investigation of driving forces and outcomes of varying strategies, such as deploying only a specific type of boundary resources.

In our study, we focused on a crisp and clear research question regarding the strategic decision and value of deploying boundary resources. However, other strategies need to be considered when evaluating boundary resources. While the results of our study indicate that boundary resources are being deployed and capitalized under certain conditions, the deeper dimensions and chains of effects of certain constructs remain unclear. As we derived our findings based on a large-scale empirical analysis, future in-depth case studies should investigate in more detail when and why certain performance effects from deploying boundary resources arise. With regard to this, future research could, on the one side, shed light on specific factors inside the firm, such as path dependency (Cohen and Levinthal 1990; Lane et al. 2006) or internal conflicts (Lucas and Goh 2009; Svahn et al. 2017), and on the other side, examine how the firm's contexts (e.g., industry, digital complementors) exactly influences the effective deployment of boundary resources. In addition, future research should particularly consider developing more insights on the currently less explored user side perspective of boundary resources (Benlian et al. 2015; Parker et al. 2017), since firms are increasingly dependent on the co-creation and co-capture of value with external players (El Sawy and Pereira 2013) that similarly represent potential users of their boundary resources in their respective digital business ecosystems.

1.9 Appendix A: Variable Description

Variable	Description & Calculation	Data source
API Variables:		
API	Binary variable that takes the value of 1 if a firm adopted at least one API in the given year and zero otherwise.	Programmable Web API directory
API access	Binary variable that takes the value of 1 if a firm adopted at least one API for access openness in the given year and zero otherwise.	Programmable Web API directory
API resource	Binary variable that takes the value of 1 if a firm adopted at least one API for resource openness in the given year and zero otherwise.	Programmable Web API directory
Antecedent variables:		
Digital knowledge	Calculated as one plus the natural logarithm of the average digital patent filings in the recent two years t and t-1. Patents are defined as digital, if they are classified in technological classed that relate to digital technologies according to the USPC scheme. Specifically, we consider the following USPC classes as related to digital technologies: 178, 333, 340, 342, 343, 358, 367, 370, 375, 379, 385, 455, 341, 380, 382, 395, 700, 701, 702, 704, 705, 706, 707, 708, 709, 710, 712, 713, 714, 345, 347, 360, 365, 369, 711, 715, 716, 717, 718, 719, 720, 725, 726.	USPTO
Digital complementors	Calculated as the average number of digital ventures in a Fama and French 48 industry per S&P 500 industry incumbent filings in the recent two years t and t-1. Digital ventures are extracted by from the CrunchBase Database.	CrunchBase
Firm performance variables:		
TSR 2y	Total Shareholder Return is calculated as the average dividend adjusted stock returns over two years (t and t+1).	Datastream
ROA 2y	Return on Assets is calculated as over two years (t and t+1) and based on DataStream item, which is calculated as net income + (interest expense on debt-interest capitalized) * (1- tax rate)) divided by the average of last year's and current year's total assets.	Datastream
Moderator variable		
Market power	Calculated as the firm's relative market share by dividing the net sales of a firm by its largest industry competitor	Datastream
Control Variables		
CEO age	Measured as the number of CEO's years.	BoardEx
IT board expertise	Measured as the number of directors that have either worked in an IT related position (e.g., CIO) or have IT related education	BoardEx
IT TMT expertise	Measured as the number of managers in the top management team that are devoted to either IT or digital technologies (e.g., CDO, CIO and CTO).	BoardEx
Size	Calculated as the natural logarithm of total assets	Datastream
R&D intensity	Calculated as the R&D expenditures divided by net sales.	Datastream
Intangibles	Calculated as intangible assets divided by property, plant, and equipment	Datastream
Leverage	Calculated as total debt divided by total assets.	Datastream
B2B-B2C mix	Calculated as the proportion of sales in segments related to consumers to total sales and then calculated the deviation from an equal relation between sales to consumers and business customers (50% each).	Datastream
Diversification	Calculated as an entropy index based on unrelated sales segment data.	Datastream
ROA	Calculated as net income + ((interest expense on debt-interest capitalized) * (1- tax rate)) / average of last year's and current year's total assets.	Datastream
TSR	Calculated as the average dividend adjusted stock returns of the current year	Datastream
Sales growth	Calculated as the yearly average of growth in net sales over the last three years.	Datastream
Firm Risk	Calculated as the standard deviation in return on equity over the last three years	Datastream
Ownership concentration	The sum of closely held ownership stakes (i.e., exceeding 5 percent)	Datastream
Net sales	Calculated as the natural logarithm of net sales.	Datastream
Variables in Additional Tests:		
Operating margin 2y	Calculated as the average operating margin over two years (t and t+1). Operating margin is calculated as operating income divided by net sales.	Datastream
Sales 2y	Calculated as the net sales (in billion Euros) over two years (t and t+1).	Datastream

2 Study 3: Leveraging "AI-as-a-Service" – Antecedents and Consequences of Using Artificial Intelligence Boundary Resources

Table B-17. Fact Sheet of Study No. 3.

Title	Leveraging "AI-as-a-Service" – Antecedent and Consequences of Using Artificial Intelligence Boundary Resources
Authors	Patryk Zapadka*[a], André Hanelt[a], Sebastian Firk[b], Jana Oehmichen[c] [a] Chair of Digital Transformation Management, University of Kassel, Kleine Rosenstr. 3, 34109 Kassel, Germany [b] Department of Accounting, University of Groningen, Nettelbosje 2, 9747 AE Groningen, Netherlands [c] Department of Innovation Management and Strategy, Nettelbosje 2, 9747 AE Groningen, Netherlands *Corresponding author. Tel.: +49 561 804 3902. E-mail address: patryk.zapadka@uni-kassel.de
Outlet	International Conference on Information Systems (ICIS), Hyderabad, India, 2020
Abstract	Increased data availability and computing power allows businesses across industries to employ AI technologies in their products and processes. Yet, leveraging AI effectively requires high investments. To reduce these investments, companies can implement AI capabilities directly via boundary resources such as application programming interfaces (APIs). However, research tells us little about antecedents and performance consequences of the use of AI boundary resources. To close this gap, we derive hypotheses from the resource-based view and the relational view of competitive advantages and test these hypotheses on a panel dataset of S&P 500 firms for the years 2010 to 2018. Our results show that firms with high levels of internal AI capabilities are particularly likely to adopt AI boundary resources for process improvements; firms with high external market pressure are positively associated to use AI boundary resources for customer solutions; and the use of AI boundary resources has a positive performance effect.
Keywords	Boundary resources, application programming interfaces, artificial intelligence, firm performance, panel data regression

2.1 Introduction

Driven by the rapidly growing availability and accessibility of big data and computing power, businesses across industries are developing and employing increasingly "intelligent" systems that are empowered by a new wave of ***artificial intelligence*** (AI) technologies (Coombs et al. 2020; Krogh 2018; Rai 2020). These AI technologies leverage recent advances in natural language processing (NLP), machine learning (ML), and computer vision (Brynjolfsson and McAfee 2014) and offer a plethora of new technological opportunities for improving organizational performance in various areas, such as product development (Davenport et al. 2012; Gillon et al. 2014), supply chain management (Koh et al. 2011; Nissen and Sengupta 2006), and data analytics (Ghasemaghaei et al. 2018; Loebbecke and Picot 2015). Accordingly, almost 85% of executives believe AI will help their companies to build or sustain competitive advantages (Ransbotham et al. 2017). Yet, leveraging AI effectively requires high investments in expertise (e.g., data science) and technological readiness (e.g., computing and big data infrastructures), which is probably why only one in twenty companies have comprehensively incorporated AI in their processes and offerings so far (Ransbotham et al. 2017). However, companies can now turn to platform providers (e.g., Google, Microsoft, IBM, or Amazon) and implement AI capabilities (e.g., cognitive computing or machine learning services) directly via ***boundary resources*** such as application programming interfaces (APIs) (Forbes 2018; Rai et al. 2019). Labelled in business practice as "AI-as-a-service", these novel offerings allow companies to use readily available AI solutions via boundary resources (hereafter referred to as AI boundary resources) and take a leap forward in terms of developing and realizing AI-related benefits without the need for major investments in infrastructure or expertise. For instance, by taking advantage of IBM's Watson Conversation Service and its underlying computing infrastructure, Autodesk was able to build a virtual agent that interacts autonomously with customers and sped up response times by 99% (IBM 2017).

Information systems (IS) research has recently devoted more attention to AI, for instance in relation to big data analytics (BDA) capabilities that are claimed to be an organizational requirement for the development of sophisticated AI systems (e.g., Chen et al. 2012; Ghasemaghaei et al. 2018; Grover et al. 2018; Günther et al. 2017; Loebbecke and Picot 2015). Here, however, the use of boundary resources for realizing AI-related benefits has not been taken into account by research so far (Grover et al. 2018; Loebbecke and Picot 2015). Boundary resources are defined as a "*means or mechanism that enables resource sharing*" (Karhu et al. 2018, p. 482). In business practice, boundary resources typically manifest as APIs or software development kits (SDKs) that allow external actors to access and utilize assets from the deploying firm (Boudreau 2012; Ghazawneh and Henfridsson 2013; Parker and van Alstyne 2018). While existing research on boundary resources provides valuable qualitative insights regarding their design (Ghazawneh and Henfridsson 2013), managerial mechanisms (Parker et al. 2017; Parker and van Alstyne 2018), and structural implications (Eaton et al. 2015) for deploying firms, factors that drive their adoption on the user-side are as unclear as are the performance implications. Apart from that, while boundary resources have been primarily investigated in the context of governance of digital platforms, we know very little about boundary resources in the context of AI. Here, a key difference is that, unlike applications in digital platform ecosystems (Ghazawneh and Henfridsson 2013), boundary resources do not only serve as an interface between a platform owner and third-party developers, where the latter use the platform to leverage their offerings within the ecosystem of the platform owner. Instead, the shared assets accessible through boundary resources become an inherent part of the user's operations and offerings. To date, no empirical studies exist that cater to the specifics of using AI boundary resources. Accordingly, our study is concerned with the following research question: *How do contextual factors influence the use of AI boundary resources and is their use beneficial for the firm?*

To answer this question, we draw on the strategic management lens (Grant 2013), specifically on the extension of the resource-based view to interfirm networks (Lavie 2006b) and the relational view of competitive advantages (Dyer and Singh 1998). We hypothesize the use of boundary resources as a new source for extracting relational rents in the context of digital innovation (Yoo et al. 2010). Thus, based on the concept of competitive advantages, boundary resources serve as a new and more efficient channel to valuable resources, which firms opt to use in digital(izing) business environments (Ghazawneh and Henfridsson 2013; Yoo et al. 2012). We employ panel data regressions to a dataset of the largest publicly listed companies between the years 2010 and 2018 according to the Standard & Poor's 500 (S&P 500) stock index. Our findings suggest that firms with high levels of internal AI capabilities are particularly likely to adopt AI boundary resources, specifically for process improvements. Moreover, high external market pressure drives the adoption of AI boundary resources, particularly for customer solutions. Regarding the consequences, we show that, while there is no effect *per se*, the differentiated use of AI boundary resources has a positive effect on firm performance.

We contribute to IS literature by modeling the use of boundary resources as a new means for extracting relational rents in the context of digital business ecosystems. By embracing the extension of the resource-based view to interfirm networks, we show that boundary resources can be utilized as a potential complement to internal capabilities and thus advance the general understanding of the new role of boundary resources in IS research. Furthermore, we add to AI research in IS literature, as we illustrate how firms utilize boundary resources to leverage AI capabilities. In addition, our research has important implications for managerial practice by informing managers considering leveraging the new potentials of external sources of knowledge and technology while reflecting about the relevant contextual conditions as well as potential benefits of boundary resources.

2.2 Theoretical Background

2.2.1 Artificial Intelligence Capabilities

AI can be defined as "*the ability of a machine to perform cognitive functions that we associate with human minds*" (Rai et al. 2019, p. iii) and refers to a "*broad collection of computer assisted systems for task performance, including but not limited to machine learning, automated reasoning, knowledge repositories, image recognition, and natural language processing*" (Krogh 2018, p. 405). Early developments in AI, such as decision support systems (El-Najdawi and Stylianou 1993) and knowledge management systems (Alavi and Leidner 2001), had significant limitations in terms of their autonomy and learning potentials. Nowadays, with the given improvements in computing, data availability, and technological methods, the utilization of AI leads to advanced developments such as *algorithmic intelligence* (Günther et al. 2017; Markus 2017), *cognitive robotics* (Aleksander 2017), and *autonomous agents* (Nissen and Sengupta 2006; Nunamaker et al. 2011). As will be explained in the following, such novel AI technologies have been researched by IS scholars in diverse organizational settings in order to explore their effect on (1) process efficiency and quality of decision-making and (2) development of novel databased products and services.

Concerning process efficiency and quality of decision-making (1), Nissen and Sengupta (2006) showed how intelligent software agents can be instantiated for improving procurement processes in the context of supply-chain management. Furthermore, Ghasemaghaei et al. (2018) indicate that data analytics competency, as a combination of multiple AI-related systems and methods, has a significant positive impact on firm decision-making performance (i.e., decision efficiency and quality). As to the development of novel databased products and services (2), there is an increasing amount of research providing insights on innovative data-driven offerings that are enabled by and draw upon AI-related capabilities like data analytics (e.g., Bardhan et al. 2020; Chen et al. 2012; Günther et al. 2017). For instance, Gillon et al. (2014) elaborated how the sportswear company Nike redesigned their product and service offerings by developing a digital platform and data-enhanced fitness services. In sum, contemporary IS research claims that big data analytics "*determines the functional scope of today's digital products and services [and] is crucial for the development of sophisticated artificial intelligence*" (Loebbecke and Picot 2015, p. 150). However, although the BDA capability building and realization processes have recently received more attention (Grover et al. 2018), boundary resources, as a new channel to valuable resources and thus a novel strategic option for building and realizing capabilities, have not been considered so far (Yoo et al. 2010).

2.2.2 Boundary Resources

Boundary resources provide easy access to shared resources and stimulate generativity in the context of digital innovation (Eaton et al. 2015; Ghazawneh and Henfridsson 2013; Yoo et al. 2012). Hence, boundary resources encourage heterogeneous actors from various contexts to leverage the shared resources and create diverse innovations such as new services or products (Boudreau 2012; Parker and van Alstyne 2018). However, in contrast to a firm's self-possession of valuable, rare, inimitable, and non-substitutable (VRIN) resources (Barney 1991) or IS capabilities (Bharadwaj 2000; Wade and Hulland 2004), boundary resources provide a new channel to access valuable resources in networked settings (Karhu et al. 2018; Lavie 2006b). Drawing on the relational view of competitive advantage (Dyer and Singh 1998) and the extension of the resource-based view to interfirm networks (Lavie

2006b), boundary resources can be utilized as a means to extract relational rents, which are defined as "*common benefit accrued to alliance partners through combination, exchange and co-development of idiosyncratic resources*" (Lavie 2006b, p. 645). While the relational value of IS has long been known, boundary resources present a ready-to-use infrastructure to access foreign resources as compared to prior phases that relied on more traditional IS artifacts (Saraf et al. 2007). In practice, on the one hand, companies can implement AI solutions through boundary resources to improve business or decision-making processes by automating tasks (Nissen and Sengupta 2006) or using new data-driven insights (Ghasemaghaei et al. 2018). For example, Carnival Cruise Line employed Microsoft's machine learning models to predict water consumption on cruise ships and thus reducing related production and storage costs (Microsoft 2017). On the other hand, firms can integrate new AI-based functionalities such as voice assistants or data-driven features into their offerings. For instance, the medical device company Medtronic utilized IBM's Watson computing and deep learning capabilities to build a predictive diabetes app that detects critical health events before they happen (Medtronic 2015).

In the evolving IS literature, scholars have examined boundary resources in terms of (1) their design, (2) managerial mechanisms, and (3) structural implications in digital business ecosystems. Regarding their design (1), Ghazawneh and Henfridsson (2013) investigated how boundary resources enable external contribution, while simultaneously maintaining control over strategic assets (Yoo et al. 2010). As to managerial mechanisms (2), Parker et al. (2017) describe how boundary resources aid companies in improving developer innovation and after a period of openness and growth, monetizing created value by exerting control over strategic assets. Comparably, Parker and van Alstyne (2018) highlight how firms, like Facebook and Microsoft, constantly absorb innovation into their platforms and open APIs to provide access to these new layers in order to stimulate developer innovation. Concerning structural implications (3), Eaton et al. (2015) investigated how boundary resources are co-created themselves and evolve over time through a process of distributed tuning. Their study reveals the dynamic nature of boundary resources and how they evolve through multifaceted actions of heterogeneous actors in a co-creation process.

Conclusively, prior research on boundary resources developed valuable insights for their design, the associated managerial mechanisms and their structural implications in digital business ecosystems. However, there are to date no insights in IS research on particular contextual conditions serving as antecedents that lead companies to use boundary resources as a potential source of new competitive advantage. Furthermore, we are lacking empirical evidence regarding performance impacts of boundary resources on the user-side, even though such insights are needed to evaluate this strategy in increasingly interconnected digital business environments. So far, IS research has not investigated the fact that boundary resources can be utilized not only by third-party developers in a platform context, but also by firms in network settings in order to leverage external services and technologies within their own organizational operations and offerings. Additionally, previous studies were predominantly carried out in the IT-industry and thus paid less attention to investigating other contexts that are affected by digital innovation, despite the fact that the decision to use boundary resources is becoming more and more relevant in times of increasing digitalization and interconnectedness of industries.

2.3 Hypotheses Development

AI boundary resources can be used in two different ways. First, AI boundary resources allow companies to access readily available AI solutions that help to improve process efficiency through task automation (Coombs et al. 2020; Markus 2017; Rai et al. 2019) or quality of decision-making by data-driven insights (Chen et al. 2012; Ghasemaghaei et al. 2018; Günther et al. 2017). Second, AI boundary resources can be utilized to improve existing offerings and develop novel databased products or services (Davenport et al. 2012; Gillon et al. 2014). Thereby, AI boundary resources may influence firm performance via the three well-established strategic roles of automating, informing, and transforming (Dehning et al. 2003). In the following, based on this understanding, we will derive and explain our hypotheses.

2.3.1 Internal Artificial Intelligence Capabilities

The decision to use AI boundary resources is driven by the firm's anticipation of the potential to extract relational rents from the utilization of boundary resources (Karhu et al. 2018; Lavie 2006b). When reflecting about the antecedents of the use of AI boundary resource, this implies that there needs to be an associated knowledge base that helps to identify and assess these benefits in the first place in the adoption decision (Roberts et al. 2012). This rationale may come from the firm's past experiences as they shape its capability to acquire new valuable external knowledge (Zahra and George 2002). With regard to the nature of boundary resources as a middle ground strategy between openness and control (Ghazawneh and Henfridsson 2013), firms that aim to develop internal knowledge by carrying out substantial R&D are likely to opt against complete external sourcing as they seek to capitalize on their knowledge built in the past. However, on the other hand, these firms are also likely to identify and value external knowledge that complements their own and therefore seek opportunities to organize this knowledge combination (Cohen and Levinthal 1990). Furthermore, firms that have already established a knowledge base in AI might be also more capable of assimilating relevant external knowledge in their organizational environment for the specific purpose of process improvements (West and Bogers 2014). Here, firms might perceive the use of AI boundary resources as a viable mechanism to complement or augment their internal AI capabilities, particularly for automating tasks or improving decision-making processes (Coombs et al. 2020; Ghasemaghaei et al. 2018; Rai et al. 2019). The following hypotheses summarizes our line of reasoning:

H1: Internal AI capabilities – represented by the amount of registered AI patents – are positively associated with the likelihood of using AI boundary resources, particularly for process improvements.

2.3.2 External Market Pressure

The decision to adopt AI boundary resources might be influenced by developments in the respective business environments. In particular, firms might feel urged to quickly utilize AI capabilities in presence of digital ventures, acting as potential digital disruptors. As digital ventures rapidly scale their business and are typically driven by a winner-takes-it-all perception (Eisenmann et al. 2006; Huang et al. 2017; Schilling 2002), they exhibit the potential to cause severe systemic effects and disrupt existing industrial models (Skog et al. 2018; Tumbas et al. 2017a). Such pressure might drive firms to use AI boundary resources as opposed to other measures. Firms may be endangered by digital ventures and, thus, might be forced to respond to the new competitive dynamics (El Sawy et al. 2010; Yoo et al. 2010) by adopting novel technologies more quickly in order to sustain their market position. Therefore, using AI boundary resources for integrating readily available AI solutions might reflect a coping mechanism of incumbent firms in market environments with high external pressure by digital ventures. Furthermore, since digital technologies have fundamentally altered consumer behavior, customers perceive themselves no longer as captives of the firm's services and, thus, have increased expectations (Lucas et al. 2013; Vial 2019). In order to respond quickly to changing demands and prevent customer loss, firms can be urged to use AI boundary resources for incorporating AI innovations (e.g., voice assistants) in their customer solutions in a timely manner. The following hypotheses summarizes our line of reasoning:

H2: External market pressure – represented by the presence of digital ventures – is positively associated with the likelihood of using AI boundary resources, particularly for customer solutions.

2.3.3 Performance Implications

In digitalizing business environments, the use of AI boundary resources can influence firm performance in several ways. First, it can lower costs and improve process efficiency as well as decision-making. Accordingly, leveraging readily available AI solutions via boundary resources can be less costly than self-development (Rai et al. 2019). Furthermore, using market ready AI solutions can help to increase process efficiency through task automation (Coombs et al. 2020; Markus 2017) or improve decision-making by leveraging databased insights (Chen et al. 2012; Ghasemaghaei et al. 2018; Günther et al. 2017). For instance, the Walt Disney Company utilizes Google's machine learning services to automatically annotate its products with movie characters, product categories and colors (Google 2018). Second, it can stabilize or increase revenues. Here, integrating sophisticated AI solutions via boundary resources into existing and future offerings may help to quickly adapt and respond to continuously changing customer expectations in digital environments (Lucas et al. 2013; Vial 2019; Yoo et al. 2010). As an example, Johnson Controls implemented Microsoft's voice assistant Cortana into its smart heating solution in order to respond to changing customer expectations (Microsoft 2018). However, the benefits of using AI boundary resources should vary according their scope of application. Hence, we expect that benefits related to efficiency are realized when firms use AI boundary resources for process improvements. Similarly, we expect firms using AI boundary resources for customer solutions to realize benefits related to sales growth. The following hypotheses summarizes our line of reasoning:

H3a: The use of AI boundary resources is positively associated with firm performance.

H3b: The use of AI boundary resources for process improvements is positively associated with performance implications related to efficiency.

H3c: The use of AI boundary resources for customer solutions is positively associated with performance implications related to sales growth.

2.4 Methodology

2.4.1 Sample Selection

We focus on a longitudinal sample of firms that were listed in the S&P 500 index in the year 2010. To cover the diffusion of the use of AI boundary resources, we investigate the years 2010 to 2018. Data related to the provider and service description of AI boundary resources was gathered from the API directory ProgrammableWeb within its AI API section. For the purpose of collecting data related to the use of AI boundary resources, we systematically hand-collected, in line with prior IS research (e.g., Adomavicius et al. 2008; Joshi et al. 2010), press releases and company announcements from newswires on the LexisNexis database. Financial data were retrieved from Datastream and data on digital ventures from the CrunchBase database. We used the United States Patent and Trademark Office (USPTO) database to gather information on AI-related patents as a proxy for internal AI capabilities. Given that the disclosure of patents involves a certain time lag, we needed to exclude the year 2018 as recent years were still incomplete. Moreover, we excluded financial firms due to their different nature when it comes to accounting variables. Furthermore, we excluded providers of AI boundary resources (e.g., Google, IBM, Salesforce, Oracle, or Red Hat) for potential users. Based on this, we end up with a final sample covering the adoption decisions of using AI through boundary resources over the period 2010 and 2017 accounting for 393 firms and 2825 firm-years.

2.4.2 Variables

2.4.2.1 Main Variables

Use of AI Boundary Resources. To measure the use of AI boundary resources, we exploited the API directory ProgrammableWeb (Evans and Basole 2016; Yu and Woodard 2008). The API directory contains all relevant information about company APIs that are described by pre-defined criteria, such as category, type, provider, introduction date and other access-related as well as technical properties. In order to gather the required information for our analysis, we screened all of the 279 API listings in the AI category from the ProgrammableWeb directory (ProgrammableWeb 2020a) and derived a list of over 160 unique AI providers and their services. Based on our S&P 500 firms, we then systematically hand-collected and coded all press releases and company announcements from newswires on LexisNexis database according the defined categories that confirmed the use of the identified AI providers and their services in the timeframe between the years 2010 and 2018. Furthermore, all news articles were coded according previously defined categories (i.e., *corporate user, AI provider, utilized AI service, application objective,* and if possible *developed AI solution*) that were initially discussed and determined by two researchers after independently performing a pilot coding of 100 randomly selected news articles. Regarding the *application objective*, we deductively derived from the current AI-related IS literature that firms were using AI to either improve business processes or develop novel customer solutions. Thus, the content of each news article was evaluated in terms of the described objective of the firm's utilization of AI APIs and its central outcome. Here, keywords such as "automated decision-making", "optimization of processes" or "cost reduction" indicated the objective *process improvements*, whereas terms like "customer offerings" or "consumer experience" indicated the objective *customer solutions*. Drawing upon this information, we created three variables to measure the adoption of using AI APIs. At first, we created a binary variable for the adoption of using AI APIs that takes the value of 1 if a firm adopted the use of an AI API and zero otherwise. Then, in order to develop a more fine-grained view, we created two additional binary variables for AI APIs that are specifically addressing whether the AI API serves for process improvements or customer solutions. Similarly, the binary variables take the value of 1 if a firm adopted the use of the respective AI API and zero otherwise.

AI Capabilities. To proxy for AI capabilities, we use data on firms' patent filings. Similar to previous research, we expect that patents serve as proxy for a firm's internal knowledge base (Hanelt et al. 2020; Prabhu et al. 2005). Hence, we assume that AI patent fillings can proxy for a firm's AI-related knowledge base and thus their AI capabilities. We took data from the USPTO (Graham et al. 2015; Marco et al. 2015). We focus on initial filings in relevant patent families to better match our under-standing of AI capabilities and exclude incremental adaptions. The raw dataset of the USPTO does not contain any unique identifier for the applicant firms. Moreover, company names may be spelled differently across subsidiaries, contain misspellings, or parts of the company names may overlap with other companies. To over-come these issues, we spend much time and effort on an adequate matching procedure. First, we standardized the applicant names by following the harmonizing procedure of Magerman et al. (2006). We also used STATA codes that are provided by the NBER and are publicly available. Second, we employed the *matchit* command in STATA 15, which allows for an algorithm-based approximating match between the names of applicants and our sample companies (Raffo and Lhuillery 2009). Within this matching procedure, we have considered the names of subsidiaries as well as merged or acquired firms. Therefore, we extracted the list of subsidiaries as disclosed in the firm's 10-k fillings to capture all affiliated subsidiaries. In the last step, we only kept matches that have crossed the threshold of 80% according to the results of the *matchit* command. We then manually checked these matches for appropriateness and only kept those matches that are clearly to be affiliated with the corresponding company. To define AI patent filings, we follow the World Intellectual Property Organization (WIPO) Artificial Intelligence Report (2019b) that describes technological classes for AI-related patents (WIPO 2019a). Hence, in line with the report, we counted the number of patents filled in CPC codes specific to AI technologies. We finally calculated *AI capabilities* as the natural logarithm of one plus the number of AI-related patent filings over the three most recent years. We use the logarithm to avoid the influence of outliers and to address skewness.

External Market Pressure. For external market pressure, we constructed a measure by focusing on new digital start-ups entering the industry. We decided to capture the intensity of the pressure that digital ventures placed on incumbent firms by defining this variable as the number of new digital ventures entering the industry per one industry incumbent. We extracted all start-ups in the CrunchBase amounting to more than 250,000 start-ups. We used the industry description in CrunchBase to classify each start-ups industry affiliation. Next, we evaluated whether each startup was indeed a digital venture by evaluating all of the different categories and short descriptions of the start-ups. Based on this, we finally constructed our measure of *external market pressure* by counting the number of new digital ventures in each industry and year and divided this number by the number of industry incumbents. We considered firms as industry incumbent that had been listed for more than three-years in the DataStream database before the start-up entered the industry. We then used external market pressure as an average over the three most recent years.

Firm Performance. To measure firm performance, we included a broad set of measures similar to prior research in the IS economics literature. Specifically, we include two top-level performance measures capturing the market-based performance and the accounting-based performance. For the market-based performance measure, we focus similar as previous research (Joshi et al. 2019) on the stock returns (*market return)* of a firm in a given year. For accounting-based performance, we focused on the return on assets (*ROA*) (Mithas et al. 2012; Pan et al. 2018). Moreover, we follow Mithas et al. (2012) by considering two exceptional drivers of firm performance: sales growth and operational efficiency. We focus on the one-year change in net sales for *sales growth* and for operational efficiency (*OPEX*), we divided the operating expenditures by the number of employees (Joshi et al. 2019; Mithas et al. 2012).

2.4.2.2 Control Variables

We selected several control variables. We include *firm size* as the natural logarithm of total assets. We then included a firm's *leverage* proxied by total debt in relation to total assets, *liquidity* measured as cash and short-term investments divided by total assets, and *CAPEX* measured as capital expenditures divided by total assets. We also included *capital intensity* measured as property, plant and equipment divided by total assets. We also consider the firm's *diversification* by calculating an entropy index based on unrelated sales segment data. We included *sales volatility* as the standard deviation of net sales over the last 3 years. We included *R&D intensity* measured as R&D expenditure by net sales. Finally, we also included the four performance variables as control variables when estimating the antecedents of using AI boundary resources. When focusing on the consequences, we excluded the performance variables as controls but added *AI capabilities* and *external market pressure* to assure that the observed effect stem from the Adoption of using AI boundary resources and not the underlying antecedents driving the adoption.

2.4.3 *Empirical Method*

To analyze the antecedents and consequences of using AI boundary resources, we need to cope with different empirical challenges. We first elaborate on our reasoning behind the choice of an estimation procedure for analyzing the antecedents of using AI boundary resources and, second, on our choice of an estimation procedure for analyzing the performance consequences.

2.4.3.1 *Antecedents of Using AI boundary resources*

To investigate the antecedents of using AI boundary resources, we have to account for the binary scale of our dependent variable. Similar to prior research (e.g., Firk et al. 2019; Mannucci and Yong 2018; Quigley and Hambrick 2012), we decided to run a general estimating equations (GEE) model as it can be applied to various distributions with different link functions (e.g., logit). Moreover, it accounts for both within and between firm variance to calculate robust estimates and thus tackles the issue of unobserved heterogeneity (Liang and Zeger 1986; Pan et al. 2018). To account for heterogeneity at the firm-level, the GEE exploits the longitudinal design of a dataset and considers the correlation in the dependent variable across firms over time by estimating the correlation structure of the error terms (e.g., Liang and Zeger 1986). The consistency of the GEE estimates, however, depends on the selection of a correlation structure that fits the dataset (Mannucci and Yong 2018). Hence, we followed prior research by applying the quasi-likelihood under the independence model criterion (QIC) measure (Cui 2007) to select the most appropriate correlation structure (Mannucci and Yong 2018). Based on comparing the QIC statistics of selectable correlation structures, we decided for an exchangeable correlation structure as it yielded the best fit according to the smallest-QIC criteria. We then specified the GEE by employing the *xtgee* command in STATA 15. Specifically, we specified a logit link function of the binomial family and selected an exchangeable correlation structure. Finally, we lagged our independent and control variables to tackle reverse causality issues and test the following models to analyze our first and second hypothesis:

IV. $$AI\ boundary\ resources_{i,t+1} = a + \beta_1(AI\ capabilites)_{i,t} + \beta_2(External\ market\ pressure)_{i,t} + \gamma(CONTROLS)_{i,t} + Y_t + I_i + \varepsilon_{i,t}$$

AI boundary resources stands for the three dependent variables AI boundary resources (all), AI boundary resources (process) and AI boundary resources (customer) that are tested separately. The item $CONTROLS_{i,t}$ represents a matrix of the control variables, the item Y_t represents year and the item I_i industry fixed effects. The remaining items are the constant term (α) and the random error term ($\varepsilon_{i,t}$).

2.4.3.2 *Performance Consequences of Using AI boundary resources*

To examine performance implications of using AI boundary resources, we follow IS economics literature in exploiting our panel-data set by estimating a firm-fixed effects regression (Mithas et al. 2012; Pan et al. 2018). The decision for a firm fixed was supported by running a Hausman (1978) test. The firm-fixed effects regression assigns each firm an individual effect to control for firm-specific unobservable factors and thus estimates only time-variant effects within a firm such as adopting the use of AI boundary resources. Hence, as firms that decide to use AI boundary resources are likely to systematically differ from other firms, it helps us to better isolate the effect of using AI boundary resources on firm performance and to mitigate omitted variable bias concerns. Moreover, we lagged all our independent and control variables to further tackle reverse causality issues. Specifically, we estimate the following firm-fixed effects regression to test the third set of hypotheses.

V. $$Firm\ performance_{i,t+1} = \alpha + \beta_1(AI\ boundary\ resources)_{i,t} + \gamma_2(CONTROLS)_{i,t} + \gamma_t + \eta_i + \varepsilon_{i,t}$$

The item *firm performance* stands for the four components of performance that are the market-based performance, accounting-based performance, sales growth, and operational efficiency. Each of these performance measures is tested separately.

2.5 Findings

2.5.1 Descriptive Results

The diffusion and adoption of firms using AI boundary resources is illustrated in Table B-18. Based on our data sample of S&P 500 firms, the share of companies that use AI boundary resources has grown significantly from 1.2% in 2010 to 31.3% in 2018. Furthermore, we find slightly more firms utilizing AI boundary resources for process improvements (23.4%) than for customer solutions (16.1%).

Table B-18. Diffusion and Adoption of the Use of AI Boundary Resources.

Year	AI boundary resources user	AI boundary resources adoptions*	AI boundary resources (process) user	AI boundary resources (process) adoptions*	AI boundary resources (customer) user	AI boundary resources (customer) adoptions*
2010	1.2%	1.2%	1.2%	1.2%	0.0%	0.0%
2011	2.4%	1.2%	1.9%	0.7%	0.5%	0.5%
2012	2.9%	0.7%	2.4%	0.5%	0.7%	0.2%
2013	6.3%	3.4%	5.1%	2.7%	1.4%	0.7%
2014	11.6%	5.3%	8.7%	3.6%	3.4%	1.9%
2015	18.1%	7.5%	11.3%	2.9%	8.0%	4.6%
2016	23.9%	8.4%	16.6%	5.3%	11.3%	3.4%
2017	28.0%	6.5%	20.2%	3.6%	14.5%	3.1%
2018	*31.3%*	*4.6%*	*23.4%*	*3.1%*	*16.1%*	*1.7%*

(*) Firms could adopt multiple AI boundary resources. Hence, the sum of adoptions exceeds the percentage of users. The year 2018 is excluded from the regression analysis due to missing data for the independent variables.

Descriptive statistics of all our regression variables are displayed in Table B-19. The descriptive statistics have been mainly calculated on the sample used for the antecedents' regressions. We further also run (untabulated) correlation analysis to look at the bivariate correlation of our regressions variables. The results indicated that all correlations were below 0.5 and most far below 0.2. An analysis of the variance inflation factors further supported that multicollinearity need not to be considered as a problem as the highest VIF value amounted to 3.89.

Table B-19. Descriptive Statistics.

Variable names	Firm-years	Mean	Q1	Q3	Std. Dev.
AI boundary resources (all)	2825	0.044	0.000	0.000	0.205
AI boundary resources (process)	2825	0.027	0.000	0.000	0.163
AI boundary resources (customer)	2825	0.018	0.000	0.000	0.132
AI capabilities[a]	2825	0.160	0.000	0.285	0.574
External market pressure	2825	0.051	0.005	0.044	0.133
Firm size[a]	2825	16.155	15.318	16.981	1.146
Market return[b,c]	2825	18.022	-0.414	32.532	31.194
ROA[b,c]	2825	7.634	4.240	11.050	7.077
OPEX[b]	2825	124.05	39.90	79.84	166.67
Sales growth[b,c]	2825	8.721	-3.030	19.127	19.194
Sales volatility[b]	2825	0.092	0.051	0.119	0.057
Liquidity[b]	2825	0.141	0.036	0.197	0.141
Diversification	2825	0.147	0.000	0.175	0.269
R&D intensity[b]	2825	0.024	0.000	0.030	0.042
Leverage[b]	2825	0.279	0.163	0.377	0.170
CAPEX[b]	2825	0.049	0.019	0.063	0.046
Capital intensity[b]	2825	0.294	0.094	0.467	0.254

Notes: a: Measured as natural logarithm. b: Winsorized at the 1st and 99th percentiles. C: Measured in percent.

2.5.2 Regression Results

2.5.2.1 Antecedents of Using AI Boundary Resources

The results of the GEE logit models estimating the influence of AI capabilities and market pressure on adopting the use of AI boundary resources are displayed in Table B-20. Regarding the influence of AI capabilities on the use of AI boundary resources, we find a positive and significant effect ($p < 0.05$) in Model 1. Specifically, a one-standard deviation increase from the mean of AI capabilities increases the likelihood of adopting the use of AI boundary resources by 15%. In Model 2, we also find the expected positive and significant influence ($p < 0.05$) of AI capabilities on adopting the use of process-related AI boundary resources. The effect here is even stronger as a one-standard deviation increase from the mean of AI capabilities would increase the likelihood of adopting the use of process-related AI boundary resources by 18%. In contrast, the influence of AI capabilities on adopting the use of customer-related AI boundary resources is not significant. Hence, we find support for our first hypothesis that AI capabilities positively influence the decision to adopt AI boundary resources and particularly such that are process-related.

Regarding the influence of external market pressure, Model 1 indicates also a positive and significant influence ($p < 0.05$) of external market pressure on adopting the use of AI boundary resources. The results indicate that the influence is quite similar to the one of AI capabilities as a one-standard deviation increase from the mean of external market pressure would increase the likelihood of adopting the use of AI boundary resources by 16%. However, in contrast to AI capabilities, we did not find a significant effect for external market pressure on adopting the use of process-related AI boundary resources in Model 2.

Table B-20. Antecedents of Adopting the Use of AI Boundary Resources.

Model	**1**	**2**	**3**
Dependent Variable	AI boundary resources (all) (t+1)	AI boundary resources (process) (t+1)	AI boundary resources (customer) (t+1)
Method	GEE (Logit)	GEE (Logit)	GEE (Logit)
AI capabilities (H1)	0.247**	0.295**	0.065
	(0.031)	(0.040)	(0.730)
External market pressure (H2)	1.131**	0.329	2.364***
	(0.039)	(0.542)	(0.003)
Firm size	0.430***	0.366***	0.487***
	(0.000)	(0.000)	(0.000)
Market return	-0.008*	-0.013**	-0.001
	(0.072)	(0.031)	(0.906)
ROA	0.027	0.028	0.018
	(0.107)	(0.123)	(0.511)
OPEX	-0.001	-0.001*	0.000
	(0.141)	(0.053)	(0.899)
Sales growth	-0.263	-0.052	-0.578
	(0.703)	(0.946)	(0.578)
Sales volatility	-7.143***	-8.050***	-6.509
	(0.007)	(0.006)	(0.140)
Liquidity	1.313	1.204	1.896
	(0.128)	(0.177)	(0.108)
Diversification	0.135	0.128	0.024
	(0.721)	(0.774)	(0.967)
R&D intensity	4.557	2.724	5.112
	(0.117)	(0.454)	(0.137)
Leverage	-0.556	-0.924	-0.103
	(0.369)	(0.201)	(0.912)
CAPEX	-6.620*	-4.649	-9.471
	(0.099)	(0.355)	(0.132)
Capital intensity	-0.066	-0.377	0.493
	(0.930)	(0.708)	(0.642)
Intercept	-11.041***	-9.442***	-15.957***
	(0.000)	(0.000)	(0.000)
Industry & year effects	yes	yes	yes
Firm-years	2825	2825	2825
Wald-Chi-Square	169.29	131.87	114.52

Notes: *p<0.10; **p<0.05; ***p<0.01. Robust standard errors clustered at the firm-level. P-values in parentheses. Industry effects comprise 10 Fama and French industry dummies and for Year effects a dummy variable for each year is included.

We therefore find a positive and significant effect ($p < 0.01$) for the influence of external market pressure on adopting the use of customer-related AI boundary resources. We find here that a one-standard deviation increase from the mean of external market pressure would increase the likelihood of adopting the use of customer-related AI boundary resources by 37%. Hence, we find support for our second hypothesis that external market pressure positively influences the decision to adopt the use of AI boundary resources and particularly such that are customer related.

2.5.2.2 *Performance Consequences of Using AI Boundary Resources*

To comprehensively test the consequences of adopting the use of AI boundary resources on firm performance, we estimate firm-fixed effects regression on the market-based performance, accounting-based performance, sales growth, and operational efficiency. The results are displayed in Table B-21.

In Panel A, we run a regression with the variable that considers adopting the use of any AI boundary resources. Here, we find a pattern that would suggest a positive influence on firm performance as we find a positive influence on market-based and accounting-based performance as well as a positive influence on sales growth and a reduction in operating expenditures. However, except from a slightly significant coefficient for accounting-based performance ($p < 0.1$), none of the coefficients are significant. Hence, our results do not support that adopting the use of AI boundary resources *per se* influence firm performance positively as suggested in Hypothesis 3. In Panel B, we focus on the influence of adopting the use of process related AI boundary resources. In Model 4, we find the expected increase in operational efficiency as adopting the use of process related AI boundary resources significantly ($p < 0.05$) decreases operating expenditures (OPEX) by 5%. In contrast, in Model 3, we do not find a significant influence of adopting the use of process related AI boundary resources on sales growth. We find, however, a positive and significant ($p < 0.05$) influence on market-based performance (market return) in Model 1 and a positive and significant ($p < 0.01$) influence on accounting-based performance (ROA). Specifically, the results suggest an increase in market-based performance by 5.21 percentage points and an increase in accounting-based performance (ROA) by 1.36 percentage points. Hence, the results suggest that adopting the use of process-related AI boundary resources is effective in increasing operational efficiency and accounting-based performance and that this decisions is positively perceived by the capital market. In Panel C, we focus on the influence of adopting customer related AI boundary resources. In Model 3, we find the expected significant ($p < 0.05$) influence on sales growth. Specifically, adopting customer related AI boundary resources is associated with an increase of 4.47 percentage points in sales growth. The effect of adopting the use of customer-related AI boundary resources on operational efficiency is as expected not significant. Interestingly, we observe that despite the growth in sales the effect on market-based performance and accounting-based performance is not significant and rather negative. Hence, while adopting customer-related AI boundary resources is an effective measure to increase sales it is not positively perceived by the capital market and does also not translate into higher accounting-based performance.

Table B-21. Consequences of Using AI Boundary Resources.

Panel A: AI boundary resources (all) and firm performance				
Model	**1**	**2**	**3**	**4**
Dependent Variable	Market Return (t+1)	ROA (t+1)	Sales growth (t+1)	OPEX (t+1)
Method	Firm-fixed effects	Firm-fixed effects	Firm-fixed effects	Firm-fixed effects
AI boundary resources (all)	1.097 (0.625)	0.852* (0.063)	1.401 (0.311)	-4.373 (0.235)
Control variables	yes	yes	yes	yes
Year effects	yes	yes	yes	yes
Firm-years	2801	2801	2801	2801
Adjusted R-square	0.22	0.53	0.37	0.87
Panel B: AI boundary resources (process) and firm performance				
Model	**1**	**2**	**3**	**4**
Dependent Variable	Market Return (t+1)	ROA (t+1)	Sales growth (t+1)	OPEX (t+1)
Method	Firm-fixed effects	Firm-fixed effects	Firm-fixed effects	Firm-fixed effects
AI boundary resources (process)	5.213* (0.051)	1.362*** (0.005)	-1.212 (0.423)	-6.744** (0.046)
Control variables	yes	yes	yes	yes
Year effects	yes	yes	yes	yes
Firm-years	2801	2801	2801	2801
Adjusted R-square	0.22	0.53	0.37	0.87
Panel C: AI boundary resources (customer) and firm performance				
Model	**1**	**2**	**3**	**4**
Dependent Variable	Market Return (t+1)	ROA (t+1)	Sales growth (t+1)	OPEX (t+1)
Method	Firm-fixed effects	Firm-fixed effects	Firm-fixed effects	Firm-fixed effects
AI boundary resources (customer)	-4.886 (0.152)	-0.020 (0.977)	4.474** (0.016)	0.766 (0.899)
Control variables	yes	yes	yes	yes
Year effects	yes	yes	yes	yes
Firm-years	2801	2801	2801	2801
Adjusted R-square	0.22	0.53	0.37	0.87

Notes Panel A-C: *p<0.10; **p<0.05; ***p<0.01. Robust standard errors clustered at the firm-level. P-values in parentheses. The control variables included in the model are: firm size, sales volatility, cash, diversification R&D intensity, leverage, capex, capital intensity and our antecedents' variables internal AI capabilities and external market pressure.

2.5.3 Robustness of Results

We run several (untabulated) robustness tests. With regard to the antecedents of AI boundary resources, we alternatively run a panel logit with random effects and found consistent results. We also tested alternative correlation structure in the GEE model such as a first-order autoregressive correlation structure and found similar results. Moreover, we also changed the link function to probit model and our results remained consistent. Finally, we specified the independent variables alternatively by considering the last 5 years instead of the last 3 years and found also consistent results. With regard to the consequences of AI boundary resources, we also considered the long-term impact by focusing on two-year measures of the performance variables, we found again highly consistent results. We also tested several alternative measures such as the operating profit margin or SG&A expenses and found results that equal the picture of our main results that process-related AI boundary resources are particularly effective in driving firm performance and efficiency.

2.6 Discussion of Findings

In this paper, drawing on a cross-industry and longitudinal dataset, we present empirical insights on the antecedents and consequences of the use of boundary resources. Based on our multiple measurements for the varying fields of applications (i.e., process improvements and customer solutions), we are able to provide differentiated and nuanced insights on the use of AI boundary resources and their outcomes.

Our findings suggest that high internal AI capabilities influence firms' decisions to use AI boundary resources, particularly for internal process improvements. This result indicates that firms that substantially develop knowledge themselves perceive AI boundary resources as a complement to their knowledge base and, thus, leverage the external knowledge based on what they already know. This finding supports insights from absorptive capacity (Roberts et al. 2012), which states that knowledge gathered in the past improves the ability to identify, assimilate, and apply valuable external knowledge (Lane et al. 2006). Furthermore, it seems that using AI boundary resources is a viable complement to internal investments in building AI-related capabilities (Grover et al. 2018). In addition, our findings are in line with previous research and highlight that firms with an already established knowledge base in AI might also be more capable of assimilating and applying relevant external knowledge in their own organizational environment (West and Bogers 2014). Thus, firms may perceive the use of AI boundary resources as a viable mechanism to complement or augment their existing capabilities, particularly in areas where AI can be leveraged for task automation or improved decision-making (Coombs et al. 2020; Ghasemaghaei et al. 2018; Rai et al. 2019).

Moreover, our findings indicate that a high level of external market pressure drives the decision to use AI boundary resources. This finding suggests that firms perceive the presence of digital ventures as a threat (Skog et al. 2018; Tumbas et al. 2017a) to which they have to respond to and, thus, decide to use AI boundary resources for rapid improvement of their technological capabilities. Interestingly, we see this effect particularly in the use of AI boundary resources for customer solutions. This might be influenced by the effect of digital technologies on customer behavior, as customers have increasingly growing expectations of the services companies provide to them (Lucas et al. 2013; Vial 2019). Therefore, using AI boundary resources for the integration of AI solutions into the firm's offerings seems to represent a strategic measure to close capability and service gaps in highly competitive markets that are driven by continuously changing customer expectations (Karimi and Walter 2015).

As to the consequences of using AI boundary resources, first, except from a slightly significant effect on accounting-based performance, our empirical results show that, on the one hand, using AI boundary resources is not *per se* beneficial for the firm. This result might indicate that firms, to date, experience difficulties in realizing the benefits of lowering the costs as well as increasing revenues by AI. Prior research has illustrated that exploiting digital innovation can be challenging as to internal (e.g., culture, structures) or external (competition, industry characteristics) conditions (Kohli and Melville 2019), especially in non-digital industries (Hanelt et al. 2020). Such challenges may lead companies to, at least initially, only apply AI in decoupled and potentially smaller initiatives that might not yield a substantial performance effect (Tumbas et al. 2018). On the other hand, second, our findings support the prediction that firms, which use AI boundary resources for differentiated objectives (i.e., process improvements or customer solutions), do profit from such strategies. Here, using AI boundary resources for process improvements particularly benefits performance in terms of efficiency. This finding indicates that boundary resources can be a valuable complement in realizing AI-related benefits in terms of data-driven task automation or decision-making (Coombs et al. 2020; Ghasemaghaei et al. 2018; Grover et al. 2018). Similarly, our findings support that firms that utilize AI boundary resources for customer solutions, benefit from performance implications related to sales growth. It seems likely that, by utilizing AI boundary resources for customer solutions, companies embrace combinatorial innovation (Yoo et al. 2012) and try to respond to new competitive dynamics (Skog et al. 2018; Tumbas et al. 2017a) as well as changing customer expectations (Vial 2019) by providing a continuous flow of new functionalities in their offerings (Gawer 2014; Yoo et al. 2010). Therefore, sales of existing offerings can be stabilized as can new revenues for innovative modules be realized (Eaton et al. 2015; Parker et al. 2017).

2.7 Implications

Our study complements prior IS work in the area of AI and boundary resources. First, our study suggests that the driving forces of using AI boundary resources depend on the firm's internal AI capabilities and its external market pressure. We find that firms that established a knowledge base in AI by themselves also engage in collecting further valuable knowledge from external sources. Therefore, boundary resources can be perceived as a technical mechanism of external knowledge acquisition in digital(izing) business environments. This illustrates the implications of the new organizing logic of layered modular architecture (Yoo et al. 2010), where complementary resources like knowledge can be leveraged externally through boundary resources and do not need to be fully understood or controlled by the firm (Ghazawneh and Henfridsson 2013; Parker et al. 2017; Yoo et al. 2012). This provides a valuable extension to IS research related to absorptive capacity (Roberts et al. 2012) and capability building and realization of AI-related competencies (Grover et al. 2018). Moreover, our findings indicate that firms' AI strategies depend on their internal and external environment and, thus, need to consider the crucial role of boundary resources for complementary capability development (Grover et al. 2018; Lavie 2006b).

Apart from that, our findings provide an interesting perspective on the user-side of boundary resources, particularly in the context of interfirm networks, where companies utilize them for incorporating external knowledge and technologies into their own organizational operations and offerings. While prior research predominantly dealt with purely digital contexts, the topic of boundary resources becomes increasingly important across industries because of their increasing interconnectedness and pervasive digitalization. Furthermore, in line with the extension of the resource-based view to interfirm networks (Lavie 2006b) and the relational view on competitive advantages (Dyer and Singh 1998), our findings suggest that boundary resources represent a new means to realize relational rents and, thus, accentuate them as a crucial strategic element in managing organizational challenges and opportunities stemming from digital innovation (Karhu et al. 2018; Yoo et al. 2010).

Additionally, our study has important implications for managerial practice. In the omnipresent discourse revolving around digital transformation, managers might reflect about the use of AI boundary resources for realizing AI-related benefits. Our study reveals that using AI boundary resources makes a difference – whether for improving the firm's processes or enhancing customer solutions. Our results highlight that AI boundary resources are particularly effective when employed for a clearly defined purpose (e.g., process improvement or product enhancement). Yet, implementing AI boundary resources into products could in the long run lead to losing control over the customer interface and related value creation as well as capture mechanisms. Consequently, although using AI boundary resources for customer solutions seems to be a convenient shortcut for implementing and leveraging readily available AI capabilities, it embodies a potentially dangerous dependency from the respective providers in the long term. However, in constantly evolving and increasingly interconnected digital business environments, managers must quickly leverage new partnerships and digital technologies. Therefore, using and exchanging boundary resources might be the new norm, which is why decision-makers have to think about new governance mechanisms to avoid the threat of losing their economic rent of direct customer access to the AI boundary resources provider.

2.8 Limitations and Future Research

Our research is not without limitations. First, to capture internal AI capabilities, our study focuses on patents, which surely does not reveal the full picture of the AI expertise among employees and managers. Hence, we believe, our study could be extended by a human capital approach, focusing specifically on the expertise of manager and board members, and ask the question, whether this corporate AI expertise also forms an antecedent of the use of AI boundary resources. In addition, future research could examine the specific interplay between boundary resources and related patent filings in more detail. Second, our sample is limited to the U.S. context, which ignores interesting aspects on a global scale. Whereas our study does show a general effect of competition, it would be interesting to understand, whether, the effect changes with global vs. local competition. Third, our study does not examine alternative theoretical interpretations. For instance, our results about the product use of AI boundary resources provide interesting insights for future research, drawing on transaction costs and resource dependence perspectives. AI applications in products might transform the product markets to platform-based markets. These markets can work on different rules such as the-winner-takes-all rules (Zhu and Iansiti 2012). Giving away the AI part in a product to a boundary resource provider might hence also lead to losing the platform-market competition game in the long run. In-depth case studies might want to challenge, whether firms truly anticipate these threats.

III. Managing Knowledge Integration in Incumbent Firm Contexts Impacted by Digital Innovation

The first two chapters of Part B have aimed, on the one hand, to structure existing research findings on knowledge integration and link them to the context of digital innovation, and, on the other hand, to shed light in particular on boundary resources and their function as a technological mechanism for scaling knowledge integration in digital(izing) business ecosystems.

In the following chapter (B.III), Study 4, by employing a grounded theory approach (Glaser and Strauss 1967) and using the automotive industry as an example, derives insights on how to manage knowledge integration in incumbent firms in order to generate digital innovation outcomes. Accordingly, by building upon and extending the previous findings, Study 4 answers RQ4 and enables the development of a comprehensive view on managing knowledge integration in incumbent firm contexts impacted by digital innovation.

1 Study 4: Digital Innovation in Industrial-Age Firms – Managing the Balancing Act of Knowledge Integration

Table B-22. Fact Sheet of Study No. 4.

Title	Digital Innovation in Industrial-Age Firms – Managing the Balancing Act of Knowledge Integration
Authors	Patryk Zapadka* Chair of Digital Transformation Management, University of Kassel, Kleine Rosenstr. 3, 34109 Kassel, Germany *Corresponding author. Tel.: +49-561-804 3902. E-mail address: patryk.zapadka@uni-kassel.de
Outlet	European Conference on Information Systems (ECIS), Marrakech, Morocco, 2020
Abstract	The pervasive digitalization of business environments across industrial-age industries forces incumbent firms to cope with changing competitive dynamics and business requirements. Particularly in the auto-motive industry, where new digital players (e.g., Uber, Lyft) and tech giants (e.g., Apple, Google) in-crease the complexity of the competitive landscape, embracing digital innovation becomes inevitable. Consequently, automotive original equipment manufacturers (OEMs) are increasingly exploiting digital technologies in their business activities. However, the organizational legacy (e.g., historically evolved structures, processes, and knowledge) of automotive OEMs is reaching its limits when valuable and heterogeneous knowledge required for digital innovation needs to be identified, assimilated and applied appropriately within the organizational environment. Prior research highlighted this as a significant managerial challenge and emphasized the crucial role of knowledge and its management in achieving digital innovation objectives. By employing a grounded theory approach and building upon the knowledge of 30 industry experts, I found empirically grounded evidence for three different yet inter-twined mechanisms (knowledge diversification, contextualization, and application) for balancing knowledge integration. The study's findings explain the interdependencies of these mechanisms and how their interaction contingently leads to digital innovation outcomes within the organizational environ-ment of automotive OEMs.
Keywords	Digital Innovation, Knowledge Management, Knowledge Integration, Grounded Theory, Industrial-Age Firms

1.1 Introduction

The ceaseless improvement of capability and affordability of digital infrastructure and technologies (e.g., social media, cloud computing, or big data analytics) has led to fundamental transformations in organizations, industries, society and the economy (Agarwal et al. 2010; Dhar and Sundararajan 2006; Lucas et al. 2013). Beside considerable changes in the way we live, communicate, and work, the extent of transformations based on digital technologies is also affecting various industrial-age industries (Yoo et al. 2012). Particularly in the automotive industry, where new digital players such as mobility providers (e.g., Uber, Lyft) and tech giants (e.g., Apple, Google) are increasing the complexity of the competitive landscape, embracing digital innovations is becoming inevitable (Henfridsson and Yoo 2014). Therefore, automotive OEMs are obliged to increasingly incorporate and exploit digital technologies (Henfridsson et al. 2009; Hylving and Schultze 2013; Hylving and Selander 2012).

However, when companies enter new contexts, such as new markets (Man and Duysters 2005) or discontinuous technologies (Lambe and Spekman 1997), integrating external knowledge is particularly important in order to cope with the new business logics that are often differing from the established one (Kathuria et al. 2011; Svahn et al. 2017; Xu et al. 2013). Consequently, firms that are entering digital contexts, such as automotive OEMs, have to identify and integrate new external knowledge in order to improve their capability for innovation in a previously unknown business area (Kathuria et al. 2011; Kohli and Melville 2019). However, standardized systems, structures, and organizational knowledge that evolved over decades and were responsible for the economic success of automotive OEMs tend to prove themselves as obstacles for managing today's digital challenges (Svahn et al. 2017). Previous research revealed that especially the organizational legacy of automotive OEMs (e.g., historically evolved structures, processes and knowledge) is reaching its limits, when heterogeneous and dispersed knowledge required for digital innovation needs to be identified, assimilated and applied appropriately within the organizational environment (Hylving and Schultze 2013; Piccinini et al. 2015; Svahn et al. 2017; Yoo 2010). This managerial challenge becomes even more aggravated by the convergent and generative nature of digital technologies that particularly intensifies the need for integrating increasingly heterogeneous knowledge sources in required for digital innovation (Yoo et al. 2012).

Focusing on a knowledge-based perspective, increasingly more information systems (IS) studies are highlighting the importance and necessity of new knowledge management capabilities required by companies that are embracing digital innovation. For instance, Kohli and Melville (2019) particularly emphasize that organizations need to develop new managerial capabilities to learn, apply, and creatively recombine external and existing knowledge in order to create new organizational capabilities for generating digital innovation outcomes. This is further underlined by Yoo's (2010, p. 224) call for further research on the question how organizations can manage the heterogeneity of required knowledge resources in producing new products and services and how this affects organizational structure and identity in the context of digital innovation. Nevertheless, from a knowledge-based view, there are to date no empirical insights on how incumbent firms such as automotive OEMs approach the dynamic balancing and integration of heterogeneous knowledge resources (Hildebrandt et al. 2015; Piccinini et al. 2015; Yoo et al. 2012). In this paper, I try to respond to this research opportunity by conducting an exploratory study based on the knowledge of 30 industry experts from automotive OEMs. Therefore, I have carried out in-depth interviews in order to address the following research question:

How do automotive OEMs manage knowledge integration from increasingly heterogeneous knowledge resources in order to produce digital innovation outcomes?

As a result, this study contributes to the literature on digital innovation in industrial-age firms (Henfridsson and Yoo 2014; Svahn et al. 2017) with a particular emphasis on the dynamic balancing and integration of heterogeneous knowledge resources (Kohli and Melville 2019; Yoo 2010; Yoo et al. 2012). For this purpose, the paper is structured as follows: First, I present the theoretical background for the study based on the current state of research on digital innovation and associated managerial challenges in the automotive industry. Furthermore, I provide theoretical background on the process of knowledge integration and how it affects automotive OEMs embracing digital innovation. Afterward, I explain the methodological approach, which was based upon grounded theory (Glaser and Strauss 1967). In the findings section, I present and discuss the identified concepts for balancing knowledge integration and their interdependencies. Finally, in the last section, implications for future research and practice, as well as limitations, will be derived and concluding thoughts presented.

1.2 Theoretical Background

1.2.1 Digital Innovation in the Automotive Industry

Being more than a century old, the automotive industry is dominated by OEMs that are providing mobility to consumers through developing, producing and selling cars – a mechanical and primarily physical product. Automotive OEMs operate in a technologically intensive and systemic industry and have institutionalized structures, processes and systems (King and Lyytinen 2004). However, as consumers increasingly embed themselves in digital ecosystems and use digital technologies on a daily basis (Yoo 2010), they also expect digital innovation within their automobiles. This environmental pressure is based on digital technologies and embodies managerial challenges for automotive OEMs, which traditionally focus on the development of mechanical parts and the assurance of their security and quality (Hylving and Selander 2012). Consequently, automotive OEMs increased their digital innovation efforts by carrying out various actions for reshaping their established business models, traditional organizational structures, and the way how they design and develop products (Henfridsson et al. 2009; Hylving and Schultze 2013; Hylving and Selander 2012). For instance, automotive OEMs have progressively integrated more digital functions into the car (e.g., navigation, radio, park distance control) through service, communication and information systems (Brandt 2013; Cho et al. 2006; Juliussen 2003). With the emergence of new digital technologies, such as artificial intelligence (AI), car-to-car communication and sensor technology, the primarily physical product of a car transforms into an intelligent, autonomously driving digital device (Henfridsson and Lindgren 2005; Rishi et al. 2008). Besides functional changes, new digital business models like car sharing services (e.g., Daimler's Car2Go, BMW's DriveNow) and driver services (e.g., GM's OnStar) also emerged and gave a new meaning to the concept of mobility (Hanelt et al. 2015; Yoo 2010). In sum, automotive OEMs are increasingly responding to the changing business environment by exploiting multifaceted digital opportunities in their product and business development activities.

However, organizational foundations of automotive OEMs such as structures, processes, knowledge, and technical systems that solidified over an extended period of time, are now giving impetus for managerial challenges in the context of digital innovation (Henfridsson and Yoo 2014; Hylving and Selander 2012; Piccinini et al. 2015; Svahn et al. 2017). These challenges are driven by competing concerns that are creating complex tensions between established structures and new requisites for digital innovation (Baldwin and Clark 1997; Henfridsson et al. 2014; Svahn et al. 2017). Here, incumbent firms are obliged to develop new managerial capabilities in order to, for instance, balance between existing and requisite innovation capabilities without compromising current product innovation practices (Henfridsson and Lindgren 2010; Henfridsson and Yoo 2014) or establish flexible governance mechanisms that allow to exercise control without limiting generativity when exploring digital options (Svahn et al. 2017; Wareham et al. 2014). Furthermore, Svahn et al. (2017) emphasized how recombining existing and acquiring new external resources drives digital innovation (Yoo et al. 2012). This is especially the case when heterogeneous and dispersed actors (Yoo et al. 2010) are leveraged for the purpose of dynamically developing novel ideas. As a result, incumbent firms are increasingly forced to engage with external contributors (Henfridsson and Lindgren 2010) and external ecosystems (Selander et al. 2013) in order to identify novel ideas within their institutional contexts (Henfridsson and Yoo 2014). Yet, this requires incumbents once again to refocus on the process of digital innovation and learn how to respond to its new logics as well as develop appropriate capabilities within their organizational environment (Kohli and Melville 2019; Svahn et al. 2017).

1.2.2 Knowledge Integration

The perception of knowledge as a firm's most valuable resource has become increasingly relevant in research over time and has recently gained more attention in IS research on digital innovation. In the knowledge-based view of a firm (Grant 1996b) the significance of knowledge is emphasized by its definition as a strategic resource and its superior potential out of all organizational resources to create sustainable competitive advantages (Coff et al. 2006). Based on this, an assumption of the knowledge-based view is that companies can be generally defined as an accumulation of knowledge (Kogut and Zander 1992). Accordingly, a company's main task is to utilize the existing knowledge as best as possible by making it in the whole organization available while constantly developing and acquiring new knowledge, which can be either created internally through research and development and learning effects or acquired externally through, for instance, business relationships (Turner and Makhija 2006). As companies enter new contexts, such as new markets (Man and Duysters 2005) or discontinuous technologies (Lambe and Spekman 1997), integrating external knowledge is particularly important in order to improve the firm's capability for innovation in a previously unknown business area (Kathuria et al. 2011). Underlining this, empirical investigations revealed that the integration of external sources of innovation, such as market or technology knowledge, is the main enabler of positive returns (Cloodt et al. 2006; Xu et al. 2013) or successful business model change (Kranz et al. 2016). Consequently, the recombination of existing with new external knowledge allows firms to seize new market or technological opportunities (Henderson and Clark 1990; Kogut and Zander 1992). Thus, knowledge integration can be defined as "*the process of absorbing knowledge from external sources and blending it with the technical, and business skills, know-how and expertise that reside in the business and IS units of a firm*" (Tiwana et al. 2003, p. 248).

The generative and convergent nature of digital technologies particularly intensifies the heterogeneity of knowledge resources required for digital innovation (Yoo et al. 2012). Therefore, firms that are embracing digital innovation are forced to increasingly acquire and integrate heterogeneous knowledge across distributed disciplines, communities and their different actors (Henfridsson et al. 2009; Yoo 2010), as it is the case for automotive OEMs entering digital contexts (Svahn et al. 2017). However, as traditional products with strong physical materiality (e.g., cars) and digital services (e.g., smartphone applications) are significantly different from each other regarding life cycles, customer expectations and the way they are developed and produced (Henfridsson et al. 2014), their convergence leads to a challenging knowledge integration problem due to the varying requirements regarding organizational capabilities and knowledge resources (Svahn et al. 2017; Yoo 2010). As a consequence, knowledge integration has been confirmed as a significant managerial challenge for automotive organizations by Piccinini et al. (2015). Their study's findings accentuate that OEMs are currently struggling with acquiring, integrating and leveraging valuable knowledge from distinct and distant areas, which is a prerequisite for exploiting opportunities amenable to digital innovation (Kohli and Melville 2019; Yoo 2010). Related to this, recent research by Hildebrandt et al. (2015) showed that traditional firms try to tap into external knowledge sources by utilizing digital technology-related M&As in order to close their emerging capability gaps in the context of digital innovation (Henfridsson et al. 2009). Further studies by Henfridsson et al. (2014) as well as Svahn et al. (2017) pointed out how automotive OEMs and their organizational alignments and practices are challenged by competing concerns between traditional manufacturing business and new digital innovation objectives. However, there are until now, to the best of my knowledge, no qualitative insights from a knowledge-based view on how incumbent firms, such as automotive OEMs, particularly manage the integration of increasingly heterogeneous knowledge sources required for achieving digital innovation outcomes (Kohli and Melville 2019; Yoo 2010; Yoo et al. 2012).

1.3 Methodology

To address the research question, I utilized a grounded theory approach with the aim of generating substantive theory for managing knowledge integration related to digital innovation in the context of incumbent firms from industrial-age industries (Glaser 1978, 1992; Glaser and Strauss 1967). Grounded theory is a qualitative research method and "*an inductive, theory discovery methodology that allows the researcher to develop a theoretical account of the general features of a topic while simultaneously grounding the account in empirical observations or data*" (Martin and Turner 1986, p. 141). This approach has been effectively used in IS research (e.g., Baskerville and Pries-Heje 1998; Gregory et al. 2015; Lehmann and Gallupe 2005; Orlikowski 1993; Pries-Heje and Plads 1992; Urquhart 2001) and is in particular useful for developing context-based, process-oriented descriptions and explanations of a particular phenomenon (Myers 1997; Urquhart 2001). Furthermore, grounded theory enables the development of theories of process, sequence and change considering organizations, positions and social interactions (Glaser and Strauss 1967) and is thus particularly appropriate for investigating the processual context of managing knowledge integration related to digital innovation within incumbent firms. I chose the automotive industry as the targeted research setting as its maturity and primarily physical product development is particularly interesting for exploring how incumbent firms manage to integrate heterogeneous knowledge from distinct and distant knowledge domains and cope with the complex tensions between present hierarchical structures and required new structures. Especially in the automotive industry, the incumbent OEMs are carrying out numerous multifaceted digital innovation projects and initiatives that can be studied in detail. For the purpose of this study, input from experts with relevant experience in managing digital innovation in automotive OEMs was required. Due to the lack of sufficient empirical literature about knowledge integration related to digital innovation, especially in the context of incumbent firms, the grounded theory method seemed suitable for addressing the research question and the development of descriptive and explanatory theory. Furthermore, by this approach, I am aiming at developing holistic insights on managing the knowledge integration process itself, rather than elaborating on singular digital innovation projects and their outcomes.

1.3.1 Data Collection

The main goal of data sampling in grounded theory is to choose participants, who will best contribute to the understanding of the problem and the research question. Accordingly, I identified appropriate organizations and departments that seemed promising in finding classes of experts in the context of digital innovation in automotive organizations. I evaluated that executives in business, IT, research and product development that were involved in the management and employment of digital technologies, such as big data analytics, mobile technologies and cloud computing, are relevant for this study. Moreover, due to the recent increase in the application of such technologies in the automotive sector, I sought experts with at least 3 years of managerial experience in the targeted departments.

Based on the selection criteria, two types of approaches were applied to find industry experts. First, I evaluated and contacted experts from the authors' personal business network. Second, I searched for experts on business-oriented social networks (e.g., LinkedIn) and contacted the ones, whose experience fitted the criteria. In total, I contacted 214 automotive experts by sending e-mails with exposés about the study's objective and the applied interview procedure. Here, I obtained a response rate of 11%. After receiving a participation confirmation from the first experts, I used the snowball sampling technique, asking them to help recruit additional interviewees, who also meet the selection criterion (Singh et al. 2009). Based on this, I conducted 30 expert interviews with practitioners, who had experience in automotive organizations relevant for this study. The interviews were carried out from 2016 to 2018. The length of each interview ranged from 30 to 112 minutes, with an average of 54 minutes. Table B-23 provides an overview of the 30 conducted interviews and the experts' profiles.

Table B-23. Overview of Expert Interviews.

Department	Participants (N=30)
Strategic IT Management	3 Senior Manager, 5 Project Manager
IT Development	4 Department Manager, 6 Project Manager
Strategic Business Management	3 Project Manager
Product Management	1 Department Manager, 1 Senior Manager, 3 Project Manager
Product Development	3 Department Manager, 1 Senior Manager

The experts had an average of five years of experience in areas related to digital innovation within automotive organizations and an average of ten years of experience in the automotive industry. They held various job positions, including head of business unit or department (e.g., product management, product and IT development), project and senior managers (e.g., digital innovation projects), IT managers and digital product development managers (e.g., connected car, digital services). The participants worked for six automotive companies that are among the world's largest automotive organizations according the OICA 2016.

1.3.2 Data Analysis

Following the guidelines on how to generate grounded theory suggested by Glaser and Strauss (1967), Eisenhardt (1989) and Urquhart et al. (2010), I applied an iterative approach of data collection, coding and analysis. Immediately after I generated and processed the first interview transcripts, I began to code the data. All data sets (i.e., interview transcripts) were managed and coded in the software tool NVivo 12. The process of coding was divided into the following three steps: open, selective and theoretical coding (Glaser 1992). In the first step, open coding, I fractured and analysed the interview transcripts line by line in order to generate as many tentative categories as possible through coding different incidences (Glaser 1978). I was able to generate over 500 of initial codes and associated tentative categories. During the development of categories, I made sure to adhere to the principle of emergence of grounded theory: categories were derived from data in a way that they must "fit" (they need to be readily, not forcibly, applicable to and indicated by the data under study) and "work" (they must be meaningfully relevant to and able to explain the behaviour under study) (Glaser and Strauss 1967; Gregory et al. 2015). The coding was not informed by an initial framework, making it emergent and solely grounded in the empirical data. In the next step, selective coding, further coding was delimited to only those categories that relate to the emerged core category (Glaser 1978). Through constant comparison between what was emerging from the data and the instances of data labelled as particular categories, I was able to substantiate and identify the core category "Balancing Knowledge Integration" and two related concepts (Contextual Conditions and Digital Innovation Outcomes), which will be presented later in the findings section (Urquhart et al. 2010). After determination of the core category (e.g., Balancing Knowledge Integration), I started to relate codes from the open coding state to the identified concepts related to the core category. In the results section, I present an overview and illustrative data samples for each concept. In order to theoretically saturate the core category and its related concepts the next step required further data collection guided by the principle of theoretical sampling, i.e., deciding on analytical grounds, where to sample from next (Glaser 1978; Glaser and Strauss 1967). Consequently, I chose further experts purposefully based on their experience and guided the respective interviews by the emerged core category. In the final stage, theoretical coding, interdependencies between concepts of the core category were examined and specified.

Based on my approach, I was able to identify different types of relationships between the core category and its concepts, including their various interdependencies (e.g., enabling, producing). After the emergence of theory in the prior stages, further engaging with other theories is necessary for theory building. In order to raise the level of conceptualization and scaling up the emerging theory, existing theories and concepts were used for comparisons (Urquhart 2007). Furthermore, through grouping higher level categories into broader themes it was possible to increase the generalizability of the theory and enable to relate the theory to the broader literature (Urquhart et al. 2010). Therefore, as the last advised step for applying grounded theory, I finalized the outcome through theoretical integration by comparing the substantive theory generated with other, previously developed theories in related field of research (Glaser 1978; Urquhart et al. 2010). Overall, the different elements of intertwined data collection and analysis, such as the process of coding, constant comparisons and theoretical sampling, facilitated each other and helped to emerge substantive theory from it.

1.4 Findings

In this section, I present the results of this study and the empirically grounded core category "Balancing Knowledge Integration", addressing the research question presented in the introduction section. Therefore, I present all of the identified concepts and their interdependencies. The study yielded five theoretical and empirically grounded concepts associated with knowledge integration related. During the analysis, the core category "Balancing Knowledge Integration" emerged and was in the focus of further examination of concepts and their respective relationships.

1.4.1 Contextual Conditions

In the concept contextual conditions, I identified external and internal factors triggering the knowledge integration process for digital innovation within the automotive organizations. Due to the generative and convergent nature of digital innovation (Yoo et al. 2012) the automotive industry experiences new competitive threats by technology organizations and start-ups, who are entering mobility-related businesses embedded in digital technologies. As one project manager stated: *"Many start-ups work on digital solutions for mobility-related services. [...] The question is: Do we want to enter the market as an automotive manufacturer? Second question: What will our role as an automotive manufacturer look like? Are we in the future - worst case – only a manufacturer and supplier?"*

Furthermore, due to the pervasiveness of digital technologies, customers are expecting increased digitalization of products. In order to respond to these changing demands automotive organizations have to meet new product requirements by customers. One project manager underlined: "*We have an international clientele and we have to think about what we can do beyond our core service and what are digital requirements of our future customers?"*

Along the external drivers, a major trigger for integration of new knowledge is the internal lack of competences and expertise in the area of digital innovation. Since automotive organizations historically focused on developing primarily physical products, entering digitally mediated environments requires the accumulation of new knowledge from diverse contexts in order to develop new digital products or business models. A department manager explained: "*Sure, we used to think that it was just an evolution of existing technologies and now we have something weird for us. Not something we can build on, instead we have to develop something new and that overstrains our current capabilities."*

Besides the lack of knowledge capabilities, the organizational legacy limits the structural and processual options towards exploring and operating new digital business opportunities. Another department manager mentioned: *„There is a lack of appropriate structures, processes, mindsets, which you need for developing and operating a digital business. [...] Historically our focus lays on generating revenue by producing and selling cars. All of our organizational structures and processes are predominantly aligned towards that traditional business."*

The identified internal and external factors constitute the eminent need for fundamental transformations of automotive manufacturers towards digital innovation. However, in order to be able to carry out those transformations appropriately and create value from them, automotive OEMs have to widen their traditional knowledge base by tapping into new knowledge contexts. This portrays the initial trigger for the knowledge integration process the organization has to go through.

1.4.2 Knowledge Integration Mechanisms

For the core category "Balancing Knowledge Integration", I identified three interdependent, yet intertwined concepts. The three interdependent concepts were derived from the adherent mechanisms of knowledge diversification, contextualization and application. Figure B:2, B:3, and B:4 give an overview of the mechanisms and their components by illustrating them with examples from the data. The grey text highlights exemplifying excerpts from interview data that served as basis for the descriptive coding.

The first mechanism, knowledge diversification, describes how automotive organizations leverage a broad range of external and internal knowledge sources for the development of new competences in the context of digital innovation (see Figure B:2). Depending on the objectives of the digital innovation activities, the automotive organizations engaged in knowledge exchange and new collaborations with technology organizations, start-ups, and research institutes, sought consultation from external knowledge providers, and hired employees with a new set of competencies and expertise related to digital technologies. With reference to this, a project manager pointed out: *"There are various new sources of knowledge that we try to open up systematically. One is that we go to digital technology conferences in order to collect new ideas. Then, there are new institutions and companies that we have strategic partnerships with. Furthermore, our engagement with digital technology start-ups is intensifying. Additionally, we try to exploit the innovation capabilities of our suppliers."*

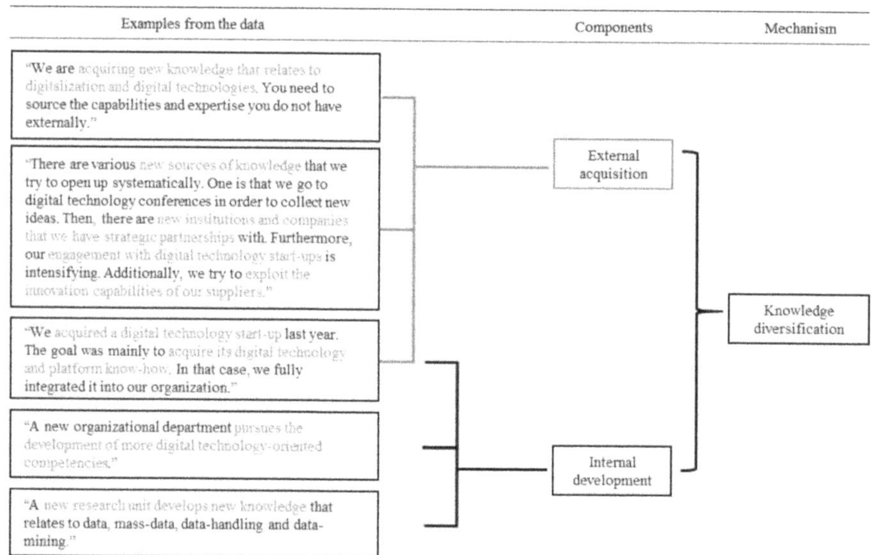

Figure B:2. The Mechanism of Knowledge Diversification.

To complement the identification and acquisition of valuable external knowledge, the automotive manufacturers created loosely coupled business units and subsidiary companies that aimed at accumulating novel knowledge and competences in the field of digital innovation. With reference to their specific structures and processes, such research units were associated to "speedboats" or "satellites". On the contrary, the experts commonly used the "tanker" as a synonym for their organizational legacy and corporate structures. However, each research unit or subsidiary focuses on a specific area of digital innovation, thus being a distinctive point of contact for organizational requests. For instance, an expert's description of the competencies of a specific digital research unit was: *"Everything that relates to data analytics can be addressed to that research unit."*

Beyond tapping into external sources, automotive organizations also aimed at activating and leveraging internal knowledge bases of employees by collecting and exchanging ideas for digital innovation in varying business departments (e.g., production, sales or product development): *"One important source of developing and integrating novel ideas are our own employees. Not only their professional expertise but also their personal experiences in other digital environments can be valuable for creating new ideas. This is why we try to employ cross-functional ideation workshops and hackathons on a regular base."*

After external acquisition and internal development of new knowledge, the second mechanism knowledge contextualization is addressing the constructive requirements of applying the knowledge and creating value from it within the organizational environment (see Figure B:3). Here, the managers needed to implement new cross-functional, multi-disciplinary committees and panels that enabled to evaluate potential opportunities amenable to digital innovation from various organizational perspectives. A senior manager described: *"Digital innovation initiatives run through new cross-functional and multi-disciplinary committees and panels. There, everyone gets the opportunity to discuss and evaluate these ideas from different organizational perspectives (from staff to top management level)."*

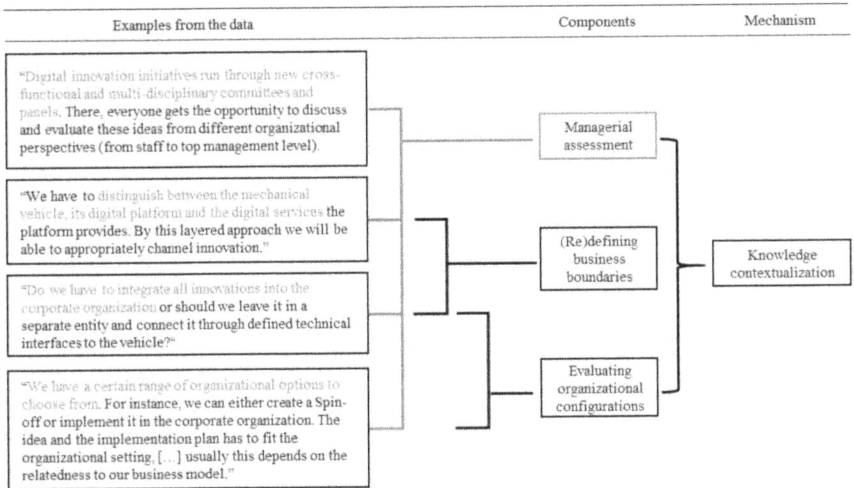

Figure B:3. The Mechanism of Knowledge Contextualization.

Moreover, the managers needed to assess the most fitting organizational setting for the newly accumulated knowledge in order to exploit it effectively. Depending on the business-

and product-relatedness of the new knowledge, the managers utilized various sense-making procedures, such as business case calculations, criteria matrices and business model canvas sheets, to derive requirements for application and the most appropriate organizational setting for it. With reference to this, a department manager stated: *"We have a certain range of organizational options to choose from. For instance, we can either create a Spin-off or implement it in the corporate organization. The idea and the implementation plan has to fit the organizational setting, [...] usually this depends on the relatedness to our business model."*

Furthermore, as managers were obliged to assess heterogeneous bodies of knowledge and how they are linked to the core business, they had to redefine business and product boundaries. As a result, they employed a modular perspective on the different parts of the core product, what led to a differentiation of its digital and physical layers and their respective relevance for generating digital innovation outcomes. Accordingly, a department manager stressed: *"We have to distinguish between the mechanical vehicle, its digital platform and the digital services the platform provides. By this layered approach we will be able to appropriately channel innovation."*

Overall, the activities related to the second mechanisms reflect the tension between existing structures and requisite new ones for successfully generating digital innovation outcomes. As a consequence, managers are increasingly confronted to evaluate existing structures and, if necessary, implement new organizational options, where previously unknown areas of knowledge can be further developed without being compromised or rejected by the organizational legacy.

By going through the third mechanism knowledge application, the automotive organizations aim at the purposeful deployment and application of the previously contextualized knowledge for generating different types of digital innovation outcomes (see Figure B:4). Based on the varying characteristics and objectives of certain organizational settings, the application and utilization of new knowledge can be multifaceted.

For instance, knowledge can create value through digital product innovations (e.g., connected car), digital business model innovations (e.g., mobility-related services or platforms): *"Our department develops digital online services, both inside and outside the vehicle in the context of Smart Mobility."*

or digital process innovations (e.g., internal data analytics capabilities): "*We are currently working on the merger of our databases, which will help us in developing new machine learning applications inside the car for our customers."*

Depending on the type of digital innovation and its operational requirements (e.g., controlled sequential or decentralized iterative development), automotive organizations have to purposefully balance the application and utilization of the newly accumulated knowledge between existing and newly created organizational settings (e.g., functional departments of the corporate organization, hybrid or loosely coupled digital innovation units or even subsidiary companies).

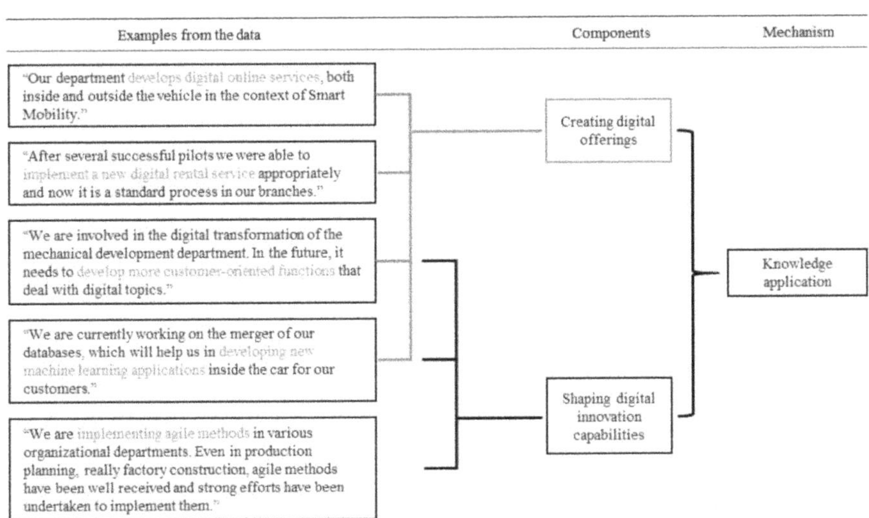

Figure B:4. The Mechanism of Knowledge Application.

1.4.3 Interdependencies and Outcomes

In order to illustrate the interdependencies of the core category and the related concepts I present in Figure B:5 an abstracted integrative process model for balancing knowledge integration.

Organizations are only able to evaluate and contextualize knowledge that they have collected. However, if firms do not acquire sufficient new knowledge, whether they are incapable of identifying it or simply do not decide to (Kogut and Zander 1992), all of the consecutive integration steps become ineffective and unsuccessful. In order to exploit the manifold opportunities digital innovation is offering, organizations are obliged to learn from and tap into a broader spectrum of heterogeneous knowledge in order to maximize potential digital innovation outcomes (Yoo 2010).

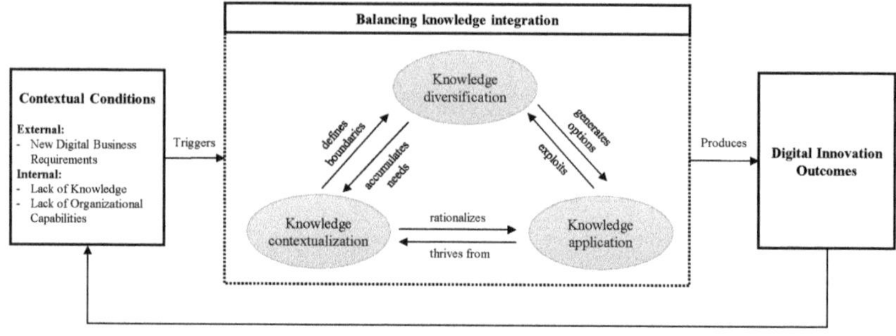

Mechanisms	Definition	Components
Knowledge diversification	The mechanism by which incumbent organizations accumulate heterogeneous and distributed knowledge related to digital innovation from internal and external sources.	• **External acquisition:** The activities of incumbent organizations towards acquiring new knowledge related to digital innovation from external sources. • **Internal development:** The activities within organizations aiming at the internal development of new knowledge related to digital innovation.
Knowledge contextualization	The mechanism by which incumbent organizations evaluate the newly accumulated knowledge regarding its value and utilization opportunities in the context of their organizational environment.	• **Managerial assessment:** The multifaceted activities that managers undertake to identify requirements and opportunities for creating value from the new knowledge within the organizational environment. • **(Re)defining business boundaries:** The activities by managers related to (re)assessing and tuning product and business objectives based on the newly accumulated knowledge. • **Evaluating organizational configurations:** The activities of managers that revolve around identifying appropriate organizational structures and processes for creating value from the new knowledge.
Knowledge application	The mechanism by which incumbent organizations leverage the contextualized knowledge in a dedicated organizational setting for developing or realizing digital innovation outcomes.	• **Creating digital offerings:** The activities of incumbent organizations related to the exploitation of new knowledge that lead to new digital products, services or business models. • **Shaping digital innovation capabilities:** The activities of incumbent organizations related to the exploitation of new knowledge that lead to new digital innovation capabilities.

Figure B:5. The Mechanisms of Balancing Knowledge Integration for Digital Innovation Outcomes.

Consequently, the knowledge contextualization constitutes a crucial link between acquisition and dedicated application of new knowledge. However, as incumbent companies are path dependent, they may evaluate the knowledge incorrectly (Kogut and Zander 1992). In the worst case, firms could evaluate the novel knowledge based on their traditional mindset and thus allocate it in organizational departments that are not capable to process or create value from it. A senior manager explained: *"We developed a new digital service related to hospitality for our car customers and had to integrate it for long-term operation back into our corporate structure. However, the only department that was somehow related to this was our real estate unit that managed our buildings."*

Knowledge application is directly dependent on the other two mechanisms. If companies accumulate either too little new knowledge or evaluate it wrongfully, they will subsequently apply it incorrectly. Furthermore, it is mandatory for companies to have flexible organizational options for knowledge deployment, from which they can choose, depending on product- or business-relatedness. As business requirements related to digital innovation trigger companies to acquire and integrate knowledge from new context, they have to go through the three mechanisms. Depending on how the mechanisms are developed and what organizational conditions are in place, a corresponding result comes out. If a company is not able to apply the new knowledge in an appropriate organizational setting, it will deplete time and financial resources for developing unsatisfactory innovation or products with significant limitations: *"With the new digital service, we had to make the compromise that we build it upon the standard branch systems. That was a major downside. If you make too many compromises, then maybe you have a project that works great internally but the customer will not accept it afterward. In the worst case, you did a great pilot project and later on, the topic is dead. That's a bit of a balancing act."*

Such outcomes, in turn, aggravate the initial situation, because of the growing market pressure and the continuing lack of appropriate knowledge utilization. Therefore, firms have to assess their knowledge capabilities and organizational settings carefully and consider how to balance a reasoned equilibrium between knowledge integration in existing structures (e.g., organizational legacy) or in newly created organizational settings (e.g., digital innovation teams, departments, subsidiaries).

1.5 Discussion and Implications

The grounded core category of balancing knowledge integration and the related mechanisms combine and extend the digital innovation and knowledge-based research by shedding light on the processual context of knowledge integration in historically evolved organizations of automotive OEMs (Henfridsson and Yoo 2014; Kohli and Melville 2019; Yoo 2010). This study's findings emphasize that knowledge integration for digital innovation is a multifaceted concept that needs to be balanced cohesively by several activities in order to successfully generate digital innovation outcomes. While prior studies examined managerial challenges, competing concerns as well as the impact of mergers & acquisitions (Hanelt et al. 2015; Hildebrandt et al. 2015; Piccinini et al. 2015; Svahn et al. 2017), I particularly focused on the knowledge integration process and identified three different but intertwined mechanisms that need to be balanced by automotive OEMs in order to achieve digital innovation objectives. The findings augment prior research insights, such as the concept of competing concerns from Svahn et al. (2017), as the knowledge integration mechanisms were also affected by managerial tensions that resided between different business requirements of traditional automotive business and digital innovation offerings (Henfridsson et al. 2014).

Furthermore, the study's insights underline that the greater extent of required knowledge for digital innovation needs to be accompanied by an increase in organizational flexibility (Svahn et al. 2017; Yoo 2010; Yoo et al. 2012). Choosing from a set of organizational options is particularly required when newly accumulated and developed knowledge related to digital innovation is assessed as valuable, but is more or less separable from the core business (e.g., mobility-related services). Nevertheless, with the emergence and increasing perception of a layered modular architecture (Yoo et al. 2010) and the recombination of the existing knowledge base with new knowledge related to digital innovation (Kogut and Zander 1992; Kohli and Melville 2019), even the organizational legacy of automotive OEMs and their traditional product boundaries are being reshaped in their structure and content. Thus, contextualization of new knowledge in terms of product- and business-relatedness is critically important for organizations in order to find the most promising organizational setting for channelling new digital innovations appropriately. Moreover, companies that want to create value from their digital innovation activities have to develop a new mindfulness towards traditional and new knowledge requirements (Kohli and Melville 2019). Because of this and the highlighted tensions in previous research, especially incumbent firms need a broader understanding of the content and meaning of relevant knowledge and more organizational options for flexible application.

This study also provides valuable insights for practitioners. The different mechanisms of knowledge integration clearly delineate the aspects that need to be taken into consideration while managing the partly conflicting requirements between digital innovation and traditional automotive business. By increasing the understanding of how the organizational legacy of automotive OEMs is influenced by the integration of novel knowledge and vice versa, managers can improve their decision-making concerning the development of new digital products or the overall digital transformation of their organizations.

Moreover, the convergence of traditional and new knowledge domains (i.e., automotive business and digital innovation) can be a distinctive source for developing innovations and sustainable competitive advantages. In order to accomplish that, at first, organizations need to expand their knowledge base and related capabilities by progressively tapping into dispersed and heterogeneous knowledge domains and sources. Secondly, managers need to be trained in the particularities and relevance of new knowledge in order to be capable of accurately assessing and contextualizing it within the own organizational environment. Finally, firms require more organizational options (e.g., flexible structures, connecting interfaces and processes) that allow digital innovation managers to explore and successfully exploit digital opportunities inside as well as outside organizational legacy. The findings suggest to create and experiment with flexible or hybrid organizing while implementing rather more than less options to learn and profit from the increasing diverse and heterogeneous knowledge bases required for digital innovation.

1.6 Limitations, Future Research and Conclusion

However, before discussing implications for future research, I have to point out the limitations of this empiric investigation. First, the study focused on automotive OEMs as they provide an interesting research setting for studying digital innovation and the combination of physical and digital components. Hence, the gathered insights cannot be applied to other types of organizations or industries without concerning the possibility of different circumstances. Nevertheless, there are general knowledge-related findings that can be utilized in similar organizational environments. As a result, the study's findings shed light on the processual and contextual conditions of knowledge integration for digital innovation and, thus, contribute to the research on digital transformation in general.

I derived the results from a somewhat limited number of 30 expert interviews. Therefore, theoretical saturation, where new data slices were not adding substantially to the emerged theory, could only be reached to a certain degree. Additional data collection might have helped to gain more detailed insights on the developed concepts and components. Nevertheless, all of the findings were identified multiple times, which supports their theoretical and practical validity. Regardless the assurance of data protection and privacy by anonymizing any content, the interviewees had to avoid the disclosure of confidential information and thus were not able to answer some questions in detailed elaboration. Furthermore, as automotive OEMs are currently undergoing various transformational activities with uncertainties and unknown outcomes, the experts could not elaborate on certain issues comprehensively.

This study serves as a guiding point for empirically conceptualizing the processual context of knowledge integration for digital innovation outcomes in automotive OEMs based on the insights provided by several field experts. Besides expanding the research activities of this study's approach, one direction for future research would be to examine the success of digital innovation activities and the related knowledge integration with quantitative methods. Subsequently, it would be advised to validate and further examine best practices and success factors on the basis of additional explorative, real-world case studies within automotive organizations. Finally, as the process of digital transformation of automotive OEMs is still at an early stage, there is clearly a need for more empirical research on the ongoing organizational development and the convergence between the knowledge bases of digital innovation and traditional automotive business.

In this study, applying a grounded theory approach, I shed light on the nuanced view of balancing knowledge integration and how it contingently leads to digital innovation outcomes in the industrial-age industry of automotive manufacturers. Drawing on the knowledge of 30 industry experts, I identified three different yet intertwined mechanisms of knowledge integration and delineated their interdependencies towards digital innovation outcomes. The findings indicate that automotive OEMs need to develop new organizational and managerial capabilities for balancing knowledge integration in order to respond to the changing business and knowledge requirements related to the dynamics of digital innovation.

C. Contributions

This cumulative dissertation had the following two important goals: First, it aimed to explore the unique nature of knowledge integration in the context of digital innovation and, second, to examine in particular how incumbent firms can manage the related challenges in their contexts. To achieve these goals, four research questions were derived with a focus on synthesizing and evaluating the existing knowledge (RQ1), examining the function and use of technological mechanisms (RQ2 and RQ3), and bringing all the findings together while particularly focusing on the context of incumbent firms (RQ4).

The first Chapter in this part (C.I) recapitulates the findings from each study in order to answer the research questions and synthesizes the respective insights in an overarching theoretical framework. The following Chapters present the implications for research and practice (C.II) and reveal the limitations of as well as the future research opportunities for this work (C.III). Finally, the thesis closes with a concluding resume about managing digital innovation in incumbent firm contexts through knowledge integration (C.IV).

I. Findings and Results

This chapter summarizes the findings of each study and provides answers to the four main research questions. At the end of this chapter, the results are related to each other through a theoretical synthesis and brought together into an overarching conceptual framework.

I.1 Findings Regarding the Understanding of Knowledge Integration and Its Interaction with Digital Innovation

The first chapter of Part B aimed to consolidate the current state of IS research on knowledge integration and examine it with respect to recent phenomena in digital innovation. Therefore, it accounted for the unique nature of knowledge integration and its interaction with digital innovation. The title, research question, and main contribution of Study 1 are shown in Table C-1.

Table C-1. Title, Research Question, and Main Contribution of Study 1.

Findings of Study 1	
Title	Knowledge Integration and Digital Innovation – Towards a Multi-Dimensional Framework
Associated research question	RQ1: What is the status quo of information systems research on knowledge integration and how is it intertwined with digital innovation?
Main contribution	Overview of the status quo of IS research on knowledge integration and its interaction with digital innovation; multi-dimensional framework comprising the determinants and dimensions of knowledge integration

Based on a systematic literature review (Webster and Watson 2002), Study 1 assessed the existing knowledge base in IS research on the topic of knowledge integration and identified the associated research streams, theoretical conceptualizations, and underlying theories. This allowed to synthesize the existing findings on knowledge integration into a multi-dimensional framework of determinants and dimensions (Crossan and Apaydin 2010). Building on this, connections with and implications for the context of digital innovation could be derived.

With regard to dimensions, IS research employs two different theoretical conceptualizations of knowledge integration – one *as a process* and one *as an outcome* (Grant 1996a, 1996b; Okhuysen and Eisenhardt 2002). Research that theorizes knowledge integration as a process is differentiated in terms of where it took place (e.g., organizational level), which knowledge sources were considered (e.g., external or internal), which actors were involved (e.g., individuals), and in what form it was conducted (e.g., collective interaction). With regard to knowledge integration as an outcome, research distinguishes its locus (e.g., product or business model), novelty (e.g., established or new knowledge), and type (e.g., tacit or explicit) (Alavi and Leidner 2001; Nonaka and Takeuchi 1995; Polanyi 1967). Overall, the results on both conceptualizations indicated that external sources of knowledge and new technological artifacts, such as digital boundary resources, have gained importance and are increasingly considered in terms of their influence on knowledge integration processes and outcomes in the context of digital innovation.

Regarding the determinants of knowledge integration, the following three distinctive constructs emerged: *social mechanisms*, *technological mechanisms,* and *managerial levers*. The first construct, social mechanisms, builds mainly on social capital theory (Nahapiet and Ghoshal 1998) and is composed of social aspects such as social interactions and activities (Daniel and Stewart 2016), social networks and relationships (Robert et al. 2008), and communication channels (Mitchell 2006) as well as shared understanding and beliefs (Bittner and Leimeister 2014). The identified elements primarily influence knowledge integration on an individual or group level. Regarding the interaction of social mechanisms with the context of digital innovation, the findings indicated that increasingly more social aspects (e.g., social interactions) are becoming permeated by and are carried out with new digital technologies (e.g., digital networks). The second construct, technological mechanisms, accounts for all technological-related elements, such as knowledge management systems (Alavi and Leidner 2001), digital networks and platforms (Zhang et al. 2011), digital boundary resources (Foerderer et al. 2019), and system complexity (Daniel and Stewart 2016). These technological elements are primarily related to a firm's IT capabilities and represent all technological artifacts that affect the knowledge integration process or outcomes. Here, especially the role of boundary resources is emphasized for the context of digital innovation as they allow firms to "*overcome knowledge boundaries and enable effective product development outcomes*" (Foerderer et al. 2019, p. 125). The third construct, managerial levers, contains knowledge management activities (Carlo et al. 2012), intra-organizational linkages (Mitchell 2006), innovation culture (Datta and Roumani 2015), and process formalization (Patnayakuni and Ruppel 2006). These managerial aspects are mostly related to dynamic capabilities (Teece et al. 1997). Here, the identified determinants shape knowledge integration primarily from a broader, organizational level. As digital innovation increasingly relies on the integration of heterogeneous and distributed knowledge (Yoo et al. 2012), a major finding was that individual as well as organizational linkages have gained importance in terms of knowledge integration as they enable accessing and leveraging distributed pockets of knowledge within as well as outside the firm. Lastly, as most of the studies employ the knowledge-based theory of the firm as a theoretical foundation, the research commonly theorizes a general influence from the underlying knowledge base of the firm (e.g., individual or organizational knowledge) on knowledge integration processes and outcomes.

Based on the results of the first study, the importance of boundary resources as a novel mechanism for knowledge integration was uncovered. In this regard, Study 2 examined the current state of IS research in the emerging stream of boundary resources and thus contributes complementary insights to RQ1 (see Table C-2).

Table C-2. Title, Research Question, and Main Contribution of Study 2.

Findings of Study 2	
Title	Digital at the Edge – Antecedents and Performance Effects of Boundary Resources Deployment
Associated research question	RQ1: What is the status quo of information systems research on knowledge integration and how is it intertwined with digital innovation?
Main contribution	Overview of emerging IS research on boundary resources with a focus on the deploying firm (provider side)

In general, boundary resources are considered as a means or mechanism that enables resource sharing and thus stimulates external innovation in digital contexts (Ghazawneh and Henfridsson 2013; Parker et al. 2017). The current IS research on the emerging topic of boundary resources has developed valuable insights into how companies can deploy and manage boundary resources and what structural implications they have for digital business ecosystems. Regarding deployment, for instance, Ghazawneh and Henfridsson (2013) examined how boundary resources can be designed to enable external contribution while simultaneously enforcing control over strategic assets (Yoo et al. 2010). They apply a boundary resources model to analyze the processes of *resourcing* (i.e., extending the scope and diversity of the firm's offering) and *securing* (i.e., improving the firm's control) in the case of Apple's iPhone platform. Furthermore, they generate qualitative insights into how the design and evolution of boundary resources can help firms cope with coexisting and contradicting forces of resourcing and securing in digital business ecosystems. Concerning the management of boundary resources, for instance, Karhu et al. (2018) delineate how open digital platforms, such as Google's Android platform, can instantiate and modify boundary resources to defend against *platform forking* from hostile market participants. They describe platform forking as the process in which external actors bypass the host's controlling boundary resources and exploit the platform's shared resources, core, and complements to create competing businesses. Considering the structural implications of boundary resources, for example, Eaton et al. (2015) analyze in the context of Apple's iOS service system and how boundary resources are co-created themselves and evolve over time through the process of what they call *distributed tuning*. Their study illustrates the dynamic nature of boundary resources and how they are shaped by the multifaceted actions of heterogeneous actors in co-creation processes. Conclusively, as boundary resources are considered a crucial element for resource integration between heterogeneous and distributed partners in digital business ecosystems (Eaton et al. 2015), they serve as technological mechanisms for integrating knowledge from both inside and outside the firm and thus are particularly important for leveraging the generative and distributed nature of digital innovation (Kohli and Melville 2019; Yoo et al. 2010).

Apart from being deployed by focal firms, boundary resources can serve as channels for organizations to integrate external resources (e.g., knowledge-based capabilities). In this context, Study 3 primarily focused on how firms can integrate digital capabilities from external providers into their own organizational operations and innovations, thus providing insights into the user-side of boundary resources (see Table C-3).

Table C-3. Title, Research Question, and Main Contribution of Study 3.

Findings of Study 3	
Title	Leveraging "AI-as-a-Service" – Antecedents and Consequences of Using Artificial Intelligence Boundary Resources
Associated research question	RQ1: What is the status quo of information systems research on knowledge integration and how is it intertwined with digital innovation?
Main contribution	Overview of emerging IS research on boundary resources, focusing particularly on the adopting firm (user side)

In digital(izing) business ecosystems, boundary resources serve as a means for resource sharing between heterogeneous and distributed partners and promote the development of new products and services in the context of digital innovation (Ghazawneh and Henfridsson 2013). Here, boundary resources can not only be utilized by third-party developers for the development of complementary or combinatorial innovations but also by firms themselves to integrate capabilities from external actors into their own organizational environment (Karhu et al. 2018; Selander et al. 2013). This enables companies to close existing capability gaps in the context of digital innovation and improve their processes or products in line with changing market requirements (Karimi and Walter 2015; Yoo et al. 2010). Selander et al. (2013), for instance, investigated how the mobile device manufacturer Sony Ericsson engaged in *capability search* and *redeem* processes across various digital business ecosystems. Their findings indicate that firms actively seek external resources (e.g., technologies or competences) and leverage them through, for instance, boundary resources to improve existing and realize new innovation capabilities in the context of digital innovation. Thus, in contrast to earlier IT artifacts (Saraf et al. 2007), boundary resources represent a modern infrastructure for dynamic knowledge integration and can be both offered or used by firms (Ghazawneh and Henfridsson 2013; Karhu et al. 2018; Selander et al. 2013).

I.2 Findings Regarding the Scaling of Knowledge Integration through Boundary Resources in Digital(izing) Business Ecosystems

The research questions of the second chapter of Part B focused on boundary resources and their impact on knowledge integration in digital(izing) business ecosystems. Therefore, Study 2 delineated how firms can deploy boundary resources with varying objectives in order to leverage their own and the external knowledge from heterogeneous and distributed partners within their digital(izing) environment. Furthermore, by conducting a large-scale quantitative assessment using panel data regressions, insights into the antecedents and outcomes of boundary resources' deployments were derived. Table C-4 displays the title, research question, and main contributions of Study 2.

Table C-4. Title, Research Question, and Main Contribution of Study 2.

Findings of Study 2	
Title	Digital at the Edge – Antecedents and Performance Effects of Boundary Resources Deployment
Associated research question	RQ2: How and when do firms use boundary resources to leverage internal knowledge? RQ3: How and when do firms use boundary resources to leverage external knowledge?
Main contributions	Conceptualization of boundary resources as a technological mechanism for scaling knowledge integration in digital(izing) business ecosystems; insights into the antecedents and consequences of firms opting to deploy boundary resources

Depending on the requirements and objectives, a firm can design boundary resources to serve different purposes. For example, companies can decide to implement boundary resources in order to share different types of resources separately with distinct target groups (Eisenmann et al. 2008). In doing so, the firm can also decide exactly how it will regulate the interaction of these resources so that different utilization scenarios arise (Eaton et al. 2015). In this way, a firm can define the degree of openness and govern the complementors' work in line with its objectives (Karhu et al. 2018). Accordingly, depending on the type of openness, external actors can utilize the resources either by reusing them in their current business activities or by developing complementary innovations upon them. In this context, Karhu et al. (2018) discerned two different types of openness – *access openness*, which aims at distributing assets among external audiences and enabling basic interaction with them, and *resource openness*, which allows access to more valuable resources of the firm and leads to higher innovation potentials for external contributors. Accordingly, boundary resources for access openness enable firms primarily to distribute their existing digital offerings to external actors, which then can reuse or integrate the shared assets within their business activities. Therefore, this type of boundary resources primarily drives the distribution and exposure of companies' assets among external parties. For instance, Visa distributes many of its financial service solutions via APIs to provide them to users in their digital business ecosystem (Visa, 2020). In contrast, boundary resources for resource openness permit external contributors to access more valuable firm assets in order to diversify the firm's offerings based on their heterogeneous knowledge and innovation capabilities (Boudreau 2012; Parker et al. 2017). As an example, Apple lets external developers access the iPhone's camera core functionality (e.g., control of exposure or focus) in order to build complementary services and thus diversify the user's experience (Apple, 2020). In summary, companies can use boundary resources, on one hand, to leverage internal knowledge by facilitating access openness and distributing existing assets among external audiences or, on the other hand, to leverage external knowledge by establishing resource openness and enabling outside contributors to innovate upon the shared assets (Eaton et al. 2015; Karhu et al. 2018). Both objectives of boundary resources, however, drive the dynamic allocation and combination of knowledge resources residing inside as well as outside the firm and thus enable firms to scale knowledge integration in digital(izing) business ecosystems.

As to the contingencies of boundary resources deployments, the findings suggest that prior digital knowledge drives a firm's decision in favor of implementing boundary resources. This finding is in line with absorptive capacity theory in that prior knowledge supports firms in developing new related knowledge in the future as well as realizing technological outcomes building upon that knowledge (Lane et al. 2006; Roberts et al. 2012). This is further underscored by the empirical findings as they revealed that firms with high levels of digital knowledge tend to particularly deploy boundary resources that provide access openness (Karhu et al., 2018). Here, boundary resources might be utilized to increase the reach of specific offerings with the help of others in order to achieve network effects (Boudreau 2012; Boudreau and Jeppesen 2015). Furthermore, these boundary resources could be an indication for exploitative learning (March 1991) from the perspective of firms that have already progressed in terms of their digital maturity. These companies seem to exploit boundary resources particularly for the commercialization (West and Bogers 2014) or implementation and exploitation (Kohli & Melville, 2019) phase of innovation. Apart from this, the results also indicate that firms decide to deploy boundary resources particularly when digital ventures are present in their environment. One conceivable reason for this might stem from the fact that digital ventures can be perceived as potential competitors or disruptors (Karimi and Walter 2015; Lucas and Goh 2009). Thus, firms might be urged to engage in digital innovation to defend against disruption (Henfridsson and Yoo 2014), eventually driving the decision to deploy boundary resources (Svahn et al., 2017). Another reason could be that incumbent firms identify digital ventures as potential complementors and thus decide to set up boundary resources to leverage their capabilities as, in digital innovation, "*a firm's ability to attract heterogeneous and unexpected firms to build various components has become strategically important*" (Yoo et al. 2010, p. 731). In this context, the findings suggest that firms tend to deploy boundary resources that aim at resource openness particularly when digital ventures are present. Consequently, utilizing boundary resources to facilitate co-creation might be an indication for explorative learning (March 1991). Accordingly, such boundary resources might support the initiation and development (Kohli & Melville, 2019) or obtaining and integration (West & Bogers, 2014) phases of innovation, in which companies seek to leverage the heterogeneous and diverse knowledge capabilities of external actors to create new offerings.

Regarding the outcomes of deploying boundary resources, the findings indicate that deploying boundary resources, on average, does not have a significant performance implication per se. This could be rooted in the claim that firms are not always capable of managing new technologies appropriately and thus do not realize the potential economic benefits. However, the results further indicate that firms with higher market power profit significantly from deploying boundary resources. A reason for this could be that firms with greater market power potentially represent more attractive partners for external contributors due to their well-known brands, client bases, and quality of offerings (Eaton et al. 2015). To this end, the results indicate that firms with high market power realize economic benefits primarily from deploying boundary resources for access openness. This could be because access openness aims at distributing already-existing digital innovations that possess a certain degree of maturity and quality. Consequently, the shared digital assets provide added value to the target audiences, which comes with greater commercialization opportunities for the deploying firm. In contrast, the firm's assets that are provided through resource openness might be far away from the commercialization phase. Furthermore, deploying boundary resources for resource openness might be more costly in terms of their maintenance as they require more complex coordination and governance of complementors' activities and contributions (Eaton et al. 2015) and thus potentially limit economic benefits. In addition, as complementors seek to co-capture value from their contributions (Karhu et al. 2018), realizing financial benefits from boundary resources for resource openness might be even more challenging.

Study 3 investigated the firm's use of boundary resources for the purpose of integrating external digital capabilities into its own internal context (e.g., operations or innovation activities). Methodologically, the study also employed a large-scale quantitative analysis using panel data regressions and focused on firms that integrated the AI-related capabilities of external providers via boundary resources. Table C-5 presents the addressed research questions and main contributions.

Table C-5. Title, Research Question, and Main Contribution of Study 3.

Findings of Study 3	
Title	Leveraging "AI-as-a-Service" – Antecedents and Consequences of Using Artificial Intelligence Boundary Resources
Associated research question	RQ2: How and when do firms use boundary resources to leverage internal knowledge? RQ3: How and when do firms use boundary resources to leverage external knowledge?
Main contributions	Improved understanding for building and realizing digital capabilities by using external boundary resources; insights into the antecedents and consequences of firms opting to use external boundary resources

With the rapid development of accessible computing power and available big data, firms across industries are developing and utilizing increasingly "intelligent systems" that are reinforced by a new wave of AI technologies (Coombs et al. 2020; Krogh 2018; Rai et al. 2019). These new technologies offer a variety of opportunities to improve organizational performance in different areas, such as product development (Davenport et al. 2012; Gillon et al. 2014), supply chain management (Koh et al. 2011; Nissen and Sengupta 2006), and data analytics (Ghasemaghaei et al. 2018; Loebbecke and Picot 2015). Yet, leveraging these new technologies requires high investments in necessary know-how (e.g., data science) and technological infrastructures (e.g., computing and big data infrastructures). To circumvent this, companies can now turn to external providers and integrate AI capabilities (e.g., cognitive computing or machine learning services) via boundary resources (Forbes 2018; Rai et al. 2019). Accordingly, boundary resources enable firms to leverage external knowledge by integrating the digital capabilities of external providers into their own internal contexts (Yoo et al. 2010). Building on this, the external AI-related assets can then either be used by integrating them with internal knowledge and, for example, optimize processes (e.g., data-driven decision making) or by anchoring them directly into products (e.g., integration of voice assistants). For example, based on IBM's AI capabilities and its underlying computing infrastructure, Autodesk has developed a virtual agent that was able to accelerate customer service response times by 99% (IBM 2017). Hence, boundary resources represent a new strategic alternative for companies to build and realize digital capabilities in their digital(izing) business ecosystems (Grover et al. 2018; Selander et al. 2013; Yoo et al. 2010).

Regarding the contingencies that drive firms to use external boundary resources, the empirical results indicate that high internal AI capabilities drive firms to use AI boundary resources, particularly for internal process improvements. Accordingly, firms that have developed their own knowledge see AI boundary resources as a complement and thus leverage the external knowledge on the basis of what they already know. This finding connects to insights from absorptive capacity (Roberts et al. 2012), which assume that prior knowledge improves the ability to identify, assimilate, and apply valuable external knowledge (Lane et al. 2006). Therefore, firms might consider the use of AI boundary resources as a practical means to supplement or enhance their existing capabilities in contexts where AI can be leveraged for improving decision making or automating tasks (Coombs et al. 2020; Ghasemaghaei et al. 2018; Rai et al. 2019). Furthermore, the findings suggest that a high level of external market pressure is positively associated with a firm's decision to use AI boundary resources, particularly those that are anchored directly into customer solutions. This might be caused by the impact of digital technologies on consumer behavior and related expectations toward the services that companies provide (Lucas et al. 2013; Vial 2019). Thus, utilizing AI boundary resources for embedding AI solutions into the firm's offerings might be a strategic measure to close capability and service gaps in highly competitive environments that are driven by constantly changing and increasing customer expectations (Karimi and Walter 2015; Selander et al. 2013).

In terms of the consequences of using AI boundary resources, first, except for a marginally significant effect on accounting-based performance, the findings show that, on one hand, using AI boundary resources is not beneficial for the firm per se. This finding might hint at the difficulties companies face when trying to realize the benefits of lowering costs as well as increasing revenues with AI-related technologies. With regard to this, previous research has indicated that the exploitation of digital innovation can be challenging due to internal (e.g., culture or structure) or external (competition, industry characteristics) conditions (Kohli and Melville 2019), particularly in non-digital contexts (Hanelt et al. 2020). These difficulties may drive firms to employ AI in decoupled and potentially smaller projects, thus limiting their performance effect (Tumbas et al. 2018). On the other hand, the results support the prediction that firms that decide to use AI boundary resources for specific objectives (i.e., process improvements or customer solutions) do profit from this choice. Here, using AI boundary resources for process improvements particularly benefits performance in terms of efficiency. This result shows that boundary resources can be a valuable complement in realizing AI-related benefits regarding data-driven task automation or decision making (Coombs et al. 2020; Ghasemaghaei et al. 2018; Grover et al. 2018). Likewise, the results support that firms that utilize AI boundary resources for customer solutions benefit from performance implications related to sales growth. Thus, by utilizing AI boundary resources for customer solutions, firms embrace combinatorial innovation (Yoo et al. 2012) and try to respond to changing customer expectations (Vial 2019) as well as new competitive dynamics (Skog et al. 2018; Tumbas et al. 2017) by providing a constant stream of new functions in their offerings (Gawer 2014; Yoo et al. 2010). As a result, the sales of existing offerings can be secured, and new revenues for innovative complements can be realized (Eaton et al. 2015; Parker et al. 2017).

I.3 Findings Regarding the Management of Knowledge Integration in Incumbent Firm Contexts Impacted by Digital Innovation

The previously summarized studies investigated knowledge integration in order to, first, understand its unique nature in digital innovation and, second, delineate how it can be scaled through boundary resources in digital(izing) business ecosystems. Both aspects lead to fundamental changes in how knowledge integration needs to be managed in incumbent firm contexts impacted by digital innovation.

Study 2, described in the previous section, focused on the role of boundary resources for knowledge integration, providing insights into these aspects. With regard to this, Table C-6 describes the research question and main contribution.

Table C-6. Title, Research Question, and Main Contribution of Study 2.

Findings of Study 2	
Title	Digital at the Edge – Antecedents and Performance Effects of Boundary Resources Deployment
Associated research question	RQ4: How can incumbent firms dynamically balance and integrate heterogeneous and dispersed knowledge resources required for digital innovation?
Main contribution	Improved understanding for the dynamic balancing and integration of heterogeneous and dispersed knowledge resources in the context of digital innovation

As incumbent firms and their offerings are increasingly embedded in digital(izing) business ecosystems (Bharadwaj et al. 2013; Tilson et al. 2010), they are required to scale and diversify their digital products to ensure innovation and growth (Boudreau 2012; Gawer and Cusumano 2014). To this end, they need to leverage their own knowledge by combining it with that of heterogeneous and widely distributed actors (El Sawy and Pereira 2013; Yoo et al. 2012). To do this, however, they need new mechanisms that can cope with the increasing scale and scope of required knowledge linkages. Here, boundary resources, as a new technological artifact, represent such a mechanism (Ghazawneh and Henfridsson 2013). Accordingly, incumbent firms can utilize boundary resources, on one hand, to distribute and expose their existing assets to outside audiences and, on the other hand, to diversify the firm's offerings by tapping into the knowledge and innovation capabilities of external actors within their digital(izing) business ecosystems (Karhu et al. 2018). Therefore, boundary resources represent a mandatory element for managing knowledge integration in incumbent firm contexts impacted by digital innovation.

Study 3, described in the previous section, provides additional insights into managing knowledge integration through boundary resources. With regard to this, Table C-7 shows the research question and main contribution.

Table C-7. Title, Research Question, and Main Contribution of Study 3.

Findings of Study 3	
Title	Leveraging "AI-as-a-Service" – Antecedents and Consequences of Using Artificial Intelligence Boundary Resources
Associated research question	RQ4: How can incumbent firms dynamically balance and integrate heterogeneous and dispersed knowledge resources required for digital innovation?
Main contributions	Insights into building and realizing digital capabilities based on boundary resources in digital(izing) business ecosystems

Due to rapid technological developments driven by digital technologies and the innovations building on them (El Sawy et al. 2010; Nambisan et al. 2017), market requirements and customer needs are in a constant state of flux (Lucas et al. 2013; Vial 2019). To keep up with these changes, incumbent firms are increasingly dependent on closing existing capability gaps as quickly as possible to ensure their innovativeness and survival (Karimi and Walter 2015; Lavie 2006a; Lucas and Goh 2009). However, some new technological areas, such as AI, require sophisticated infrastructural (Tilson et al. 2010) as well as knowledge-based capabilities (Kohli and Melville 2019) and therefore might be challenging for established companies to rapidly tap into, especially for those coming from non-digital contexts (Hanelt et al. 2020). In order to avoid negative outcomes, incumbent firms can utilize boundary resources to leverage external knowledge (e.g., digital capabilities) from providers in their digital(izing) business ecosystems (Rai et al. 2019; Yoo et al. 2010). Here, established companies can not only anchor the external capabilities directly into their offerings (e.g., Bardhan et al. 2020; Günther et al. 2017) but also integrate them with their own intra-organizational knowledge and, for example, optimize business processes (e.g., Ghasemaghaei et al. 2018; Günther et al. 2017). Conclusively, incumbent firms can utilize boundary resources as a kind of all-purpose tool and modern infrastructure for rapidly and diversely linking the firm's own and external knowledge in digital(izing) business ecosystems to dynamically build up necessary capabilities and meet constantly changing market requirements in the digital age (El Sawy and Pereira 2013; Yoo et al. 2012).

Study 4, by employing a grounded theory approach (Glaser and Strauss 1967) and drawing upon the automotive industry as an example, aimed at providing in-depth insights into the knowledge integration process of incumbent firms that are impacted by digital innovation. Table C-8 displays the title, research question, and main contribution.

Table C-8. Title, Research Question, and Main Contribution of Study 4.

Findings of Study 4	
Title	Digital Innovation in Industrial-Age Firms – Managing the Balancing Act of Knowledge Integration
Associated research question	RQ4: How can incumbent firms dynamically balance and integrate heterogeneous and dispersed knowledge resources required for digital innovation?
Main contributions	Insights into the interplay of the contextual conditions, mechanisms, and outcomes of managing knowledge integration in incumbent firm contexts impacted by digital innovation

The study's findings highlight that knowledge integration for digital innovation is a multilayered process that needs to be balanced cohesively by several interdependent activities in order to achieve digital innovation outcomes. Here, the study particularly sheds light on internal and external contextual conditions and three different but intertwined knowledge integration mechanisms as well as associated outcomes related to the process of integrating knowledge in incumbent firms impacted by digital innovation. In this context, the identified internal (e.g., capability gaps) and external (e.g., digital business requirements) factors established the need for fundamental transformations of automotive manufacturers toward digital innovation. In order to be able to realize those transformations properly and create value from them, the incumbent firms had to increase the breadth of their traditional knowledge base by tapping into new, unrelated, and distant knowledge areas. This represented the initial trigger for the process of knowledge integration that the organization had to carry out. Furthermore, the findings indicated three different but intertwined knowledge integration mechanisms of *knowledge diversification*, *knowledge contextualization*, and *knowledge application*. The first mechanism represents how the organization's knowledge base is increasing in breadth based on the acquisition of external as well as the development of internal knowledge related to digital technologies and innovations that build upon them. The second mechanism, *knowledge contextualization,* reflects the cross-functional assessment of the previously diversified knowledge and the evaluation of the organizational configurations required to leverage it appropriately. Apart from this, the previously described diversification of knowledge enabled the identification of new business opportunities (e.g., new digital services) stemming from the layered architecture of digital technologies (Yoo et al. 2010) as well as the generative nature of digital innovation (Yoo et al. 2012) and thus created the need for a (re)definition of business boundaries (e.g., traditional vs. new digital business models). Finally, the third mechanism, *knowledge application,* reflects the exploitation of the previously diversified and contextualized knowledge for realizing digital innovation outcomes. Here, the incumbent firms either created new digital offerings (e.g., digital services) or shaped digital innovation capabilities that enabled them to leverage digital technologies and build innovations upon them (e.g., machine learning applications).

However, as these mechanisms are interdependent, the incumbent firms have to manage them appropriately in order to realize beneficial outcomes. To achieve this, organizations require, first, the ability to acquire external valuable knowledge (Roberts et al. 2012). If they are not capable of such or do not decide to do so (Kogut and Zander 1992), the subsequent mechanisms become irrelevant. Second, as the next mechanism of knowledge contextualization represents a crucial link between the development and application of new knowledge, organizations require knowledge-based competencies to properly assess the value of external knowledge and the conditions (e.g., organizational structures or processes) in which it needs to be applied (Lane et al. 2006; Svahn et al. 2017). Finally, the mechanism of knowledge application that leads to the creation of digital innovation outcomes is directly reliant on the preceding mechanisms. Consequently, if organizations develop too little new knowledge or evaluate it wrongfully, its application can become faulty and thus, in the worst case, further aggravate the deficits and challenges the company is facing in the context of digital innovation. Apart from this, as the knowledge required for digital innovation becomes increasingly heterogeneous (Yoo et al. 2012), incumbent firms require flexible organizational options for deploying it depending on product- or business-relatedness in order to exploit it appropriately (Yoo et al. 2010). In sum, as the business requirements related to digital innovation trigger incumbent firms to acquire and integrate new knowledge from distant and unrelated contexts, they have to go through the three mechanisms. Depending on how they are developed and managed as well as what organizational conditions are in place, a corresponding result will be generated, either improving or further aggravating the initial situation of the organization. Accordingly, incumbent firms need to assess their knowledge capabilities and organizational conditions carefully and consider how to balance a reasoned equilibrium between integrating new knowledge in existing structures (e.g., organizational legacy) or in newly developed settings (e.g., digital innovation teams, departments, or subsidiaries).

After recapitulating the results of the three Chapters in Part B and the four studies included in this cumulative thesis, Figure C:1 provides an overview of the main findings and how they relate to the overall goals of this thesis.

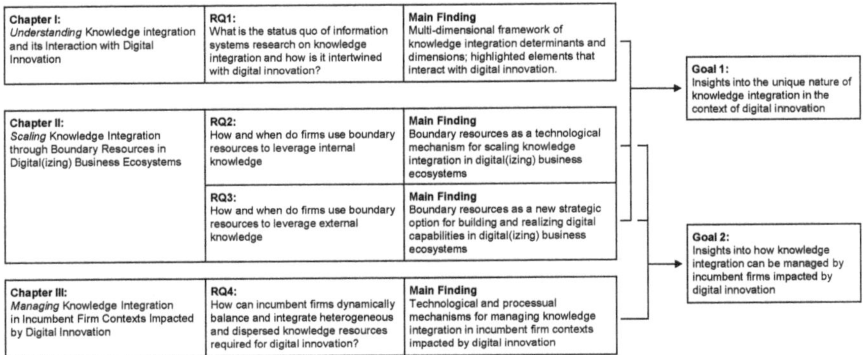

Figure C:1. Integrated Findings and Relation to Overall Goals.

I.4 Synthesis: A Knowledge Integration Perspective on Digital Innovation in Incumbent Firm Contexts

In the last decade alone, the rapid rise and increasing diffusion of pervasive digital technologies have fundamentally influenced and transformed our society and economy (Bharadwaj et al. 2013; Tilson et al. 2010). In this context, digital technologies have not only become an integral part of our daily lives (Yoo 2010) but also a major driver of the innovations that have been made possible by them (Yoo et al. 2012). Their fundamental properties, such as reprogrammability and a layered architecture, play a vital role as they enable new offerings that can be continuously improved and are capable of creating complementary and combinatorial innovations based on them (Yoo et al. 2010; Yoo et al. 2012). Because of this driving force and the opportunities it creates, companies are increasingly required to integrate digital technologies into their innovation processes and outcomes (Nambisan et al. 2017) regardless of whether or not they have existing competencies in this area. As a result, incumbent firms in particular need to redevelop their existing knowledge base in order to cope with the technological discontinuity (Hill and Rothaermel 2003; Kranz et al. 2016). Here, the convergent and generative nature of digital innovation reinforces the need for new knowledge capabilities by not only uniting originally separate industries and products but also enabling increasingly heterogeneous and widely distributed actors to innovate on it (Yoo et al. 2010). This increases the amount and the diversity of knowledge that incumbent firms must dynamically balance and integrate not only to adapt to competitive changes but also to take advantage of the many new opportunities for collaboration (El Sawy and Pereira 2013; Yoo et al. 2012).

However, these changes encounter the existing realities of incumbent firms and therefore lead to different difficulties depending on the internal or external conditions prevailing in their contexts (Piccinini et al. 2015; Svahn et al. 2017). On one hand, looking at the internal conditions, companies need to have certain knowledge-based capabilities to be able to identify and integrate valuable external knowledge in the context of digital innovation (Kohli and Melville 2019). Despite that, the integration of digital components into existing products plays an important role for established companies (Yoo et al. 2010), as it can create a fundamentally different innovation infrastructure that enables new complementary or combinatorial developments (Porter and Heppelmann 2014; Yoo et al. 2012). On the other hand, the external context in which companies find themselves also plays a vital role in how and what knowledge must be integrated (Kohli and Melville 2019; Lyytinen et al. 2016). Driven by the force of digital innovation and the increasing interconnectedness of products, processes, and services, companies are increasingly finding themselves in digital(izing) business ecosystems (Bharadwaj et al. 2013; El Sawy and Pereira 2013). Here, the joint creation of value with heterogeneous and widely distributed players is becoming increasingly important in order to remain successful through innovation and growth (Boudreau 2012; Parker and van Alstyne 2018). Accordingly, it is precisely these new actors as digital audiences that offer diverse opportunities to ignite the generative nature of digital innovation and make it exploitable for incumbent firms (El Sawy and Pereira 2013; Yoo et al. 2012). To this end, established companies can leverage external actors by distributing their own digitized products among them and utilize network effects (Gawer and Cusumano 2014) or by diversifying their offerings based on their heterogeneous knowledge and innovation capabilities (Ghazawneh and Henfridsson 2013). Apart from this, digital(izing) business ecosystems provide incumbent firms with new strategic options to overcome gaps in their technological competences by integrating the digital capabilities (e.g., AI-related infrastructure) of external partners and thus be able to react rapidly to changes in market requirements or customer demands (Karimi and Walter 2015; Selander et al. 2013; Yoo et al. 2010). However, depending on the contextual conditions described above, there are two basic mechanisms by which incumbent firms must manage the intensified demands for knowledge integration in relation to digital innovation. While one of these mechanisms is rather procedural in nature and aims more at managing the increased knowledge requirements in the internal context of the firm, the other is rather technical in nature and seeks to exploit the new generative possibilities in the context of digital(izing) business ecosystems.

Looking first at the internal context, incumbent firms that are, particularly at an early stage of their digital maturity, affected by the convergent aspects of digital innovation need to manage the procedural mechanism of knowledge integration through three interdependent and mutually influencing steps. Accordingly, in the first step, knowledge diversification, companies need to rebuild their existing knowledge base, especially when they are from non-digital contexts (Hanelt et al. 2020), and address the knowledge domains related to the digital technologies and innovations that build on them. Depending on how developed their knowledge base is in this context, their need to acquire valuable external knowledge can vary (Kranz et al. 2016). Despite this, it is crucial for incumbent firms to foster the development of new knowledge within their organizational context as the success of digital innovation relies increasingly on the recombination of knowledge inside and outside the firm (Kohli and Melville 2019). This knowledge diversification creates the requirement for assessing the novel or newly combined knowledge in terms of its value and best possible place of use, leading to the second step, knowledge contextualization. Here, incumbent firms particularly need to examine the new knowledge based on cross-functional evaluation as well as product and business relatedness to find the best possible organizational setting in which it can be applied and exploited. Consequently, when conducting the preceding steps appropriately, the final step, knowledge application, enables the beneficial exploitation of the previously developed and contextualized knowledge. However, especially during the interaction of internal preconditions and the execution of these steps, managerial tensions between traditional business logics and the required digital ones can arise (e.g., Svahn et al. 2017), which incumbent firms must consider when trying to manage knowledge integration appropriately. If these tensions cannot be solved through, for instance, the creation of fitting organizational settings for exploiting the diversified knowledge, the initial knowledge-related deficits and associated challenges of incumbent firms in the context of digital innovation can be further exacerbated. Thus, it is particularly important to manage these three steps in a balanced way so that sufficient new knowledge can be acquired but also integrated in suitable organizational structures (e.g., Lyytinen et al. 2016) in order to ultimately be exploited in a value-creating way.

With respect to the external context and the generativity enabled by digital innovation, incumbent firms are increasingly dependent on distributing their products based on network effects (Boudreau and Jeppesen 2015; Gawer 2014) and collaborating with a growing number of heterogeneous and widely distributed actors in their digital(izing) business ecosystems to ensure growth and innovation (Boudreau 2012; Gawer and Cusumano 2014). However, to manage the increasing quantity and complexity of knowledge integration with distributed partners in an efficient and value-creating way, established companies rely on utilizing the technological mechanism of boundary resources, such as APIs (Eaton et al. 2015; Ghazawneh and Henfridsson 2013). These new technological artifacts present multiple options to leverage internal as well external knowledge for the purpose of digital innovation.

On one hand, with regard to leveraging internal knowledge-based assets, companies can use boundary resources to define different types of openness and, in doing so, either distribute and expose their digital assets among external audiences to achieve network effects (i.e., access openness) or allow external contributors interaction with the firm's digital products to diversify them through complementary and combinatorial innovations (Karhu et al. 2018; Yoo et al. 2012). On the other hand, depending on internal conditions and needs, incumbent firms can also leverage external knowledge in their digital(izing) business ecosystems by obtaining the required digital capabilities (e.g., AI-related infrastructure or services) from partners via boundary resources (Rai et al. 2019). Such capabilities can then be used either to integrate them with their own knowledge and, for example, improve internal business processes (e.g., task automation) (Coombs et al. 2020) or to anchor them directly in products or services in order to respond rapidly to changing market conditions or customer demands (Karimi and Walter 2015; Lucas et al. 2013).

In summary, both mechanisms are required by incumbent firms to build new knowledge-based capabilities in the context of digital innovation that enables them, on one hand, to manage the changing and expanding knowledge base within their organizations and, on the other hand, to exploit the new possibilities of generativity in their digital(izing) business ecosystems. Conclusively, while the procedural mechanism supports incumbent firms rather in the *dynamic balancing* of the increasing amount and diversity of knowledge that needs to be integrated within their organizations, the technological mechanism of boundary resources primarily enables the *dynamic integration* of internal as well as external knowledge within their digital(izing) business ecosystems. However, even though each mechanism tends to address different organizational areas – one the internal and the other the external context of the firm – only by leveraging both in combination can incumbent firms become capable of mastering the challenges and exploiting the opportunities in the wake of digital innovation.

Figure C:2 integrates these findings and provides a knowledge integration perspective on managing digital innovation in incumbent firm contexts.

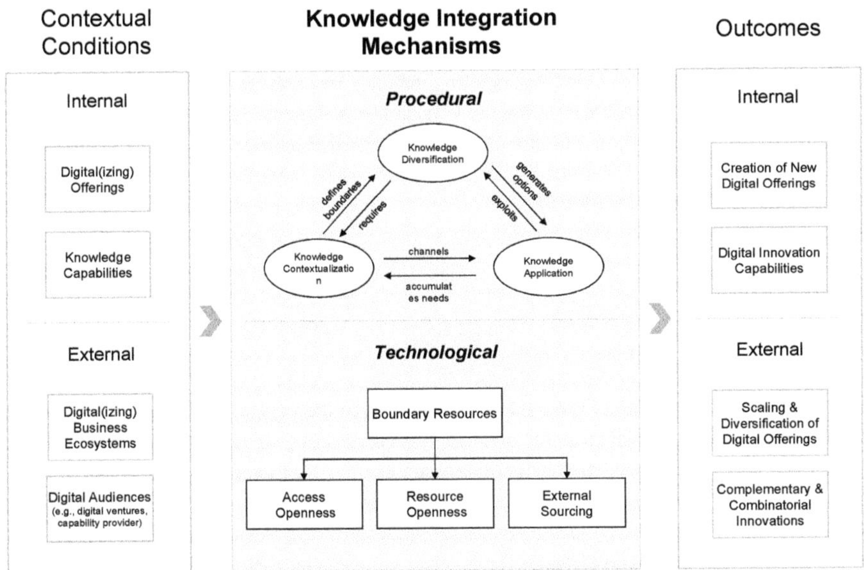

Note: Illustration of most relevant concepts and interactions examined in this thesis, therefore not exhaustive.

Figure C:2. Integrated Findings of the Knowledge Integration Mechanisms Required for Managing Digital Innovation in Incumbent Firm Contexts.

II. Implications

Based on the previously outlined findings, this chapter presents the key contributions of this thesis for the three IS research areas of knowledge integration, boundary resources, and digital innovation and derives important implications for managerial practice.

II.1 Implications for Research

This thesis sheds light on the unique nature of knowledge integration and how it can be managed by incumbent firms in the context of digital innovation. With regard to this, particularly the role of boundary resources as a technological mechanism for knowledge integration has been examined. Accordingly, this thesis aimed to derive valuable contributions to research in the aforementioned areas.

Considering the interaction of knowledge integration with the context of digital innovation, this thesis offers valuable insights. First, apart from traditional knowledge management systems, new technological elements such as boundary resources (Ghazawneh and Henfridsson 2013) or software-related aspects such as system complexity (Daniel and Stewart 2016) have become increasingly relevant to the processes and outcomes of knowledge integration, thus underscoring the increasing diffusion and adoption of digital technologies by organizations (Bharadwaj et al. 2013). For example, companies increasingly deploy boundary resources to allow external developers to access their digital products in order to develop complementary or combinatorial innovations upon them (Foerderer et al. 2019; Yoo et al. 2012). This in turn indicates a major shift in organizational knowledge management from developing and controlling the firm's knowledge base to enabling others to innovate upon it and orchestrate their heterogeneous and distributed knowledge capabilities (Boudreau 2012; Eaton et al. 2015). Second, it was found that digital technologies have become increasingly embedded in the social activities and interactions of organizational actors. As a result, knowledge integration within digitally enabled teams (Robert et al. 2008) is increasingly shifting into the virtual space of digital networks and platforms (Zhang et al. 2011). As these virtual interactions and distributed activities can now take place at any time and in any place, the process of knowledge integration becomes more flexible and dynamic and thus requires organizations to develop new knowledge management capabilities (Kohli and Melville 2019; Yoo et al. 2012). Finally, knowledge integration is increasingly built on individual and organizational linkages between distributed knowledge resources of heterogeneous actors, both inside and outside the firm (Kohli and Melville 2019). Hence, managerial levers such as organizational linkages or an innovation-oriented culture are becoming increasingly mandatory in the context of digital innovation (Datta and Roumani 2015; Mitchell 2006).

Regarding the specific impact of digital innovation on knowledge integration in incumbent firms, it was found that associated processes were affected by managerial tensions that were related to different business requirements between traditional businesses (e.g., the automotive industry) and digital innovation (Henfridsson et al. 2014), thus supporting prior research insights, such as the concept of competing concerns from Svahn et al. (2017).

Furthermore, the findings underscore that the greater extent of required knowledge for digital innovation needs to be supported by an increase in organizational flexibility (Svahn et al. 2017; Yoo et al. 2010; Yoo et al. 2012). Accordingly, selecting from various organizational options is especially critical when new knowledge related to digital innovation is assessed as valuable but is more or less separable from the core business (e.g., mobility-related services in the automotive industry). However, due to the force of digital innovation (Kogut and Zander 1992; Kohli and Melville 2019) even industrial-age organizations (e.g., automotive OEMs) and their traditional product boundaries are being reshaped in structure and content (Svahn et al. 2017). Therefore, the evaluation of new knowledge concerning its product- and business-relatedness is critically important for incumbent firms in order to find the most favorable organizational setting for exploiting its potential in the context of digital innovation. In summary, the findings accentuate the convergent and generative nature of digital innovation, which makes knowledge integration a permanent, dynamic, and multifaceted issue. Therefore, the diversity and complexity of knowledge integration processes as well as outcomes are increasing in the digital era and thus require more in-depth investigations into, for instance, new technological mechanisms such as boundary resources.

As knowledge integration processes and outcomes become increasingly influenced and shaped by digital technologies, their nature becomes more complex and dynamic and thus demands the utilization of new technological mechanisms such as boundary resources for coping with it. Here, based on the particular investigation of how and when companies utilize boundary resources to leverage internal and external knowledge in the context of digital innovation, this thesis has important insights to offer. The findings on boundary resources provide an interesting contextual differentiation to boundary resources research. Previous research has thus far considered only purely digital contexts. For example, the work by Karhu et al. (2018) was set in the context of a digital platform business. However, as digitalization permeates organizations across industries (Tilson et al. 2010), the decision to use boundary resources is becoming relevant in all types of business contexts. To this end, it was found that boundary resources have experienced a widespread dissemination across a broad range of industries and different contexts. Especially in contexts that traditionally do not belong to IT or digital industries, the decision to adopt boundary resources might be part of a larger process of digital transformation. Companies that are starting to explore and develop their digital business strategies (Bharadwaj et al. 2013) might learn in parallel with or through the use of boundary resources. In addition, based on inexperience and uncertainty, firms might also follow trends and hypes and thus engage in utilizing boundary resources. All these factors might have an influence on their decision to use boundary resources. In this context, history might be influencing in a variety of ways, such as due to socio-technical or socio-cognitive inertia (Besson and Rowe 2012). For example, firms that were successful in the past in non-digital contexts might strongly follow a supply chain logic, which opposes the platform logic in digital(izing) business environments (Gawer and Phillips 2013). Therefore, the specific organizational conditions that surround boundary resources become more relevant in the era of digitalization and provide valuable insights into managerial decisions about and the effectiveness of boundary resources deployment.

Accordingly, even though prior research has generated valuable insights into how boundary resources, in general, can be designed and deployed, the strategic reasoning behind this as well as the consequences, particularly from a knowledge-based perspective, have received less attention. To this end, the findings in Studies 2 and 3 illustrated the dynamics of coopetition in the digital age (El Sawy and Pereira 2013). Traditionally, research theorizes a potential competition between internal and external sources of innovation (West and Bogers 2014). However, the properties of digital technologies, including the architecture consisting of loosely coupled layers (Yoo et al. 2010), as well as the nature of digital innovation, including its combinatorial and distributed characteristics (Yoo et al. 2012), are particularly creating demands for combining and leveraging internal as well as external knowledge. Accordingly, it was found that firms possessing a knowledge base related to digital innovation (i.e., digital knowledge) and that are surrounded by potential complementors (e.g., digital ventures) are driven to use boundary resources to leverage knowledge from external sources (without contracting or formally acquiring it). Thus, boundary resources can be considered as technical infrastructure for external knowledge acquisition in digital(izing) business ecosystems (Cohen and Levinthal 1990; Ghazawneh and Henfridsson 2013). This outlines the implications of digital technologies and their layered architecture (Yoo et al. 2010), where complementary resources such as knowledge can be leveraged externally and do not need to be fully understood or controlled by the firm (Ghazawneh and Henfridsson 2013; Parker et al. 2017; Yoo et al. 2012). Accordingly, this observation provides a valuable extension to the IS research related to absorptive capacity (Roberts et al. 2012) and, in general, improves the understanding on the new nature of knowledge integration in the context of digital innovation (Mitchell 2006).

Concerning the development and realization of digital capabilities in the digital era, the findings provide an interesting perspective especially for digital(izing) business ecosystems, where companies can utilize boundary resources to incorporate external knowledge and technologies into their own organizational operations and offerings (Yoo et al. 2010). To this end, previous research on knowledge recombination (i.e., knowledge integration) has identified that IT has a significant impact on related processes and outcomes (Dong and Yang 2019). Yet, related studies have primarily investigated more traditional IT systems that had been used either internally or externally with very specific business partners. Nowadays, however, the topic of boundary resources is becoming increasingly relevant across industries due their growing interconnectedness and pervasive digitalization (Bharadwaj et al. 2013; Yoo et al. 2010). Accordingly, boundary resources such as APIs, with their external focus and ready-to-use infrastructure, might therefore significantly drive knowledge integration, especially in terms of diversity (Dong and Yang 2019). Alternatively, boundary resources can be considered as a viable approach to expose internal digital knowledge. To this end, they reinforce a firm's desorptive capacity as a crucial capability for achieving technology transfer across organizational boundaries (Müller-Seitz 2012; Ziegler et al. 2013), a perspective that has thus far been missing in the discourse of IS research. Conclusively, the two-way nature of boundary resources makes the simultaneous perspective on the inflows as well as the outflows of knowledge particularly important (West and Bogers 2014).

Apart from the specific insights into knowledge integration and boundary resources, additional implications, in broader terms, could be derived for the context of digital innovation. Digital(izing) business ecosystems are increasingly requiring openness by a firm's business and innovation activities (El Sawy and Pereira 2013; Yoo et al. 2012). Firms that open up, however, reduce their ability to control their assets as well as the operations of external actors (Parker and van Alstyne 2018). Thus, as firms are confronted with the new competitive and cooperative dynamics of digital(izing) business ecosystems, they are forced to decide whether to open up toward external contribution and, if they do so, how they can ensure control over their strategic assets (Yoo et al. 2010). This decision creates a managerial tension since firms are increasingly dependent on outside heterogeneous capabilities and resources in the context of digital innovation but at the same time need to guard their assets from external exploitation (Karhu et al. 2018; Yoo et al. 2010). To this end, boundary resources have been suggested as a theoretical concept to manage or solve this tension (Eaton et al. 2015; Ghazawneh and Henfridsson 2013). Thus, the utilization of boundary resources can be understood as an intermediate strategy residing between complete openness and tight control, which displays the firm's balancing act of stimulating external contribution while simultaneously maintaining control over strategic assets (Ghazawneh and Henfridsson 2013).

In this context, prior works have revealed important insights into what happens inside firms or ecosystems in the time after the deployment of boundary resources. However, the strategic reasoning to do so as well as the consequences for the deploying firm have received less attention. In this regard, the findings in this thesis provide valuable extensions. Here, firms that hold digital knowledge are opting toward this intermediate strategy. On one hand, these firms want to leverage their knowledge. On the other, they are likely to also want to maintain some sort of control. Furthermore, firms that are surrounded by digital ventures tend to opt for the middle ground strategy. These companies might consider advantages in opening up to some amount to allow cooperation while simultaneously they also might be conscious about giving away too much to their potential competitors. Boundary resources are a viable strategy to exercise some sort of control over external actors that do not fall into the traditional sphere of suppliers or partners that might be controlled via contracting. In sum, as indicated by the findings, particularly when firms hold digital knowledge and face digital ventures in their surroundings, the middle-ground strategy of using boundary resources seems to be compelling as it enables openness but also allows the firm to exert a certain degree of power in leveraging internal and external knowledge. Therefore, firms in such conditions open up progressively yet in a narrow manner to secure important assets. This strategy, however, only pays off financially for firms with a high degree of market power. Firms without such a position might potentially benefit more from alternative strategies that seek even more openness to reach greater audiences, for instance, by providing open-source licenses (Karhu et al., 2018). Following this line of reasoning, the firm's decision to open up for value co-creation and co-capture with external actors as well as the implementation of associated technical artifacts (e.g., APIs) are as important as the potential assets (brands, customers, platforms, etc.) a firm provides within interactions with these actors.

An overview of the key implications for researchers that focus on knowledge integration, boundary resources, and digital innovation is provided in Table C-9.

Table C-9. Implications for Research.

Field	Main implication	Explanation
Knowledge Integration	(1) Digital technologies are increasingly permeating knowledge integration processes and outcomes.	Digital technologies (e.g., digital platforms) are reshaping the way in which knowledge integration is carried out and the type of outcomes it produces (e.g., complementary or combinatorial innovations).
	(2) The nature of knowledge integration becomes increasingly dynamic and complex in the context of digital innovation.	Knowledge integration in the context of digital innovation is moving, on one hand, increasingly into the virtual space and is thus becoming more flexible and scalable and, on the other hand, relies more on the integration of the heterogeneous knowledge resources and activities of distributed partners.
	(3) Knowledge integration builds upon new procedural and technological mechanisms for managing the requirements of and exploiting opportunities in the context digital innovation.	The changing nature of knowledge integration intensifies related requirements and forces organizations to employ new procedural as well as technological mechanisms to cope with the associated challenges.
Boundary Resources	(1) Boundary resources represent a technological mechanism for leveraging internal as well as external knowledge.	Complex and dynamic interactions in digital(izing) business ecosystems require technological infrastructure on which they can be carried out in order to scale and diversify innovations.
	(2) The beneficial utilization of boundary resources depends on internal as well as external conditions.	Internal knowledge capabilities as well as external complementors drive firms' decision whether to utilize boundary resources, and particularly market power allows for realizing benefits.
Digital Innovation	(1) Incumbent firm contexts impacted by digital innovation require new organizational capabilities related to knowledge integration.	Changes in knowledge integration processes and outcomes driven by digital technologies force incumbent firms to employ new procedural as well as technological mechanisms in order to manage the associated requirements and exploit the opportunities of digital innovation.
	(2) Boundary resources represent a crucial element for strategic frameworks of digital innovation.	Digital(izing) business ecosystems force firms to dynamically interact and exchange knowledge resources as well as capabilities with external partners in order to cope with the requirements of and exploit opportunities stemming from digital innovation.

II.2 Implications for Practice

In addition to the theoretical contributions, the findings of this thesis and the four studies included herein have four important implications for digital innovation managers in incumbent firm contexts.

The first implication refers to the unique nature of knowledge integration and its interaction with digital innovation. As knowledge integration processes and outcomes become permeated by digital technologies, their nature becomes increasingly more complex and dynamic. Consequently, managers wanting to create value from their digital innovation initiatives have to develop a new mindfulness toward traditional and new knowledge requirements (Kohli and Melville 2019; Yoo et al. 2012). To this end, managers need to be aware of the various determinants and dimensions of knowledge integration when they try to exploit heterogeneous and distributed knowledge resources for achieving digital innovation outcomes.

Second, particularly in incumbent firm contexts, where partly conflicting requirements between digital innovation and traditional businesses emerge (Henfridsson et al. 2014), managers need to assess the interaction of knowledge integration and internal (e.g., organizational capabilities) as well as external (e.g., the presence of complementors) conditions (Kohli and Melville 2019) to improve their decision making in relation to developing new digital products or the overall digital transformation of their organizations. Apart from this, the convergence of traditional and new knowledge domains (e.g., automotive business and digital innovation) can also serve as a distinctive source for developing innovations and sustainable competitive advantages (Coff et al. 2006). To achieve both, organizations need to diversify their knowledge base and related capabilities by increasingly tapping into heterogeneous and distributed knowledge domains related to digital innovation (El Sawy and Pereira 2013; Yoo et al. 2010). Here, managers need to employ new procedural mechanisms in order to be capable of accurately assessing and contextualizing the new knowledge within the organizational environment (Kohli and Melville 2019). Furthermore, firms require more organizational options (e.g., flexible structures, connecting interfaces and processes) that allow digital innovation managers to explore and exploit digital opportunities inside as well as outside organizational boundaries (Yoo et al. 2010; Yoo et al. 2012). Here, particularly new technological mechanisms, such as boundary resources, should be utilized by managers to scale the required knowledge integration across the firm's boundaries in digital(izing) business ecosystems. Accordingly, managers should try to create and experiment with flexible or hybrid organizing while employing rather more than fewer options to learn and profit from the increasing diverse and heterogeneous knowledge bases required for digital innovation. Thus, understanding and employing appropriate procedural and technological mechanisms, such as boundary resources (Ghazawneh and Henfridsson 2013), become strategically important and improve the likelihood of success for current and future digital innovation efforts.

Third, as firms become embedded in digital(izing) business ecosystems, they are increasingly forced to co-create and co-capture value with heterogeneous and distributed actors. To cope with the increasing amount and complexity of required interactions and exchange of knowledge resources as well as digital capabilities, managers might think about utilizing boundary resources, such as APIs. However, to exploit boundary resources beneficially, managers need to assess the firm's own situation as well as its potential development with regard to openness and consider the strategic moves of competitors. This is particularly important as the utilization of boundary resources does not come with performance implications per se. When the goal is to financially profit from APIs, the right conditions need to be in place. Here, particularly firms with a high degree of market power can realize positive returns. This, however, is primarily driven by leveraging internal knowledge. Therefore, it is crucial that managers of incumbent firms take their market position and bargaining power into account when they assess whether the profits from deploying boundary resources have the potential to compensate for the costs. Furthermore, firms in digital(izing) business environments need to recognize that they are embedded in an ecosystem of increasingly heterogeneous and diverse actors with different requirements and demands. Therefore, managers need to focus on optimizing the quality of co-creation on their part and be extra-sensitive to hubris and false assumptions. Nevertheless, managers should not consider boundary resources as a substitute for their own R&D efforts but as a means to garner valuable complements and profits from knowledge integration (Yoo et al. 2010; Yoo et al. 2012). Here, especially digital ventures should be viewed as potential complementors rather than threats.

Finally, with increasingly turbulent and competitive environments driven by digital innovation (El Sawy et al. 2010), companies must quickly build and realize digital capabilities to respond to changing market conditions. However, the infrastructural and knowledge-based requirements in some technological areas (e.g., AI) can be very high, particularly for firms from non-digital contexts (Hanelt et al. 2020). To stay competitive and be able to swiftly leverage technological advancements in the context of digital innovation, companies can decide to obtain digital capabilities from external providers via boundary resources (Rai et al. 2019; Yoo et al. 2010). As in the case of internal deployments, managers need to assess internal as well as external conditions and find a clearly defined purpose (e.g., process improvement or product enhancement) in order to make the utilization of external boundary resources beneficial. Nevertheless, implementing external capabilities could in the long run lead to potentially adverse consequences related to value creation and capture mechanisms. Therefore, even though using external boundary resources seems to be a convenient shortcut for implementing and leveraging readily available digital capabilities, it embodies a potentially dangerous dependency on the respective providers in the long term. However, in constantly evolving and increasingly digital(izing) business ecosystems, managers must quickly leverage new partnerships and digital technologies. Therefore, using and exchanging boundary resources might be the new norm, which is why practitioners have to think about new governance mechanisms to mitigate the risk of increasing dependency on their capability providers.

Table C-10 provides an overview of the key implications for incumbent firm managers that are engaged in digital innovation activities.

Table C-10. Implications for Practice.

Implication	Explanation
Consider various determinants and dimensions of knowledge integration when trying to realize outcomes from digital innovation.	Digital technologies increasingly permeate the processes and outcomes of knowledge integration and thus make them more complex and dynamic. Accordingly, these changes need to be taken into account when trying to manage knowledge integration for the purpose of digital innovation.
Employ appropriate procedural and technological mechanisms to effectively manage knowledge integration in the context of digital innovation.	Managing knowledge integration in the context of digital innovation requires the employment of new procedural and technological mechanisms in order to master the increasing requirements of and opportunities in the context of digital innovation.
Leverage boundary resources for scaling knowledge integration in digital(izing) business ecosystems based on internal as well as external conditions.	Digital Innovation increasingly requires leveraging knowledge from inside as well as outside the firm. By enabling the dynamic integration of heterogeneous and distributed knowledge resources, boundary resources can help firms to cope, under specific internal as well external conditions, with the growing scope and scale of knowledge that needs to be integrated for digital innovation purposes.
Build and realize digital capabilities quickly but with a clearly defined purpose and the right conditions in place.	Environmental turbulence is increasing in digital(izing) business ecosystems and thus requires firms to quickly build and realize digital capabilities in order to respond to changing market dynamics. Accordingly, boundary resources can be utilized as a ready-to-use infrastructure in order to rapidly access and leverage external capabilities for digital innovation purposes.

III. Limitations and Future Research

The findings of this cumulative thesis as well as the implications for research and practice come with different limitations and offer potential for future research. Thus, the next chapter delineates these limitations (III.1) and presents future research opportunities (III.2) for the specific research streams of knowledge integration as well as boundary resources and, on a broader level, for the context of digital innovation.

III.1 Limitations

Researchers and practitioners should consider the following limitations when interpreting the results of this thesis. These limitations arise, on one hand, from the nature of the chosen research topics and their associated particularities. With regard to this, the central research topic of knowledge integration represents a complex and multifaceted phenomenon, which has been explored by various interdisciplinary research fields (e.g., organization science or strategic management) (Grant 1996b; Nonaka 1994). Accordingly, knowledge integration is associated with varying theoretical lenses and distinctive conceptualizations (Alavi and Leidner 2001). One reason for this stems from the lack of a common understanding and partly contradictory opinions in research as to what the notion of knowledge itself actually means. Despite this, there are also different variations in terminology with respect to knowledge integration (e.g., knowledge combination or configuration) (Grant 1996a; Henderson and Clark 1990; Kogut and Zander 1992). Due to this, the consideration of all associated research streams and their contents is only possible to a limited extent. In contrast, the topic of boundary resources, as the second focused research topic in this thesis, represents an evolving research stream in the IS field. Hence, although a certain amount of insight on this topic already exists, the associated body of knowledge is still developing and growing dynamically, which makes it difficult to take the latest research into account.

On the other hand, aside from the unique nature of the research topics in this thesis, limitations arise based on the chosen research designs and methods that were employed in the four studies. With regard to this, Study 1 conducted a systematic literature review (Webster and Watson 2002) to shed light on the current state of IS research on the topic of knowledge integration. As the study aimed to derive focused implications for the context of digital innovation, the scope of the literature review was limited to the IS discipline. Although this enabled the researcher to derive specific insights into the research field of digital innovation, an interdisciplinary review might have yielded additional insights, particularly in regard to complementing the developed multi-dimensional framework (Crossan and Apaydin 2010). Furthermore, as there are multiple varying terminologies associated with the concept of knowledge integration (e.g., knowledge reconfiguration) (Henderson and Clark 1990), the scope was limited to the most common one and thus potentially led to the exclusion of related studies.

Furthermore, there are some caveats regarding Studies 2 and 3, which employed panel data regressions on large-scale quantitative datasets, worth mentioning. First, the data samples were restricted to publicly listed companies in the U.S. market based on the S&P 500 stock index. Although the S&P 500 stock index represents a widespread set of companies across various industries in a renowned market, the generalizability of the findings is limited. In addition, boundary resources deployment could be influenced by the fact that the most valuable and impactful tech companies in the world (e.g., Google or Amazon) originate from and are headquartered in the U.S. Therefore, future research in other international markets could help to validate and expand the empirical findings. Moreover, the study focused on APIs as boundary resources and considered only a certain number of companies (S&P 500). Apart from the focus on specific boundary resources, the analysis was reduced to two major antecedents – one for the internal (i.e., knowledge capabilities) and the other for the external context of the firm (i.e., the presence of digital ventures). Each antecedent was represented by a certain proxy (e.g., AI-related patents). Hence, the findings could be extended, for instance, by a human capital approach focusing specifically on the expertise of managers and board members and ask the question as to whether this corporate expertise also forms an antecedent for using boundary resources.

Lastly, Study 4 employed a grounded theory approach (Glaser and Strauss 1967) and focused on the automotive industry as it provides an interesting research setting for studying the impact of digital innovation on incumbent firms. However, the developed insights cannot be applied uniformly to other types of organizations or industries without considering the possibility of different circumstances. Nevertheless, there are general knowledge-related findings that can be utilized in similar organizational environments. Moreover, the results were derived from a somewhat limited number of 30 expert interviews. Therefore, theoretical saturation, where new data slices were not adding substantially to the emerged theory, could only be reached to a certain degree. With regard to this, additional data collection might have helped to gain more detailed insights into the developed concepts and components. Nevertheless, all of the findings were identified multiple times, which supports their theoretical and practical validity.

III.2 Future Research Opportunities

The findings of this thesis as well as the aforementioned limitations offer ample opportunities for further research in the area of knowledge integration and boundary resources in relation to the context of digital innovation.

First, developing aspects of digital innovation, such as digital networks (Zhang et al. 2011), boundary resources (Ghazawneh and Henfridsson 2013), and digitally enabled teams (Robert et al. 2008), are to some extent represented in the current state of the research on knowledge integration and deliver important insights to managers for coping with current digitalization challenges related to internal and external knowledge management. However, due to the distributed nature of digital innovation, there is currently a lack of insights into strategies for and approaches to the development of the required knowledge management capabilities for coping with the increasingly heterogeneous and distributed knowledge resources needed for digital innovation (Kohli and Melville 2019; Yoo et al. 2012). Moreover, despite the existing findings on knowledge integration, the current literature in this area has not yet dealt in depth with the particularities of digital knowledge (as opposed to other types of knowledge), which is subject to knowledge integration in contexts of digital innovation. Recent works show that these particularities influence knowledge integration and its processes (Hanelt et al. 2020). In addition, the loose coupling between different elements in digital innovation, afforded by standardized interfaces, points to the need to distinguish the particular degree of knowledge integration. Recent case study research proposes that in digital innovation, diverse knowledge might be utilized without deep integration and that balancing different types of knowledge integration might be a key managerial challenge in the digital age. In general, it can be claimed based on the findings of this thesis that, until today, the body of knowledge with a specific focus on the integration of heterogeneous knowledge resources still requires fundamental investigation.

Second, another direction for future research could be the examination of knowledge integration with respect to its success in related digital innovation activities based on quantitative methods. Subsequently, it would be interesting to validate and further examine best practices and success factors on the basis of additional explorative, in-depth case studies within the incumbent firm context that have been impacted by digital innovation. Furthermore, as the process of the digital transformation of incumbent firms is still at an early stage, more empirical research on the ongoing organizational development and the convergence between the knowledge bases of digital innovation and traditional automotive business is required. Consequently, research needs to draw its attention toward the examination of integrating heterogeneous and distributed knowledge resources in the context of digital innovation in order to shed light into this, albeit elusive, highly significant topic.

Third, with regard to the research on boundary resources, multiple avenues for future research could be identified. Although the findings in this thesis focused on the strategic decision to use and the value of using boundary resources for leveraging internal as well as external knowledge, other aspects need to be considered when evaluating boundary resources. For instance, while the results indicate that boundary resources are being utilized and capitalized upon under specific conditions, the deeper dimensions and chains of the effects of certain constructs remain unclear. Accordingly, as the related insights were based on a large-scale empirical analysis, future in-depth case studies should investigate in more detail when and why certain knowledge-based outcomes from the utilization of boundary resources arise. In this context, future studies could, on one hand, focus on specific factors inside the firm, such as path dependency (Cohen and Levinthal 1990; Lane et al. 2006) or internal conflicts (Lucas and Goh 2009; Svahn et al. 2017) and, on the other hand, examine how a firm's external contexts (e.g., industry, digital complementors) influence the utilization of boundary resources and their respective outcomes.

Finally, future research should especially aim at providing more insights into the currently under-explored user side perspective of boundary resources (Benlian et al. 2015; Parker et al. 2017) since firms are increasingly dependent on value co-creation and co-capture with external actors (El Sawy and Pereira 2013), which also represent potential users of boundary resources in digital(izing) business ecosystems. Therefore, more research is necessary to understand boundary resources more comprehensively. An avenue for future research could be to repeat Study 3 with a larger scale of companies for the purpose of developing more generalized findings. Moreover, the analysis of additional boundary resources, such as software development kits (SDKs) might promise fruitful insights, which could complement the understanding on different deployment strategies related to other types of boundary resources. With regard to this, future studies could also dive in depth into and focus on the empirical investigation of the driving forces behind and outcomes of differing strategies, such as deploying only a specific type of boundary resource. Furthermore, the two studies related to boundary resources (Studies 2 and 3) do not examine alternative theoretical interpretations. For instance, the results in Study 3 related to using AI boundary resources for product enhancement provide interesting insights for future research, drawing on transaction costs and resource dependence perspectives. Accordingly, the increasing integration of AI capabilities into products might transform the associated product markets to platform-based markets in the long term. Thus, these markets can be influenced by new rules such as those of the winner-takes-all category (Zhu and Iansiti 2012). However, leaving the AI capabilities in a product to a boundary resource provider might lead to losing the platform-market competition game in the long run. In-depth case studies could try to uncover whether firms truly anticipate these threats.

IV. Conclusion

This cumulative dissertation has intended to shed light on the unique nature of knowledge integration and how it can be managed by incumbent firms in the context of digital innovation. To achieve this, four research questions were derived and subsequently answered in four studies described in Chapters I, II, and III of Part B.

The first chapter of Part B provided a systematic classification of knowledge integration and evaluated its interaction with digital innovation, thus answering RQ1 with regard to the current state of IS research. It was revealed that knowledge integration is being shaped by various determinants and represents a multi-dimensional concept – a concept whose processes and results are increasingly permeated by digital technologies in the digital era. This technological permeation, however, makes the integration of knowledge more perpetual, dynamic, and complex. Consequently, not only are the associated requirements changing but also the way in which knowledge needs to be integrated. As a result, new technological mechanisms such as boundary resources are required by firms in order to cope with the increasingly demanding task of integrating knowledge in the context of digital innovation.

Building on this, the second chapter of Part B offered an in-depth view on boundary resources as a technological mechanism for knowledge integration. It was found that boundary resources can be used by firms, under certain internal and external conditions, as a technological infrastructure for scaling knowledge integration in digital(izing) business ecosystems. Accordingly, on one hand, boundary resources can be utilized to leverage a firm's existing knowledge by exposing it to external actors for reuse and innovation. On the other hand, boundary resources can also be utilized by firms to access and leverage external knowledge from outside players in order to create value within their organizations. Thus, both ways indicate a fundamental shift in organizational knowledge management from developing and controlling the firm's knowledge base to enabling others to innovate upon it and orchestrating heterogeneous knowledge capabilities.

Finally, the third chapter of Part B provided insights into how to manage the challenges associated with knowledge integration in incumbent firm contexts impacted by digital innovation. It was found that, in addition to the technological means, established companies need new procedural mechanisms within their organizations to manage their transforming and expanding knowledge base in a value-creating way. These procedural mechanisms, however, are affected by tensions between established business logics and the new ones required for digital innovation. This, in turn, forces incumbent firms to balance knowledge integration between existing structures and new, digital ones. Conclusively, to withstand the impact and exploit the opportunities of digital innovation, established companies need to implement, on one hand, new procedural mechanisms that support the *dynamic balancing* of the increasing amount and diversity of knowledge that needs to be integrated and, on the other hand, novel technological mechanisms such as boundary resources that enable the *dynamic integration* of internal and external knowledge resources in digital(izing) business ecosystems.

References

Abrahamson, E. 1991. "Managerial Fads and Fashions: The Diffusion and Rejection of Innovations," *Academy of Management Review* (16:3), pp. 586-612.

Adomavicius, Bockstedt, Gupta, and Kauffman, R. J. 2008. "Making Sense of Technology Trends in the Information Technology Landscape: A Design Science Approach," *Management Information Systems Quarterly* (32:4), pp. 779-809.

Agarwal, R., Gao, G., DesRoches, C., and Jha, A. K. 2010. "Research Commentary —The Digital Transformation of Healthcare: Current Status and the Road Ahead," *Information Systems Research* (21:4), pp. 796-809.

Alavi, M., and Leidner, D. E. 2001. "Review: Knowledge Management and Knowledge Management Systems: Conceptual Foundations and Research Issues," *Management Information Systems Quarterly* (25:1), pp. 107-136.

Aleksander, I. 2017. "Partners of Humans: A Realistic Assessment of the Role of Robots in the Foreseeable Future," *Journal of Information Technology* (32:1), pp. 1-9.

Amazon 2018. *Amazon Alexa Official Site: What Is Alexa?* https://developer.amazon.com/en-US/alexa. Accessed 25 September 2020.

Andersson, M., Lindgren, R., and Henfridsson, O. 2008. "Architectural Knowledge in Inter-organizational IT Innovation," *The Journal of Strategic Information Systems* (17:1), pp. 19-38.

Apple 2020. *Cameras and Media Capture | Apple Developer Documentation.* https://developer.apple.com/documentation/avfoundation/cameras_and_media_capture. Accessed 3 October 2020.

Armstrong, C. P., and Sambamurthy, V. 1999. "Information Technology Assimilation in Firms: The Influence of Senior Leadership and IT Infrastructures," *Information Systems Research* (10:4), pp. 304-327.

Baldwin, C. Y., and Clark, K. B. 1997. "Managing in an Age of Modularity," *Harvard Business Review* (75:5), pp. 84-93.

Ballinger, G. A. 2004. "Using Generalized Estimating Equations for Longitudinal Data Analysis," *Organizational Research Methods* (7:2), pp. 127-150.

Balsmeier, B., Fleming, L., and Manso, G. 2017. "Independent Boards and Innovation," *Journal of Financial Economics* (123:3), pp. 536-557.

Banker, R. D., and Kauffman, R. 2004. "50th Anniversary Article: The Evolution of Research on Information Systems: A Fiftieth-Year Survey of the Literature in Management Science," *Management Science* (50:3), pp. 281-298.

Bardhan, I., Chen, H., and Karahanna, E. 2020. "Connecting Systems, Data, and People: A Multidisciplinary Research Roadmap for Chronid Disease Management," *Management Information Systems Quarterly* (44), pp. 185-200.

Barney, J. B. 1991. "Firm Resources and Sustained Competitive Advantage," *Journal of Management* (17:1), pp. 99-120.

Baskerville, R., and Myers 2009. "Fashion Waves in Information Systems Research and Practice," *Management Information Systems Quarterly* (33:4), pp. 647-662.

Baskerville, R., and Pries-Heje, J. 1998. "Information Technology Diffusion Building Positive Barriers," *European Journal of Information Systems* (7:1), pp. 17-28.

Benkler, Y. 2006. *The Wealth of Networks: How Social Production Transforms Markets and Freedom*, Yale University Press.

Benlian, A., Hilkert, D., and Hess, T. 2015. "How open is this Platform? The Meaning and Measurement of Platform Openness from the Complementers' Perspective," *Journal of Information Technology* (30:3), pp. 209-228.

Besson, P., and Rowe, F. 2012. "Strategizing Information Systems-enabled Organizational Transformation: A Transdisciplinary Review and New Directions," *The Journal of Strategic Information Systems* (21:2), pp. 103-124.

Best Buy 2020. *Best Buy Developer Portal*. https://developer.bestbuy.com/. Accessed 3 October 2020.

Bharadwaj, A. S. 2000. "A Resource-Based Perspective on Information Technology Capability and Firm Performance: An Empirical Investigation," *Management Information Systems Quarterly* (24:1), pp. 169-196.

Bharadwaj, A. S., El Sawy, O. A., Pavlou, P. A., and Venkatraman, N. 2013. "Digital Business Strategy: Toward a Next Generation of Insights," *Management Information Systems Quarterly* (37:2), pp. 471-482.

Bhattacherjee, A. 2012. *Social Science Research: Principles, Methods, and Practices*, University of South Florida.

Bittner, E. A. C., and Leimeister, J. M. 2014. "Creating Shared Understanding in Heterogeneous Work Groups: Why It Matters and How to Achieve It," *Journal of Management Information Systems* (31:1), pp. 111-144.

Boland, R. J., Lyytinen, K., and Yoo, Y. 2007. "Wakes of Innovation in Project Networks: The Case of Digital 3-D Representations in Architecture, Engineering, and Construction," *Organization Science* (18:4), pp. 631-647.

Boudreau, K. J. 2010. "Open Platform Strategies and Innovation: Granting Access vs. Devolving Control," *Management Science* (56:10), pp. 1849-1872.

Boudreau, K. J. 2012. "Let a Thousand Flowers Bloom? An Early Look at Large Numbers of Software App Developers and Patterns of Innovation," *Organization Science* (23:5), pp. 1409-1427.

Boudreau, K. J., and Jeppesen, L. B. 2015. "Unpaid Crowd Complementors: The Platform Network Effect Mirage," *Strategic Management Journal* (36:12), pp. 1761-1777.

Brandt, T. 2013. "Information Systems in Automobiles – Past, Present, and Future Uses," in *Proceedings of the 19th Americas Conference on Information Systems*.

Brynjolfsson, E., and McAfee, A. 2011. *Race Against the Machine: How the Digital Revolution is Accelerating Innovation, Driving Productivity, and Irreversibly Transforming Employment and the Economy*, Digital Frontier Press.

Brynjolfsson, E., and McAfee, A. 2014. *The Second Machine Age: Work, Progress, and Prosperity in a Time of Brilliant Technologies*, Langara College.

Carlo, J. L., Lyytinen, K., and Rose, G. 2012. "A Knowledge-based Model of Radical Innovation in Small Software Firms," *Management Information Systems Quarterly* (36:3), pp. 865-895.

Chatterjee, D., Grewal, R., and Sambamurthy, V. 2002. "Shaping up for E-Commerce: Institutional Enablers of the Organizational Assimilation of Web Technologies," *Management Information Systems Quarterly* (26:2), pp. 65-89.

Chen, H., Chiang, R. H., and Storey 2012. "Business Intelligence and Analytics: From Big Data to Big Impact," *Management Information Systems Quarterly* (36:4), pp. 1165-1188.

Cho, K., Bae, C. H., Chu, Y., and Suh, M. 2006. "Overview of Telematics: A System Architecture Approach," *International Journal of Automotive Technology* (7:4), pp. 509-517.

Christensen, C. M. 1997. *The Innovator's Dilemma: When New Technologies Cause Great Firms to Fail*, Harvard Business School Press.

Cloodt, M., Hagedoorn, J., and van Kranenburg, H. 2006. "Mergers and Acquisitions: Their Effect on the Innovative Performance of Companies in High-Tech Industries," *Research Policy* (35:5), pp. 642-654.

Coff, R. W., Coff, D. C., and Eastvold, R. 2006. "The Knowledge-leveraging Paradox How to Achieve Scale without Making Knowledge Imitable," *Academy of Management Review* (31:2), pp. 452-465.

Cohen, W. M., and Levinthal, D. A. 1990. "Absorptive Capacity A New Perspective on Learning and Innovation," *Administrative Science Quarterly* (35:1), pp. 128-152.

Coombs, C., Hislop, D., Taneva, S. K., and Barnard, S. 2020. "The Strategic Impacts of Intelligent Automation for Knowledge and Service Work: An Interdisciplinary Review," *The Journal of Strategic Information Systems*, pp. 1-30.

Cooper, V., and Molla, A. 2017. "Information Systems Absorptive Capacity for Environmentally Driven IS-enabled Transformation," *Information Systems Journal* (27:4), pp. 379-425.

Crossan, M. M., and Apaydin, M. 2010. "A Multi-Dimensional Framework of Organizational Innovation: A Systematic Review of the Literature," *Journal of Management Studies* (47:6), pp. 1154-1191.

Cui, J. 2007. "QIC Program and Model Selection in GEE Analyses," *The Stata Journal* (7:2), pp. 209-220.

Custódio, C., Ferreira, M. A., and Matos, P. 2019. "Do General Managerial Skills Spur Innovation?" *Management Science* (65:2), pp. 459-476.

Daniel, S., Midha, V., Bhattacherjee, A., and Singh, S. P. 2018. "Sourcing Knowledge in Open Source Software Projects: The Impacts of Internal and External Social Capital on Project Success," *The Journal of Strategic Information Systems* (27:3), pp. 237-256.

Daniel, S., and Stewart, K. 2016. "Open Source Project Success: Resource Access, Flow, and Integration," *The Journal of Strategic Information Systems* (25:3), pp. 159-176.

Datta, P., and Roumani, Y. 2015. "Knowledge-acquisitions and Post-acquisition Innovation Performance: A Comparative Hazards Model," *European Journal of Information Systems* (24:2), pp. 202-226.

Davenport, T. H., Barth, P., and Bean, R. 2012. “How Big Data is Different,” *MIT sloan management review* (54:1), pp. 43-46.

Dehning, Richardson, and Zmud, R. 2003. “The Value Relevance of Announcements of Transformational Information Technology Investments,” *Management Information Systems Quarterly* (27:4), pp. 637-656.

Dhar, V., and Sundararajan, A. 2006. “Does it Matter in Business Education? Interviews with Business School Deans.,” *Center For Digital Economy Research* (Working Paper No. CeDER-06-08).

Dibbern, Winkler, and Heinzl 2008. “Explaining Variations in Client Extra Costs between Software Projects Offshored to India,” *Management Information Systems Quarterly* (32:2), pp. 333-366.

Dong, J. Q., and Yang, C.-H. 2019. “Information Technology and Innovation Outcomes: Is Knowledge Recombination the Missing Link?” *European Journal of Information Systems* (28:6), pp. 612-626.

Dyer, J. H., and Singh, H. 1998. “The Relational View: Cooperative Strategy and Sources of Interorganizational Competitive Advantage,” *Academy of Management Review* (23:4), pp. 660-679.

Eaton, B., Elaluf-Calderwood, S., Sørensen, C., and Yu, Y. 2015. “Distributed Tuning of Boundary Resources: The case of Apple's iOS service system,” *Management Information Systems Quarterly* (39:1), pp. 217-243.

eBay 2020. *eBay Developers Program*. https://developer.ebay.com/. Accessed 2 October 2020.

Eisenhardt, K. M. 1989. “Building Theories from Case Study Research,” *Academy of Management Review* (14:4), pp. 532-550.

Eisenmann, T., Parker, G., and van Alstyne, M. W. 2006. “Strategies for Two-sided Markets,” *Harvard Business Review* (84:10), p. 92.

Eisenmann, T. R., Parker, G. G., and van Alstyne, M. W. 2008. “Opening Platforms: How, When and Why?” Harvard Business School.

Ejodame, K., and Oshri, I. 2018. “Understanding Knowledge Re-integration in Backsourcing,” *Journal of Information Technology* (33:2), pp. 136-150.

El Sawy, O. A., Malhotra, A., Park, Y., and Pavlou, P. A. 2010. “Research Commentary — Seeking the Configurations of Digital Ecodynamics: It Takes Three to Tango,” *Information Systems Research* (21:4), pp. 835-848.

El Sawy, O. A., and Pereira, F. 2013. *Business Modelling in the Dynamic Digital Space*, Heidelberg: Springer.

El-Najdawi, M. K., and Stylianou, A. C. 1993. “Expert Support Systems: Integrating AI Technologies,” *Communications of the ACM* (36:12), 55-103.

Evans, P. C., and Basole, R. C. 2016. “Revealing the API Ecosystem and Enterprise Strategy via Visual Analytics,” *Communications of the ACM* (59:2), pp. 26-28.

FedEx 2020. *FedEx Developer Resource Center Home*. https://www.fedex.com/en-us/developer.html. Accessed 3 October 2020.

Firk, S., Schmidt, T., and Wolff, M. 2019. "CFO Emphasis on Value-based Management: Performance Implications and the Challenge of CFO Succession," *Management Accounting Research* (44), pp. 26-43.

Foerderer, J., Kude, T., Schuetz, S. W., and Heinzl, A. 2019. "Knowledge Boundaries in Enterprise Software Platform Development: Antecedents and Consequences for Platform Governance," *Information Systems Journal* (29:1), pp. 119-144.

Forbes 2018. *The Rise Of Artificial Intelligence As A Service In The Public Cloud.* https://www.forbes.com/sites/janakirammsv/2018/02/22/the-rise-of-artificial-intelligence-as-a-service-in-the-public-cloud/#1007de54198e. Accessed 26 April 2020.

Forbes 2019. *The World's Largest Public Companies.* https://www.forbes.com/global2000/list/.

Ford 2020. *Ford Connected Vehicle API.* https://developer.ford.com/fordconnect. Accessed 3 October 2020.

Gawer, A. 2014. "Bridging Differing Perspectives on Technological Platforms: Toward an Integrative Framework," *Research Policy* (43:7), pp. 1239-1249.

Gawer, A., and Cusumano, M. A. 2014. "Industry Platforms and Ecosystem Innovation," *Journal of Product Innovation Management* (31:3), pp. 417-433.

Gawer, A., and Phillips, N. 2013. "Institutional Work as Logics Shift: The Case of Intel's Transformation to Platform Leader," *Organization Studies* (34:8), pp. 1035-1071.

Ghasemaghaei, M., Ebrahimi, S., and Hassanein, K. 2018. "Data Analytics Competency for Improving Firm Decision Making Performance," *The Journal of Strategic Information Systems* (27:1), pp. 101-113.

Ghazawneh, A., and Henfridsson, O. 2013. "Balancing Platform Control and External Contribution in Third-party Development: The Boundary Resources Model," *Information Systems Journal* (23:2), pp. 173-192.

Ghezzi, A., Gastaldi, L., Lettieri, E., Martini, A., and Corso, M. 2016. "A Role for Startups in Unleashing the Disruptive Power of Social Media," *International Journal of Information Management* (36:6), pp. 1152-1159.

Gillon, K., Aral, S., Lin, C.-Y., Mithas, S., and Zozulia, M. 2014. "Business Analytics: Radical Shift or Incremental Change?" *Communications of the Association for Information Systems* (34).

Glaser, B. G. 1978. *Theoretical Sensitivity: Advances in the Methodology of Grounded Theory*, Sociology Press.

Glaser, B. G. 1992. *Emergence vs Forcing: Basics of Grounded Theory Analysis*, Sociology Press.

Glaser, B. G., and Strauss, A. L. 1967. *The Discovery of Grounded Theory: Strategies for Qualitative Research*, Aldine Transaction.

Goh, J., Pan, S. L., and Zuo, M. 2013. "Developing the Agile IS Development Practices in Large-Scale IT Projects: The Trust-Mediated Organizational Controls and IT Project Team Capabilities Perspectives," *Journal of the Association for Information Systems* (14:12), pp. 722-756.

Gold, A. H., Malhotra, A., and Segars, A. H. 2001. "Knowledge Management An Organizational Capabilities Perspective," *Journal of Management Information Systems* (18:1), pp. 185-214.

Google 2018. *Cloud AutoML - Custom Machine Learning Models*. https://cloud.google.com/automl. Accessed 4 September 2020.

Gopal, A., and Gosain, S. 2010. "Research Note —The Role of Organizational Controls and Boundary Spanning in Software Development Outsourcing: Implications for Project Performance," *Information Systems Research* (21:4), pp. 960-982.

Graham, S. J., Marco, A. C., and Miller, R. 2015. "The USPTO Patent Examination Research Dataset: A Window on the Process of Patent Examination," *SSRN Electronic Journal*.

Grant, R. M. 1996a. "Prospering in Dynamically-Competitive Environments: Organizational Capability as Knowledge Integration," *Organization Science* (7:4), pp. 375-387.

Grant, R. M. 1996b. "Toward a Knowledge-based Theory of the Firm," *Strategic Management Journal* (17), pp. 109-122.

Grant, R. M. 2013. *Contemporary Strategy Analysis*, John Wiley & Sons.

Gray, P. H. 2000. "The effects of knowledge management systems on emergent teams: towards a research model," *The Journal of Strategic Information Systems* (9:2-3), pp. 175-191.

Gregor 2006. "The Nature of Theory in Information Systems," *Management Information Systems Quarterly* (30:3), pp. 611-642.

Gregory, R. W., Keil, M., Muntermann, J., and Mähring, M. 2015. "Paradoxes and the Nature of Ambidexterity in IT Transformation Programs," *Information Systems Research* (26:1), pp. 57-80.

Grimpe, C., and Hussinger, K. 2014. "Resource Complementarity and Value Capture in Firm Acquisitions: The Role of Intellectual Property Rights," *Strategic Management Journal* (35:12), pp. 1762-1780.

Grover, V., Chiang, R. H., Liang, T.-P., and Zhang, D. 2018. "Creating Strategic Business Value from Big Data Analytics: A Research Framework," *Journal of Management Information Systems* (35:2), pp. 388-423.

Günther, W. A., Rezazade Mehrizi, M. H., Huysman, M., and Feldberg, F. 2017. "Debating Big Data: A Literature Review on Realizing Value from Big Data," *The Journal of Strategic Information Systems* (26:3), pp. 191-209.

Gupta, A., and Misangyi, V. F. 2018. "Follow the Leader (or not): The Influence of Peer Ceos' Characteristics on Interorganizational Imitation," *Strategic Management Journal* (39:5), pp. 1437-1472.

Hall, B. H., Jaffe, A. B., and Trajtenberg, M. 2001. "The NBER Patent Citation Data File: Lessons, Insights and Methodological Tools," *National Bureau of Economic Research*.

Hanelt, A., Firk, S., Hildebrandt, B., and Kolbe, L. M. 2020. "Digital M&A, Digital Innovation, and Firm Performance: an Empirical Investigation," *European Journal of Information Systems*, pp. 3-26.

Hanelt, A., Piccinini, E., Gregory, R. W., Hildebrandt, B., and Kolbe, L. M. 2015. "Digital Transformation of Primarily Physical Industries - Exploring the Impact of Digital Trends on

Business Models of Automobile Manufacturers," in *Proceedings of the 12th International Conference on Wirtschaftsinformatik*.

Hanseth, O., and Lyytinen, K. 2010. "Design Theory for Dynamic Complexity in Information Infrastructures: The Case of Building Internet," *Journal of Information Technology* (25:1), pp. 1-19.

Hausman, J. A. 1978. "Specification Tests in Econometrics," *Econometrica* (46:6), pp. 1251-1271.

Heckman, J. 1979. "Sample Selection Bias as a Specification Error," *Econometrica* (47:1), pp. 153-161.

Henderson, R. M., and Clark, K. B. 1990. "Architectural Innovation: The Reconfiguration of Existing Product Technologies and the Failure of Established Firms," *Administrative Science Quarterly* (35:1), pp. 9-30.

Henfridsson, O., and Lindgren, R. 2005. "Multi-contextuality in Ubiquitous Computing Investigating the Car Case Through Action Research," *Information and Organization* (15:2), pp. 95-124.

Henfridsson, O., and Lindgren, R. 2010. "User Involvement in Developing Mobile and Temporarily Interconnected Systems," *Information Systems Journal* (20:2), pp. 119-135.

Henfridsson, O., Mathiassen, L., and Svahn, F. 2014. "Managing Technological Change in the Digital Age: The Role of Architectural Frames," *Journal of Information Technology* (29:1), pp. 27-43.

Henfridsson, O., and Yoo, Y. 2014. "The Liminality of Trajectory Shifts in Institutional Entrepreneurship," *Organization Science* (25:3), pp. 932-950.

Henfridsson, O., Yoo, Y., and Svahn, F. 2009. "Path Creation in Digital Innovation: A Multi-Layered Dialectics Perspective," *Sprouts: Working Papers on Information Systems* (9:20), pp. 1-25.

Hevner, A., March, Park, and Ram 2004. "Design Science in Information Systems Research," *Management Information Systems Quarterly* (28:1), pp. 75-105.

Hildebrandt, B., Hanelt, A., Firk, S., and Kolbe, L. M. 2015. "Entering the Digital Era - The Impact of Digital Technology-related M&As on Business Model Innovations of Automobile OEMs," in *Proceedings of the 36th International Conference on Information Systems*.

Hill, C. W. L., and Rothaermel, F. T. 2003. "The Performance of Incumbent firms in the Face of Radical Technological Innovation," *Academy of Management Review* (28:2), pp. 257-274.

Howard-Grenville, J. A., and Carlile, P. R. 2006. "The Incompatibility of Knowledge Regimes: Consequences of the Material World for Cross-Domain Work," *European Journal of Information Systems* (15:5), pp. 473-485.

Huang, J., Henfridsson, O., Liu, M. J., and Newell, S. 2017. "Growing on Steroids: Rapidly Scaling the User Base of Digital Ventures Through Digital Innovation," *Management Information Systems Quarterly* (41:1), pp. 301-314.

Huang, J. C., Newell, S., and Pan, S. L. 2001. "The Process of Global Knowledge Integration: A Case Study of a Multinational Investment Bank's Y2K," *European Journal of Information Systems* (10:3), pp. 161-174.

Huber, G. P. 1991. "Organizational Learning: The Contributing Processes and the Literatures," *Organization Science* (2:1), pp. 88-115.

Hylving, L., and Schultze, U. 2013. "Evolving the Modular Layered Architecture in Digital Innovation: The Case of the Car's Instrument Cluster," in *Proceedings of the 34th International Conference on Information Systems*.

Hylving, L., and Selander, L. 2012. "Under the Pressure of Openness: Exploring Digital Innovation in User Interface Design," in *Proceedings of the 20th European Conference on Information Systems*.

IBM 2017. *How Autodesk Sped Up Customer Response Times by 99% with Watson*. https://www.ibm.com/blogs/watson/2017/10/how-autodesk-sped-up-customer-service-times-with-watson/. Accessed 26 April 2020.

Iyer, B., and Subramaniam, M. 2015a. "Are You Using APIs to Gain Competitive Advantage?" *Harvard Business Review Digital Articles*, pp. 2-4.

Iyer, B., and Subramaniam, M. 2015b. "The Strategic Value of APIs," *Harvard Business Review Digital Articles*, pp. 2-4.

Jacobides, M. G., Cennamo, C., and Gawer, A. 2018. "Towards a Theory of Ecosystems," *Strategic Management Journal* (39:8), pp. 2255-2276.

Javadi, E., Gebauer, J., and Mahoney, J. T. 2013. "The Impact of User Interface Design on Idea Integration in Electronic Brainstorming: An Attention-Based View," *Journal of the Association for Information Systems* (14:1), pp. 1-21.

Jayatilaka, B., Schwarz, A., and Hirschheim, R. 2003. "Determinants of ASP Choice: An Integrated Perspective," *European Journal of Information Systems* (12:3), pp. 210-224.

Jernigan, S., Ransbotham, S., and Kiron, D. 2016. "Data Sharing and Analytics Drive Success with IOT," *Sloan Management Review*.

John Deere 2020. *Develop with Deere*. https://developer.deere.com/#!welcome. Accessed 2 October 2020.

Johnson Controls 2021. *GLAS*. https://glas.johnsoncontrols.com/. Accessed 26 February 2021.

Joshi, A., van Peteghem, M., Mithas, S., Bollen, L., and Haes, S. de 2019. "Board IT Competence and Firm Performance," in *Proceedings of the 40th International Conference on Information Systems*.

Joshi, K. D., Chi, L., Datta, A., and Han, S. 2010. "Changing the Competitive Landscape: Continuous Innovation Through IT-Enabled Knowledge Capabilities," *Information Systems Research* (21:3), pp. 472-495.

Juliussen, E. 2003. "The Future of Automotive Telematics," *Business Briefing: Global Automotive Manufacturing & Technology*, Business Briefing: Global Automotive Manufacturing & Technology.

Karhu, K., Gustafsson, R., and Lyytinen, K. 2018. "Exploiting and Defending Open Digital Platforms with Boundary Resources: Android's Five Platform Forks," *Information Systems Research* (29:2), pp. 479-497.

Karimi, J., and Walter, Z. 2015. "The Role of Dynamic Capabilities in Responding to Digital Disruption: A Factor-Based Study of the Newspaper Industry," *Journal of Management Information Systems* (32:1), pp. 39-81.

Kathuria, A., Fontaine, A., and Prietula, M. 2011. "Acquiring IT Competencies through Focused Technology Acquisitions," in *Proceedings of the 32nd International Conference on Information Systems*.

Kearns, G. S., and Sabherwal, R. 2006. "Strategic Alignment Between Business and Information Technology: A Knowledge-Based View of Behaviors, Outcome, and Consequences," *Journal of Management Information Systems* (23:3), pp. 129-162.

King, J. L., and Lyytinen, K. (eds.) 2004. *Automotive Informatics: Information Technology and Enterprise Transformation in the Automobile Industry*, Cambridge, Massachusetts: MIT Press.

Kogut, B., and Zander, U. 1992. "Knowledge of the Firm, Combinative Capabilities, and the Replication of Technology," *Organization Science* (3:3), pp. 383-397.

Koh, S., Gunasekaran, A., and Goodman, T. 2011. "Drivers, Barriers and Critical Success Factors for ERPII Implementation in Supply Chains: A Critical Analysis," *The Journal of Strategic Information Systems* (20:4), pp. 385-402.

Kohli, R., and Melville, N. P. 2019. "Digital Innovation: A Review and Synthesis," *Information Systems Journal* (29:1), pp. 200-223.

Kranz, J. J., Hanelt, A., and Kolbe, L. M. 2016. "Understanding the Influence of Absorptive Capacity and Ambidexterity on the Process of Business Model Change - the Case of On-premise and Cloud-computing Software," *Information Systems Journal* (26:5), pp. 477-517.

Krogh, G. von 2018. "Artificial Intelligence in Organizations: New Opportunities for Phenomenon-Based Theorizing," *Academy of Management Discoveries* (4:4), pp. 404-409.

Lambe, C. J., and Spekman, R. E. 1997. "Alliances, External Technology Acquisition, and Discontinuous Technological Change," *Journal of Product Innovation Management* (14:2), pp. 102-116.

Lane, P. J., Koka, B. R., and Pathak, S. 2006. "The Reification of Absorptive Capacity: A Critical Review and Rejuvenation of the Construct," *Academy of Management Review* (31:4), pp. 833-863.

Langlois, R. N. 2007. "Computers and Semiconductors," in *Technological Innovation and Economic Performance*, B. Steil, D. G. Victor and R. R. Nelson (eds.), Princeton University Press, pp. 265-284.

Lavie, D. 2006a. "Capability Reconfiguration: An Analysis of Incumbent Responses to Technological Change," *Academy of Management Review* (31:1), pp. 153-174.

Lavie, D. 2006b. "The Competitive Advantage of Interconnected Firms: An Extension of the Resource-Based View," *Academy of Management Review* (31:3), pp. 638-658.

Lee, J., and Berente, N. 2012. "Digital Innovation and the Division of Innovative Labor: Digital Controls in the Automotive Industry," *Organization Science* (23:5), pp. 1428-1447.

Lehmann, H., and Gallupe, B. 2005. "Information Systems for Multinational Enterprises - Some Factors at Work in Their Design and Implementation," *Journal of International Management* (11:2), pp. 163-186.

Lempinen, H., and Rajala, R. 2014. "Exploring Multi-Actor Value Creation in IT Service Processes," *Journal of Information Technology* (29:2), pp. 170-185.

Leonard-Barton, D. 1992. "Core Capabilities and Core Rigidities: A Paradox in Managing New Product Development," *Strategic Management Journal* (13:S1), pp. 111-125.

Levy, Y., and Ellis, T. J. 2006. "A Systems Approach to Conduct an Effective Literature Review in Support of Information Systems Research," *Informing Science: The International Journal of an Emerging Transdiscipline* (9), pp. 181-212.

Liang, K.-Y., and Zeger, S. L. 1986. "Longitudinal Data Analysis Using Generalized Linear Models," *Biometrika Trust* (73:1), pp. 13-22.

Lindberg, A., Berente, N., Gaskin, J., and Lyytinen, K. 2016. "Coordinating Interdependencies in Online Communities: A Study of an Open Source Software Project," *Information Systems Research* (27:4), pp. 751-772.

Liu, J., Nandhakumar, J., and Zachariadis, M. 2018. "When Guanxi Meets Structural Holes: Exploring the Guanxi Networks of Chinese Entrepreneurs on Digital Platforms," *The Journal of Strategic Information Systems* (27:4), pp. 311-334.

Loebbecke, C., and Picot, A. 2015. "Reflections on Societal and Business Model Transformation Arising from Digitization and Big Data Analytics: A Research Agenda," *The Journal of Strategic Information Systems* (24:3), pp. 149-157.

Lucas, H. C., and Goh, J. M. 2009. "Disruptive Technology: How Kodak Missed the Digital Photography Revolution," *The Journal of Strategic Information Systems* (18:1), pp. 46-55.

Lucas, J. H. C., Agarwal, R., Clemons, E. K., El Sawy, O. A., and Weber, B. 2013. "Impactful Research on Transformational Information Technology: An Opportunity to Inform New Audiences," *Management Information Systems Quarterly* (37:2), pp. 371-382.

Lyytinen, K., Yoo, Y., and Boland, R. J. 2016. "Digital Product Innovation within Four Classes of Innovation Networks," *Information Systems Journal* (26:1), pp. 47-75.

Macys 2020. *macys.com - App Gallery/Sample apps*. http://developer.macys.com/App_Gallery_Sample_apps. Accessed 3 October 2020.

Magerman, T., van Looy, B., and Song, X. 2006. "Data Production Methods for Harmonized Patent Statistics: Patentee Name Harmonization," *SSRN Electronic Journal*.

Majchrzak, A., Malhotra, A., and John, R. 2005. "Perceived Individual Collaboration Know-How Development Through Information Technology–Enabled Contextualization: Evidence from Distributed Teams," *Information Systems Research* (16:1), pp. 9-27.

Majchrzak, A., Wagner, C., and Yates, D. 2013. "The Impact of Shaping on Knowledge Reuse for Organizational Improvement with Wikis," *Management Information Systems Quarterly* (37:2), pp. 455-469.

Man, A.-P. de, and Duysters, G. 2005. "Collaboration and Innovation: A Review of the Effects of Mergers, Acquisitions and Alliances on Innovation," *Technovation* (25:12), pp. 1377-1387.

Mannucci, P. V., and Yong, K. 2018. "The Differential Impact of Knowledge Depth and Knowledge Breadth on Creativity over Individual Careers," *Academy of Management Journal* (61:5), pp. 1741-1763.

March, J. G. 1991. "Exploration and Exploitation in Organizational Learning," *Organization Science* (2:1), pp. 71-87.

March, S. T., and Smith, G. F. 1995. "Design and Natural Science Research on Information Technology," *Decision Support Systems* (15:4), pp. 251-266.

Marco, A. C., Myers, A. F., Graham, S. J., D'Agostino, P. A., and Apple, K. 2015. "The USPTO Patent Assignment Dataset: Descriptions and Analysis," *SSRN Electronic Journal*.

Markus, M. L. 2017. "Datification, Organizational Strategy, and IS Research: What's the Score?" *The Journal of Strategic Information Systems* (26:3), pp. 233-241.

Martin, P. Y., and Turner, B. A. 1986. "Grounded Theory and Organizational Research," *The Journal of Applied Behavioral Science* (22:2), pp. 141-157.

Medtronic 2015. *IBM Watson Health Sugar.IQ Mobile App*. https://www.medtronic.com/us-en/transforming-healthcare/aligning-value/collaboration-in-healthcare/leveraging-actionable-data/ibm-watson-sugar-iq.html. Accessed 31 August 2020.

Mehta, N., and Bharadwaj, A. S. 2015. "Knowledge Integration in Outsourced Software Development: The Role of Sentry and Guard Processes," *Journal of Management Information Systems* (32:1), pp. 82-115.

Microsoft 2017. *Carnival Maritime is Testing the Waters with Machine Learning in the Cortana Intelligence Suite*. https://customers.microsoft.com/en-us/story/carnivalmaritime. Accessed 31 August 2020.

Microsoft 2018. *Creating Smarter Heating and Cooling Systems with Cloud-connected IoT Solution*. https://customers.microsoft.com/de-de/story/johnson-controls. Accessed 30 April 2020.

Mitchell 2006. "Knowledge Integration and Information Technology Project Performance," *Management Information Systems Quarterly* (30:4), 919-939.

Mithas, S., Tafti, Bardhan, I., and Goh 2012. "Information Technology and Firm Profitability: Mechanisms and Empirical Evidence," *Management Information Systems Quarterly* (36:1), pp. 205-224.

Müller-Seitz, G. 2012. "Absorptive and Desorptive Capacity-related Practices at the Network Level: The case of SEMATECH," *R&D Management* (42:1), pp. 90-99.

Myers, M. D. 1997. "Qualitative Research in Information Systems," *Management Information Systems Quarterly* (21:2), pp. 241-242.

Nahapiet, J., and Ghoshal, S. 1998. "Social Capital, Intellectual Capital, and the Organizational Advantage," *Academy of Management Review* (23:2), pp. 242-266.

Nambisan, S., Lyytinen, K., Majchrzak, A., and Song, M. 2017. "Digital Innovation Management: Reinventing Innovation Management Research in a Digital World," *Management Information Systems Quarterly* (41:1), pp. 223-238.

Newell, S. 2015. "Managing Knowledge and Managing Knowledge Work: What we know and what the Future holds," *Journal of Information Technology* (30:1), pp. 1-17.

Newell, S., Swan, J. A., and Galliers, R. D. 2000. "A Knowledge-focused Perspective on the Diffusion and Adoption of Complex Information Technologies: the BPR Example," *Information Systems Journal* (10:3), pp. 239-259.

Nissen, and Sengupta 2006. "Incorporating Software Agents into Supply Chains: Experimental Investigation with a Procurement Task," *Management Information Systems Quarterly* (30:1), pp. 145-166.

Nonaka, I. 1994. "A Dynamic Theory of Organizational Knowledge Creation," *Organization Science* (5:1), pp. 14-37.

Nonaka, I., and Takeuchi, H. 1995. *The Knowledge Creating Company: How Japanese Companies Create the Dynamics of Innovation*, Oxford University Press.

Nunamaker, J. F., Derrick, D. C., Elkins, A. C., Burgoon, J. K., and Patton, M. W. 2011. "Embodied Conversational Agent-Based Kiosk for Automated Interviewing," *Journal of Management Information Systems* (28:1), pp. 17-48.

Okhuysen, G. A., and Eisenhardt, K. M. 2002. "Integrating Knowledge in Groups: How Formal Interventions Enable Flexibility," *Organization Science* (13:4), pp. 370-386.

Orlikowski, W. J. 1993. "CASE Tools as Organizational Change Investigating Incremental and Radical Changes in Systems Development," *Management Information Systems Quarterly* (17:3), pp. 309-340.

Orlikowski, W. J., and Baroudi, J. J. 1991. "Studying Information Technology in Organizations: Research Approaches and Assumptions," *Information Systems Research* (2:1), pp. 1-28.

Oshri, I., van Fenema, P., and Kotlarsky, J. 2008. "Knowledge Transfer in Globally Distributed Teams: The Role of Transactive Memory," *Information Systems Journal* (18:6), pp. 593-616.

Pagani, M. 2013. "Digital Business Strategy and Value Creation: Framing the Dynamic Cycle of Control Points," *Management Information Systems Quarterly* (37:2), pp. 617-632.

Pan, S. L., and Leidner, D. E. 2003. "Bridging Communities of Practice with Information Technology in Pursuit of Global Knowledge Sharing," *The Journal of Strategic Information Systems* (12:1), pp. 71-88.

Pan, Y., Huang, P., and Gopal, A. 2018. "Board Independence and Firm Performance in the IT Industry: The Moderating Role of New Entry Threats," *Management Information Systems Quarterly* (42:3), pp. 979-1000.

Parker, G. G., and van Alstyne, M. W. 2018. "Innovation, Openness, and Platform Control," *Management Science* (64:7), pp. 3015-3032.

Parker, G. G., van Alstyne, M. W., and Jiang, X. 2017. "Platform Ecosystems: How Developers Invert the Firm," *Management Information Systems Quarterly* (41:1), pp. 255-266.

Patnayakuni, R., and Ruppel, C. 2006. "Managing the Complementarity of Knowledge Integration and Process Formalization for Systems Development Performance," *Journal of the Association for Information Systems* (7:8), pp. 545-567.

Penrose, E. 1959. *The Theory of the Growth of The Firm*, Basil Blackwell.

Peppard, J. 2007. "The Conundrum of IT Management," *European Journal of Information Systems* (16:4), pp. 336-345.

Peppard, J. 2018. "Rethinking the Concept of the IS Organization," *Information Systems Journal* (28:1), pp. 76-103.

Peppard, J., and Ward, J. 2004. "Beyond Strategic Information Systems: Towards an IS Capability," *The Journal of Strategic Information Systems* (13:2), pp. 167-194.

Piccinini, E., Hanelt, A., and Gregory, R. W. 2015. "Transforming Industrial Business: The Impact of Digital Transformation on Automotive Organizations," in *Proceedings of the 36th International Conference on Information Systems.*

Polanyi, M. 1962. *Personal Knowledge: Towards a Post-critical Philosophy*, Routledge.

Polanyi, M. 1967. *The Tacit Dimension*, Anchor.

Porter, M. E., and Heppelmann, J. E. 2014. "How Smart, Connected Products are Transforming Competition.," *Harvard Business Review* (92:11), pp. 64-88.

Prabhu, J. C., Chandy, R. K., and Ellis, M. E. 2005. "The Impact of Acquisitions on Innovation: Poison Pill, Placebo, or Tonic?" *Journal of Marketing* (69:1), pp. 114-130.

Preston, D. S., and Karahanna, E. 2009. "Antecedents of IS Strategic Alignment: A Nomological Network," *Information Systems Research* (20:2), pp. 159-179.

Pries-Heje, J., and Plads, T. J. 1992. "Three Barriers for Continuing Use of Computer-Based Tools in Information Systems Development: A Grounded Theory Approach," *Scandinavian Journal of Information Systems* (4:1), pp. 120-136.

Prieto, I. M., and Easterby-Smith, M. 2006. "Dynamic Capabilities and the Role of Organizational Knowledge: An Exploration," *European Journal of Information Systems* (15:5), pp. 500-510.

ProgrammableWeb 2019. *Ford API*. https://www.programmableweb.com/api/ford.

ProgrammableWeb 2020a. *API Category: Artificial Intelligence*. https://www.programmableweb.com/category/artificial-intelligence. Accessed 30 April 2020.

ProgrammableWeb 2020b. *Citrix Online GoToMeeting*. https://www.programmableweb.com/api/citrix-online-gotomeeting. Accessed 3 October 2020.

Quigley, T. J., and Hambrick, D. C. 2012. "When the Former Ceo Stays on as Board Chair: Effects on Successor Discretion, Strategic Change, and Performance," *Strategic Management Journal* (33:7), pp. 834-859.

Raffo, J., and Lhuillery, S. 2009. "How to Play the "Names Game": Patent Retrieval Comparing Different Heuristics," *Research Policy* (38:10), pp. 1617-1627.

Rai, A. 2020. "Explainable AI: from Black Box to Glass Box," *Journal of the Academy of Marketing Science* (48:1), pp. 137-141.

Rai, A., Constantinides, P., and Sarker, S. 2019. "Next-Generation Digital Platforms: Towards Human-AI Hybrids," *Management Information Systems Quarterly* (43), pp. 3-8.

Ransbotham, S., Kiron, D., Gerbert, P., and Reeves, M. 2017. "Reshaping Business with Artificial Intelligence," *MIT sloan management review* (59), pp. 1-17.

Ravichandran, T., Han, S., and Mithas, S. 2017. "Mitigating Diminishing Returns to R&D: The Role of Information Technology in Innovation," *Information Systems Research* (28:4), pp. 812-827.

Rishi, S., Stanley, B., and Gyimesi, K. 2008. "Automotive 2020: Clarity Beyond the Chaos," IBM Institute for Business Value.

Robert, L. P., Dennis, A. R., and Ahuja, M. K. 2008. "Social Capital and Knowledge Integration in Digitally Enabled Teams," *Information Systems Research* (19:3), pp. 314-334.

Roberts, N., Galluch, P. S., Dinger, M., and Grover, V. 2012. "Absorptive Capacity and Information Systems Research Review, Synthesis, and Directions for Future Research," *Management Information Systems Quarterly* (36:2), pp. 625-648.

Rowe, F. 2014. "What Literature Review is Not: Diversity, Boundaries and Recommendations," *European Journal of Information Systems* (23:3), pp. 241-255.

Saraf, N., Langdon, C. S., and Gosain, S. 2007. "IS Application Capabilities and Relational Value in Interfirm Partnerships," *Information Systems Research* (18:3), pp. 320-339.

Schilling, M. A. 2002. "Technology Success and Failure in Winner-Take-All Markets: The Impact of Learning Orientation, Timing, and Network Externalities," *Academy of Management Journal* (45:2), pp. 387-398.

Schryen, G. 2015. "Writing Qualitative IS Literature Reviews - Guidelines for Synthesis, Interpretation, and Guidance of Research," *Communications of the Association for Information Systems* (37).

Sedera, D., and Gable, G. G. 2010. "Knowledge Management Competence for Enterprise System Success," *The Journal of Strategic Information Systems* (19:4), pp. 296-306.

Selander, L., Henfridsson, O., and Svahn, F. 2013. "Capability Search and Redeem across Digital Ecosystems," *Journal of Information Technology* (28:3), pp. 183-197.

Shao, Z., Feng, Y., and Hu, Q. 2016. "Effectiveness of Top Management Support in Enterprise Systems Success: A Contingency Perspective of Fit between Leadership Style and System Life-cycle," *European Journal of Information Systems* (25:2), pp. 131-153.

Sharma, and Yetton 2007. "The Contingent Effects of Training, Technical Complexity, and Task Interdependence on Successful Information Systems Implementation," *Management Information Systems Quarterly* (31:2), pp. 219-238.

Shaver, J. M. 1998. "Accounting for Endogeneity When Assessing Strategy Performance: Does Entry Mode Choice Affect FDI Survival?" *Management Science* (44:4), pp. 571-585.

Simon, H. A. 1996. *The Sciences of the Artificial*, MIT Press.

Singh, R., Keil, M., and Kasi, V. 2009. "Identifying and Overcoming the Challenges of Implementing a Project Management Office," *European Journal of Information Systems* (18:5), pp. 409-427.

Skog, D. A., Wimelius, H., and Sandberg, J. 2018. "Digital Disruption," *Business & Information Systems Engineering* (60:5), pp. 431-437.

Slaughter, S. A., and Kirsch, L. J. 2006. "The Effectiveness of Knowledge Transfer Portfolios in Software Process Improvement: A Field Study," *Information Systems Research* (17:3), pp. 301-320.

Song, P., Xue, L., Rai, A., and Zhang, C. 2018. "The Ecosystem of Software Platform: A Study of Asymmetric Cross-Side Network Effects and Platform Governance," *Management Information Systems Quarterly* (42:1), pp. 121-142.

Song, P., Xue, L., Zhang, C., and Rai, A. 2017. "APIs in Software Platform: Implications for Innovation and Imitation," in *Proceedings of the 38th International Conference on Information Systems*.

Spender, J.-C. 1996a. "Making Knowledge the Basis of a Dynamic Theory of the Firm," *Strategic Management Journal* (17:S2), pp. 45-62.

Spender, J.-C. 1996b. "Organizational Knowledge, Learning and Memory: Three Concepts in Search of a Theory," *Journal of Organizational Change Management* (9:1), pp. 63-78.

Spiegel, O., Abbassi, P., Zylka, M. P., Schlagwein, D., Fischbach, K., and Schoder, D. 2016. "Business Model Development, Founders' Social Capital and the Success of Early Stage Internet Start-ups: A Mixed-method Study," *Information Systems Journal* (26:5), pp. 421-449.

Srivardhana, T., and Pawlowski, S. D. 2007. "ERP Systems as an Enabler of Sustained Business Process Innovation: A Knowledge-based View," *The Journal of Strategic Information Systems* (16:1), pp. 51-69.

Svahn, F., Mathiassen, L., and Lindgren, R. 2017. "Embracing Digital Innovation in Incumbent Firms: How Volvo Cars Managed Competing Concerns," *Management Information Systems Quarterly* (41:1), pp. 239-253.

Sydow, J., Schreyögg, G., and Koch, J. 2009. "Organizational Path Dependence: Opening the Black Box," *Academy of Management Review* (34:4), pp. 689-709.

Tanriverdi 2005. "Information Technology Relatedness, Knowledge Management Capability, and Performance of Multibusiness Firms," *Management Information Systems Quarterly* (29:2), pp. 311-334.

Teece, D. J., Pisano, G., and Shuen, A. 1997. "Dynamic Capabilities and Strategic Management," *Strategic Management Journal* (18:7), pp. 509-533.

Teo, T. S. H., and Pian, Y. 2003. "A Contingency Perspective on Internet Adoption and Competitive Advantage," *European Journal of Information Systems* (12:2), pp. 78-92.

Tilson, D., Lyytinen, K., and Sørensen, C. 2010. "Digital Infrastructures: The Missing IS Research Agenda," *Information Systems Research* (21:4), pp. 748-759.

Tilson, D., Sørensen, C., and Lyytinen, K. 2012. "Change and Control Paradoxes in Mobile Infrastructure Innovation: The Android and iOS Mobile Operating Systems Cases," in *Proceedings of the 45th Hawaii International Conference on System Science*, pp. 1324-1333.

Tiwana, A., Bharadwaj, A. S., and Sambamurthy, V. 2003. "The Antecedents of Information Systems Development Capability in Firms: A Knowledge Integration Perspective," in *Proceedings of the 24th International Conference on Information Systems*.

Tiwana, A., and Kim, S. K. 2015. "Discriminating IT Governance," *Information Systems Research* (26:4), pp. 656-674.

Tiwana, A., Konsynski, B., and Bush, A. A. 2010. "Research Commentary - Platform Evolution: Coevolution of Platform Architecture, Governance, and Environmental Dynamics," *Information Systems Research* (21:4), pp. 675-687.

Tiwana, A., and McLean, E. R. 2005. "Expertise Integration and Creativity in Information Systems Development," *Journal of Management Information Systems* (22:1), pp. 13-43.

Todorova, G., and Durisin, B. 2007. "Absorptive Capacity: Valuing a Reconceptualization," *Academy of Management Review* (32:3), pp. 774-786.

Tripsas, M. 2009. "Technology, Identity, and Inertia Through the Lens of "The Digital Photography Company"," *Organization Science* (20:2), pp. 441-460.

Tumbas, S., Berente, N., and vom Brocke, J. 2017a. "Born Digital: Growth Trajectories of Entrepreneurial Organizations Spanning Institutional Fields," in *Proceedings of the 38th International Conference on Information Systems*.

Tumbas, S., Berente, N., and vom Brocke, J. 2017b. "Digital Capabilities for Buffering Tensions of Structure, Space, and Time during Entrepreneurial Growth," in *Proceedings of the 38th International Conference on Information Systems*.

Tumbas, S., Berente, N., and vom Brocke, J. 2018. "Digital Innovation and Institutional Entrepreneurship: Chief Digital Officer Perspectives of their Emerging Role," *Journal of Information Technology* (33:3), pp. 188-202.

Turner, K. L., and Makhija, M. V. 2006. "The Role Of Organizational Controls In Managing Knowledge," *Academy of Management Review* (31:1), pp. 197-217.

Um, S., and Yoo, Y. 2016. "The Co-evolution of Digital Ecosystems.," in *Proceedings of the 37th International Conference on Information Systems*.

UPS 2020. *UPS Developer Kit APIs*. https://www.ups.com/us/en/services/technology-integration/developer-api.page? Accessed 3 October 2020.

Urquhart, C. 2001. "An Encounter with Grounded Theory," in *Qualitative Research in IS*, IGI Global, pp. 104-140.

Urquhart, C. 2007. "The Evolving Nature of Grounded Theory Method: The Case of the Information Systems Discipline," in *The SAGE Handbook of Grounded Theory*, A. Bryant and K. Charmaz (eds.), 1 Oliver's Yard, 55 City Road, London England EC1Y 1SP United Kingdom: SAGE Publications, pp. 339-359.

Urquhart, C., Lehmann, H., and Myers, M. D. 2010. "Putting the 'Theory' Back into Grounded Theory: Guidelines for Grounded Theory Studies in Information Systems," *Information Systems Journal* (20:4), pp. 357-381.

van de Ven 2005. "Running in Packs to Develop Knowledge-Intensive Technologies," *Management Information Systems Quarterly* (29:2), pp. 365-377.

van den Hooff, B., van Leeuw Weenen, F. de, Soekijad, M., and Huysman, M. 2010. "The Value of Online Networks of Practice: The Role of Embeddedness and Media Use," *Journal of Information Technology* (25:2), pp. 205-215.

Vermerris, A., Mocker, M., and van Heck, E. 2014. "No Time to Waste: The Role of Timing and Complementarity of Alignment Practices in Creating Business Value in IT Projects," *European Journal of Information Systems* (23:6), pp. 629-654.

Vermeulen, F., and Barkema, H. 2001. "Learning Through Acquisitions," *Academy of Management Journal* (44:3), pp. 457-476.

Vial, G. 2019. "Understanding Digital Transformation: A Review and a Research Agenda," *The Journal of Strategic Information Systems* (28:2), pp. 118-144.

Visa 2020. *Working with Visa APIs*. https://developer.visa.com/pages/working-with-visa-apis. Accessed 25 September 2020.

Wade, and Hulland 2004. "Review: The Resource-Based View and Information Systems Research: Review, Extension, and Suggestions for Future Research," *Management Information Systems Quarterly* (28:1), pp. 107-142.

Walmart 2020. *Developer Portal*. https://developer.walmart.com/#/home. Accessed 3 October 2020.

Walsham, G. 1995. "Interpretive Case Studies in IS Research: Nature and Method," *European Journal of Information Systems* (4:2), pp. 74-81.

Wang, C. L., Ahmed, P. K., and Rafiq, M. 2008. "Knowledge Management Orientation Construct Development and Empirical Validation," *European Journal of Information Systems* (17:3), pp. 219-235.

Wang, W., and Benbasat, I. 2013. "Research Note —A Contingency Approach to Investigating the Effects of User-System Interaction Modes of Online Decision Aids," *Information Systems Research* (24:3), pp. 861-876.

Wang, Y., and Haggerty, N. 2009. "Knowledge Tansfer in Virtual Settings: The Role of Individual Virtual Competency," *Information Systems Journal* (19:6), pp. 571-593.

Wareham, J., Fox, P. B., and Cano Giner, J. L. 2014. "Technology Ecosystem Governance," *Organization Science* (25:4), pp. 1195-1215.

Webster, J., and Watson, R. T. 2002. "Analyzing the Past to Prepare for the Future Writing a Literature Review," *Management Information Systems Quarterly* (26:2), xiii-xxiii.

Weill, P., and Olson, M. H. 1989. "An Assessment of the Contingency Theory of Management Information Systems," *Journal of Management Information Systems* (6:1), pp. 59-86.

Wernerfelt, B. 1984. "A Resource-based View of the Firm," *Strategic Management Journal* (5:2), pp. 171-180.

West, J., and Bogers, M. 2014. "Leveraging External Sources of Innovation: A Review of Research on Open Innovation," *Journal of Product Innovation Management* (31:4), pp. 814-831.

WIPO 2019a. "Data Collection Method and Clustering Scheme: Background Paper," Technology Trends 2019 Artificial Intelligence, World Intellectual Property Organization.

WIPO 2019b. "Technology Trends 2019: Artificial Intelligence," World Intellectual Property Organization.

Wu, I.-L., and Hu, Y.-P. 2012. "Examining Knowledge Management Enabled Performance for Hospital Professionals A Dynamic Capability View and the Mediating Role of Process Capability," *Journal of the Association for Information Systems* (13:12), pp. 976-999.

Wulf, J., and Blohm, I. 2017. "Service Innovation through Application Programming Interfaces-Towards a Typology of Service Designs.," in *Proceedings of the 38th International Conference on Information Systems*.

Wynn, and Williams 2012. "Principles for Conducting Critical Realist Case Study Research in Information Systems," *Management Information Systems Quarterly* (36:3), pp. 787-810.

Xu, S., Wu, F., and Cavusgil, E. 2013. "Complements or Substitutes? Internal Technological Strength, Competitor Alliance Participation, and Innovation Development," *Journal of Product Innovation Management* (30:4), pp. 750-762.

Yayla, A. A., and Hu, Q. 2011. "The Impact of Information Security Events on the Stock Value of Firms: The Effect of Contingency Factors," *Journal of Information Technology* (26:1), pp. 60-77.

Yoo, Y. 2010. "Computing in Everyday Life: A Call for Research on Experiential Computing," *Management Information Systems Quarterly* (34:2), pp. 213-231.

Yoo, Y., Boland, R. J., Lyytinen, K., and Majchrzak, A. 2012. "Organizing for Innovation in the Digitized World," *Organization Science* (23:5), pp. 1398-1408.

Yoo, Y., Henfridsson, O., and Lyytinen, K. 2010. "Research Commentary —The New Organizing Logic of Digital Innovation: An Agenda for Information Systems Research," *Information Systems Research* (21:4), pp. 724-735.

Yu, S., and Woodard, C. J. 2008. "Innovation in the Programmable Web: Characterizing the Mashup Ecosystem.," in *International Conference on Service-Oriented Computing*, Springer, pp. 136-147.

Zack, M. 1998. "An Architecture for Managing Explicated Knowledge," *Sloan Management Review* (39:4), pp. 45-58.

Zahra, S. A., and George, G. 2002. "Absorptive Capacity: A Review, Reconceptualization, and Extension," *Academy of Management Review* (27:2), pp. 185-203.

Zapadka, P. 2020. "Digital Innovation in Industrial-Age Firms: Managing the Balancing Act of Knowledge Integration," in *Proceedings of the 28th European Conference on Information Systems*.

Zhang, X., Venkatesh, V., and Brown, S. A. 2011. "Designing Collaborative Systems to Enhance Team Performance," *Journal of the Association for Information Systems* (12:8), pp. 556-584.

Zhu, F., and Iansiti, M. 2012. "Entry into Platform-based Markets," *Strategic Management Journal* (33:1), pp. 88-106.

Zhu, K. X., and Zhou, Z. Z. 2012. "Research Note - Lock-In Strategy in Software Competition: Open-Source Software vs. Proprietary Software," *Information Systems Research* (23:2), pp. 536-545.

Ziegler, N., Ruether, F., Bader, M. A., and Gassmann, O. 2013. "Creating Value through External Intellectual Property Commercialization: A desorptive capacity view," *The Journal of Technology Transfer* (38:6), pp. 930-949.

Zittrain, J. 2006. "The Generative Internet," *Harvard Law Review* (119), pp. 1974-2040.

Zmud, R., Shaft, T., Zheng, W., and Croes, H. 2010. "Systematic Differences in Firm's Information Technology Signaling: Implications for Research Design," *Journal of the Association for Information Systems* (11:3), pp. 149-181.

Zollo, M. 2002. "Deliberate Learning and the Evolution of Dynamic Capabilities," *Organization Science* (13:3), pp. 339-351.

Appendix

Appendix A. Overview of the Authors' Contribution in the Studies Included in this Thesis.

No	Section	Title	Author	Authors' contribution
1	B.I	Knowledge Integration and Digital Innovation – Towards a Multi-Dimensional Framework	**Patryk Zapadka**	**95**
			Lutz M. Kolbe	5
2	B.II	Digital at the Edge – Antecedents and Performance Effects of Boundary Resources Deployment	**Patryk Zapadka**	**40**
			Andre Hanelt	40
			Sebastian Firk	20
3	B.II	Leveraging "AI-as-a-Service" – Antecedents and Consequences of Using Artificial Intelligence Boundary Resources	**Patryk Zapadka**	**50**
			Andre Hanelt	25
			Sebastian Firk	15
			Jana Oehmichen	10
4	B.III	Digital Innovation in Industrial-Age Firms – Managing the Balancing Act of Knowledge Integration	**Patryk Zapadka**	**100**

Appendix B. Overview of the Author's Published Articles as of March 2021.

Authors Publication	Ranking
Zapadka, P.; Hanelt, A.; Firk, S.; Oehmichen, J. (2020). Leveraging "AI-as-a-Service" - Antecedents and Consequences of Using Artificial Intelligence Boundary Resources, Proceedings of the International Conference on Information Systems (ICIS), Hyderabad, India.	A
Zapadka, P. (2020). Digital Innovation in Industrial-Age Firms: Managing the Balancing Act of Knowledge Integration, Proceedings of the European Conference on Information Systems (ECIS), Marrakech, Morocco. *Best Paper Nominee	B
Brendel, A. B.; **Zapadka, P.**; Kolbe, L. M. (2018): Design Science Research in Green IS - Analyzing the Past to Guide Future Research, Proceedings of the European Conference on Information Systems (ECIS), Portsmouth, England	B
Brendel, A. B.; Brennecke, J. T.; **Zapadka, P.**; Kolbe, L. M. (2017): A Decision Support System for Computation of Carsharing Pricing Areas and its Influence on the Vehicle Distribution, Proceedings of the International Conference on Information Systems (ICIS), Seoul, South Korea	A
The study ranking was assessed according to VHB Jourqual 3.	

Göttinger Wirtschaftsinformatik

Herausgeber: Prof. Dr. J. Biethahn† • Prof. Dr. L. M. Kolbe • Prof. Dr. M. Schumann

Band 31: Christian Stummeyer
Integration von Simulationsmethoden und hochintegrierter betriebswirtschaftlicher PPS-Standardsoftware im Rahmen eines ganzheitlichen Entwicklungsansatzes
ISBN 3-89712-874-8

Band 32: Stefan Wegert
Gestaltungsansätze zur IV-Integration von elektronischen und konventionellen Vertriebsstrukturen bei Kreditinstituten
ISBN 3-89712-924-8

Band 33: Ernst von Stegmann und Stein
Ansätze zur Risikosteuerung einer Kreditversicherung unter Berücksichtigung von Unternehmensverflechtungen
ISBN 3-89873-003-4

Band 34: Gerald Wissel
Konzeption eines Managementsystems für die Nutzung von internen sowie externen Wissen zur Generierung von Innovationen
ISBN 3-89873-194-4

Band 35: Wolfgang Greve-Kramer
Konzeption internetbasierter Informationssysteme in Konzernen
Inhaltliche, organisatorische und technische Überlegungen zur internetbasierten Informationsverarbeitung in Konzernen
ISBN 3-89873-207-X

Band 36: Tim Veil
Internes Rechnungswesen zur Unterstützung der Führung in Unternehmensnetzwerken
ISBN 3-89873-237-1

Band 37: Mark Althans
Konzeption eines Vertriebscontrolling-Informationssystems für Unternehmen der liberalisierten Elektrizitätswirtschaft
ISBN 3-89873-326-2

Band 38: Jörn Propach
Methoden zur Spielplangestaltung öffentlicher Theater
Konzeption eines Entscheidungsunterstützungssystems auf der Basis Evolutionärer Algorithmen
ISBN 3-89873-496-X

Cuvillier Verlag Göttingen
Nonnenstieg 8 • 37075 Göttingen

Göttinger Wirtschaftsinformatik

Herausgeber: Prof. Dr. J. Biethahn† • Prof. Dr. L. M. Kolbe • Prof. Dr. M. Schumann

Band 39: Jochen Heimann
DV-gestützte Jahresabschlußanalyse
Möglichkeiten und Grenzen beim Einsatz computergeschützter Verfahren zur Analyse und Bewertung von Jahresabschlüssen
ISBN 3-89873-499-4

Band 40: Patricia Böning Spohr
Controlling für Medienunternehmen im Online-Markt
Gestaltung ausgewählter Controllinginstrumente
ISBN 3-89873-677-6

Band 41: Jörg Koschate
Methoden und Vorgehensmodelle zur strategischen Planung von Electronic-Business-Anwendungen
ISBN 3-89873-808-6

Band 42: Yang Liu
A theoretical and empirical study on the data mining process for credit scoring
ISBN 3-89873-823-X

Band 43: Antonios Tzouvaras
Referenzmodellierung für Buchverlage
Prozess- und Klassenmodelle für den Leistungsprozess
ISBN 3-89873-844-2

Band 44: Marina Nomikos
Hemmnisse der Nutzung Elektronischer Marktplätze aus der Sicht von kleinen und mittleren Unternehmen eine theoriegeleitete Untersuchung
ISBN 3-89873-847-7

Band 45: Boris Fredrich
Wissensmanagement und Weiterbildungsmanagement
Gestaltungs- und Kombinationsansätze im Rahmen einer lernenden Organisation
ISBN 3-89873-870-1

Band 46: Thomas Arens
Methodische Auswahl von CRM Software
Ein Referenz-Vorgehensmodell zur methodengestützten Beurteilung und Auswahl von Customer Relationship Management Informationssystemen
ISBN 3-86537-054-3

Cuvillier Verlag Göttingen

Nonnenstieg 8 • 37075 Göttingen

Göttinger Wirtschaftsinformatik

Herausgeber: Prof. Dr. J. Biethahn† • Prof. Dr. L. M. Kolbe • Prof. Dr. M. Schumann

Band 47: Andreas Lackner
Dynamische Tourenplanung mit ausgewählten Mataheuristiken
Eine Untersuchung am Beispiel des kapazitätsrestriktiven dynamischen Tourenplanungsproblems mit Zeitfenstern
ISBN 3-86537-084-5

Band 48: Tobias Behrensdorf
Service Engineering in Versicherungsunternehmen
unter besonderer Berücksichtigung eines Vorgehensmodells zur Unterstützung durch Informations- und Kommunikationstechnologien
ISBN 3-86537-110-8

Band 49: Michael Range
Aufbau und Betrieb konsumentenorientierter Websites im Internet
Vorgehen und Methoden unter besonderer Berücksichtigung der Anforderungen von kleinen und mittleren Online-Angeboten
ISBN 3-86537-490-5

Band 50: Gerit Grübler
Ganzheitliches Multiprojektmanagement
Mit einer Fallstudie in einem Konzern der Automobilzulieferindustrie
ISBN 3-86537-544-8

Band 51: Birte Pochert
Konzeption einer unscharfen Balanced Scorecard
Möglichkeiten der Fuzzyfizierung einer Balanced Scorecard zur Unterstützung des Strategischen Managements
ISBN 3-86537-671-1

Band 52: Manfred Peter Zilling
Effizienztreiber innovativer Prozesse für den Automotive Aftermarket
Implikationen aus der Anwendung von kollaborativen und integrativen Methoden des Supply Chain Managements
ISBN 3-86537-790-4

Band 53: Mike Hieronimus
Strategisches Controlling von Supply Chains
Entwicklung eines ganzheitlichen Ansatzes unter Einbeziehung der Wertschöpfungspartner
ISBN 3-86537-799-8

Band 54: Dijana Bergmann
Datenschutz und Datensicherheit unter besonderer Berücksichtigung des elektronischen Geschäftsverkehrs zwischen öffentlicher Verwaltung und privaten Unternehmen
ISBN 3-86537-894-3

Cuvillier Verlag Göttingen

Nonnenstieg 8 • 37075 Göttingen

Göttinger Wirtschaftsinformatik

Herausgeber: Prof. Dr. J. Biethahn† • Prof. Dr. L. M. Kolbe • Prof. Dr. M. Schumann

Band 55: Jan Eric Borchert
Operatives Innovationsmanagement in Unternehmensnetzwerken
Gestaltung von Instrumenten für Innovationsprojekte
ISBN 3-86537-984-2

Band 56: Andre Daldrup
Konzeption eines integrierten IV-Systems zur ratingbasierten Quantifizierung des regulatorischen und ökonomischen Eigenkapitals im Unternehmenskreditgeschäft unter Berücksichtigung von Basel II
ISBN 978-3-86727-189-9

Band 57: Thomas Diekmann
Ubiquitous Computing-Technologien im betrieblichen Umfeld
Technische Überlegungen, Einsatzmöglichkeiten und Bewertungsansätze
ISBN 978-3-86727-194-3

Band 58: Lutz Seidenfaden
Ein Peer-to-Peer-basierter Ansatz zur digitalen Distribution wissenschaftlicher Informationen
ISBN 978-3-86727-321-3

Band 59: Sebastian Rieger
Einheitliche Authentifizierung in heterogenen IT-Strukturen für ein sicheres e-Science-Umfeld
ISBN 978-3-86727-329-9

Band 60: Ole Björn Brodersen
Eignung schwarmintelligenter Verfahren für die betriebliche Entscheidungsunterstützung
Untersuchungen der Particle Swarm Optimization und Ant Colony Optimization anhand eines stochastischen Lagerhaltungs- und eines universitären Stundenplanungsproblems
ISBN 978-3-86727-777-5

Band 61: Jan Sauer
Konzeption eines wertorientierten Managementsystems unter besonderer Berücksichtigung des versicherungstechnischen Risikos
ISBN 978-3-86727-858-4

Band 62: Adam Melski
Datenmanagement in RFID-gestützten Logistiknetzwerken
RFID-induzierte Veränderungen, Gestaltungsmöglichkeiten und Handlungsempfehlungen
ISBN 978-3-86955-041-1

Cuvillier Verlag Göttingen

Nonnenstieg 8 • 37075 Göttingen

Göttinger Wirtschaftsinformatik

Herausgeber: Prof. Dr. J. Biethahn† • Prof. Dr. L. M. Kolbe • Prof. Dr. M. Schumann

Band 63: Thorsten Caus
Anwendungen im mobilen Internet
Herausforderungen und Lösungsansätze für die Entwicklung und Gestaltung mobiler Anwendungen
ISBN 978-3-86955-399-3

Band 64: Nils-Holger-Schmidt
Environmentally Sustainable Information Management
Theories and concepts for Sustainability, Green IS, and Green IT
ISBN 978-3-86955-825-7

Band 65: Lars Thoroe
RFID in Reverse-Logistics-Systemen
ISBN 978-3-86955-902-5

Band 66: Stefan Bitzer
Integration von Web 2.0-Technologien in das betriebliche Wissensmanagement
ISBN 978-3-86955-918-6

Band 67: Matthias Kießling
IT-Innovationsmanagement
Gestaltungs- und Steuerungsmöglichkeiten
ISBN 978-3-95404-104-6

Band 68: Marco Klein
HR Social Software
Unternehmensinterne Weblogs, Wikis und Social Networking Services für Prozesse des Personalmanagements
ISBN 978-3-95404-247-0

Band 69: Malte Schmidt
Migration vom Barcode zur passiven RFID-Technologie in der automobilen Logistik
Exemplarische Untersuchung am Beispiel eines Automobilherstellers
ISBN 978-3-95404-441-2

Band 70: Janis Kossahl
Konzeptuelle Grundlagen zur Etablierung einer Informationsplattform in der Energiewirtschaft
Ein Beitrag zur Energiewende aus der Perspektive der Wirtschaftsinformatik
ISBN 978-3-95404-524-2

Cuvillier Verlag Göttingen
Nonnenstieg 8 • 37075 Göttingen

Göttinger Wirtschaftsinformatik

Herausgeber: Prof. Dr. J. Biethahn† • Prof. Dr. L. M. Kolbe • Prof. Dr. M. Schumann

Band 71: Stefan Friedemann
IT-gestützte Produktionsplanung mit nachwachsenden Rohstoffen unter Berücksichtigung von Unsicherheiten
ISBN 978-3-95404-606-5

Band 72: Arne Frerichs
Unternehmensfinanzierung mit Peer-to-Peer-gestützter Mittelvergabe
ISBN 978-3-95404-624-9

Band 73: Ullrich C. C. Jagstaidt
Smart Metering Information Management
Gestaltungsansätze für das Informationsmanagement und für Geschäftsmodelle der Marktakteure in der Energiewirtschaft
ISBN 978-3-95404-696-6

Band 74: Sebastian Busse
Exploring the Role of Information Systems in the Development of Electric Mobility
Understanding the Domain and Designing the Path
ISBN 978-3-95404-727-7

Band 75: Christoph Beckers
Management von Wasserinformationen in der Fleischindustrie
Analyse von Sytemanforderungen zur produktspezifischen Ausweisung von Water Footprints
ISBN 978-3-95404-809-0

Band 76: Hendrik Hilpert
Informationssysteme für die Nachhaltigkeitsberichterstattung in Unternehmen
Empirische Erkenntnisse und Gestaltungsansätze zur Datengrundlage, Erfassung und Berichterstattung von Treibhausgasemissionen
ISBN 978-3-95404-908-0

Band 77: Simon Thanh-Nam Trang
Adoption, Value Co-Creation, and Governance of Inter-Organizational Information Technology in Wood Networks
ISBN 978-3-7369-9031-9

Band 78: Stefan Gröger
IT-Unterstützung zur Verbesserung der Drittmittel-Projekt-Bewirtschaftung an Hochschulen - Referenzprozessgestaltung, Artefakt-Design und Nutzenpotenziale
ISBN 978-3-7369-9077-7

Cuvillier Verlag Göttingen

Nonnenstieg 8 • 37075 Göttingen

Göttinger Wirtschaftsinformatik

Herausgeber: Prof. Dr. J. Biethahn† • Prof. Dr. L. M. Kolbe • Prof. Dr. M. Schumann

Band 79: Johannes Schmidt
Demand-Side Integration Programs for Electric Transport Vehicles unter Berücksichtigung von Unsicherheiten
ISBN 978-3-7369-9123-1

Band 80: Christian Tornack
IT-gestütztes Nachfolgemanagement in Großunternehmen
ISBN 978-3-7369-9161-3

Band 81: Shanna Appelhanz
Tracking & Tracing-Systeme in Wertschöpfungsnetzwerken für die industrielle stoffliche Nutzung nachwachsender Rohstoffe
ISBN 978-3-7369-9207-8

Band 82: Henning Krüp
IT Corporate Entrepreneurship – Identifying Factors for IT Innovations in Non-IT Companies
ISBN 978-3-7369-9253-5

Band 83: Andre Hanelt
Managing the Digital Transformation of Business Models – An Incumbent Firm Perspective
ISBN 978-3-7369-9254-2

Band 84: Björn Pilarski
Mobile Personalinformationssysteme
Empirische Erkenntnisse und Gestaltungsansätze zum Einsatz mobiler Anwendungen im Personalmanagement
ISBN 978-3-7369-9291-7

Band 85: Everlin Piccinini
Digital Transformation of Business - Understanding this Phenomenon in the Context of the Automotive Industry
ISBN 978-3-7369-9323-5

Band 86: Matthias Eisel
Analyzing the Range Barrier to Electric Vehicle Adoption - The Case of Range Anxiety
ISBN 978-3-7369-9379-2

Cuvillier Verlag Göttingen
Nonnenstieg 8 • 37075 Göttingen

Göttinger Wirtschaftsinformatik

Herausgeber: Prof. Dr. J. Biethahn† • Prof. Dr. L. M. Kolbe • Prof. Dr. M. Schumann

Band 87: Gerrit Remané
Digital Business Models in the Mobility Sector: Using Components and Types to Understand Existing and Design New Business Models
ISBN 978-3-7369-9544-4

Band 88: Thierry Jean Ruch
Consumerization of IT –
Studies to Explore the Phenomenon and Implications for IT Management, Information Security, and Organizational Security
ISBN 978-3-7369-9558-1

Band 89: Carolin Ebermann
Die Förderung von nachhaltigem Mobilitätsverhalten durch erhöhte User-Experience und den Einsatz von Informationssystemen
ISBN 978-3-7369-9568-0

Band 90: Sebastian Zander
Interorganizational Information Systems for the Efficient Utilization of Renewable Resources - Insights from Networks in the Wood Industry
ISBN 978-3-7369-9584-0

Band 91: Ilja Nastjuk
The Dark and the Bright Side of Digitalization -
The Case of Sustainable Mobility
ISBN 978-3-7369-9586-4

Band 92: Aaron Mengelkamp
Informationen zur Bonitätsprüfung auf Basis von Daten aus sozialen Medien
ISBN 978-3-7369-9628-1

Band 93: Alfred Benedikt Brendel
Applied Design Science Research in the Context of Smart and Sustainable Mobility
The Case of Vehicle Supply and Demand Management in Shared Vehicle Services
ISBN 978-3-7369-9685-4

Band 94: Markus Mandrella
IT-Based Value Co-Creation in Inter-Organizational Networks
Theory Integration, Extension, and Adaptation to the Wood Industry
ISBN 978-3-7369-9695-3

Cuvillier Verlag Göttingen

Nonnenstieg 8 • 37075 Göttingen

Göttinger Wirtschaftsinformatik

Herausgeber: Prof. Dr. J. Biethahn† • Prof. Dr. L. M. Kolbe • Prof. Dr. M. Schumann

Band 95: Benjamin Brauer
Persuasive User-Centric Green IS
Exploring the Role and Paving the Way of Information Systems to Induce Pro-Environmental Behavior Change
ISBN 978-3-7369-9764-6

Band 96: Sebastian Hobert
Empirische Erkenntnisse und Gestaltungsansätze zum Einsatz von Wearable Computern im Industriesektor
ISBN 978-3-7369-9794-3

Band 97: Björn Hildebrandt
Digitalization of Mobility - Understanding the Transformational Impacts of Pervasive Digital Technologies on Business Models in the Mobility Sector
ISBN 978-3-7369-9827-8

Band 98: Jasmin Decker
Micro Learning und Mobile Learning in Unternehmen – Empirische Erkenntnisse und Gestaltungsempfehlungen zum Einsatz mobiler Lernanwendungen
ISBN 978-3-7369-9835-3

Band 99: Jan Moritz Anke
IT-gestützte Lern- und Assessmentmodule für nachhaltiges Wirtschaften
Empirische Erkenntnisse und Gestaltungsansätze zum Einsatz IT-gestützter Lern- und Assessmentmodule
ISBN 978-3-7369-9986-2

Band 100: Daniel Leonhardt
Organizing for Digital Innovation – The Role of the IT Function
ISBN 978-3-7369-7060-1

Band 101: Schahin Tofangchi
Towards a Theory for Designing Machine Learning Systems for Complex Decision Making Problems
ISBN 978-3-7369-7200-1

Band 102: Stephan Diederich
Designing Anthropomorphic Conservational Agents in Enterprises: A Nascent Theory and Conceptual Framework for Fostering a Human-Like Interaction
ISBN 978-3-7369-7216-2

Cuvillier Verlag Göttingen
Nonnenstieg 8 • 37075 Göttingen

Göttinger Wirtschaftsinformatik

Herausgeber: Prof. Dr. J. Biethahn† • Prof. Dr. L. M. Kolbe • Prof. Dr. M. Schumann

Band 103: Bernd Herrenkind
Driving the Future Diffusion of Mobility
Investigating User Acceptance of Autonomous Driving in Shared Mobility Services
ISBN 978-3-7369-7214-8

Band 104: Sromona Chatterjee
Computer Vision and Machine Learning in Sustainable Mobility:
The Case of Road Surface Defects
ISBN 978-3-7369-7258-2

Band 105: Fabian Nischak
Ecosystems in the Era of Digital Innovation:
Exploring the Transformational Impact of Pervasive Digital Technologies on Industrial-Age Business Contexts and Incumbent Firms
ISBN 978-3-7369-7328-2

Band 106: Pascal Freier
Empirische Erkenntnisse und Gestaltungsansätze für Entscheidungsunterstützungssysteme in der Ablaufplanung im Kontext von Cyber-Physischen Systemen
ISBN 978-3-7369-7349-7

Band 107: Daniel Hodapp
How Incumbent Firms Navigate Nascent Digital Platform Ecosystems in the Internet of Thing: A Contextualized Perspective on Value Co-Creation in Platform Ecosystems
ISBN 978-3-7369-7362-6

Band 108: David Marz
Technology Acceptance in the Context of Digital Transformation
Studies on How and Why People Use Connected Objects
ISBN 978-3-7369-7370-1

Band 109: Hannes Kurtz
Digital Business Strategy: An Investigation of Generic Types,
Performance Implications, an Path Dependence
ISBN 978-3-7369-7402-9

Cuvillier Verlag Göttingen

Nonnenstieg 8 • 37075 Göttingen

www.ingramcontent.com/pod-product-compliance
Ingram Content Group UK Ltd.
Pitfield, Milton Keynes, MK11 3LW, UK
UKHW021652190726
13853UKWH00001B/221

9 783736 974630